Real and Financial Integration in Asia

This book investigates the impact of both real and financial integration on growth and on welfare, and enquires whether increases in either or both forms build the linkage between the real and financial economy. It contributes to the following two areas: (1) Research into economic developments in East Asia, the most dynamic and populous region in the world, is important in itself for researchers, policymakers, journalists, business people and others. East Asia's economic developments influence people's lives, not only in East Asia but also in other parts of the world. (2) Many aspects of East Asian experiences in economic development are unique, making research into East Asia attractive and important to discern the mechanisms of economic development.

The first part of this study begins with chapters that address the measurement of regional integration compared with the engagement with the global economy and how this influences the aggregate behaviour of the economies. The second part turns to consideration of the financial sector and the efficiency and performance of banking in the region. This allows a discussion of whether, in the current crisis, the banking sector was an important channel of financial shock into real behaviour. The third part turns to the corporate sector. Using data on firms, the type of finance used by firms, its impact on their performance, and ownership-structure influence over productivity growth are discussed. Based on the findings, the book presents several policy recommendations and future research agendas for further economic integration in East Asia.

Shandre M. Thangavelu is an active researcher on human capital development, technology transfer, foreign direct investment, trade, government infrastructure investment, productivity and economic growth. He has written extensively on technology transfer and economic growth and has published his research in major international journals. His recent publications are in the *Journal of Economic Development*, *Empirical Economics*, *Applied Economics*, *World Economy* and the *Journal of Economic Studies*. Recently, he was attached as the Head of the Economics Unit, MOM, under the Economist Service to the Ministry of Trade and Industry and Ministry of Manpower. Recently, he was appointed as the Managing Editor for the *Asian Economic Journal* (AEJ).

Aekapol Chongvilaivan is a Fellow and Coordinator of the Regional Economic Studies Programme at the Institute of Southeast Asian Studies (ISEAS), Singapore. His current research covers a wide range of economics areas, such as fragmentation and outsourcing in South-East Asia, international trade, regional economic integration and applied econometrics, among others. His research has been published in several international, refereed journals, including *Economic Inquiry*, *Southern Economic Journal*, the *Journal of Institutional and Theoretical Economics*, *Applied Economics* and *The World Economy*. He has served as an editor of the *ASEAN Economic Bulletin* and Coordinator of the Singapore APEC Study Centre.

Routledge-ERIA Studies in Development Economics

Economic Consequences of Globalization
Evidence from East Asia
Edited by Shujiro Urata, Chin Hee Hahn and Dionisius Narjoko

Real and Financial Integration in Asia
Edited by Shandre M. Thangavelu and Aekapol Chongvilaivan

Real and Financial Integration in Asia

Edited by
Shandre M. Thangavelu and
Aekapol Chongvilaivan

Routledge
Taylor & Francis Group
LONDON AND NEW YORK

ERIA

First published 2013
by Routledge
2 Park Square, Milton Park, Abingdon, Oxon, OX14 4RN

Simultaneously published in the USA and Canada
by Routledge
711 Third Avenue, New York, NY 10017

Routledge is an imprint of the Taylor & Francis Group, an informa business

British Library Cataloguing in Publication Data
A catalogue record for this book is available from the British Library

Library of Congress Cataloging in Publication Data
Real and financial integration in Asia/edited by Shandre Mugan Thangavelu and Aekapol Chongvilaivan.
p. cm. – (Routledge-ERIA studies in development economics; 2)
Includes bibliographical references and index.
1. Finance – Asia. 2. Monetary policy – Asia. 3. International economic integration – Asia. I. Thangavelu, Shandre, 1969–. II. Chongvilaivan, Aekapol.
HG187.A2R43 2012
332′.042095 – dc23
2012004129

ISBN: 978-0-415-68643-3 (hbk)
ISBN: 978-0-203-10495-8 (ebk)

Typeset in Times New Roman by
Florence Production Ltd, Stoodleigh, Devon

Contents

Figures

Tables

Contributors

Tony Cavoli is a Senior Lecturer in the School of Commerce, Deputy Director of the Australian Centre for Asian Business at the University of South Australia and Senior Research Fellow at the Center for Emerging Markets Policies at George Mason University.

Aekapol Chongvilaivan is a Fellow and Coordinator of the Regional Economic Studies Programme at the Institute of Southeast Asian Studies (ISEAS), Singapore.

Jenny Corbett is Professor of Economics and the Executive Director of the Australia–Japan Research Centre, Crawford School of Public Policy at the Australian National University. She is also Reader in the Economy of Japan at the University of Oxford.

Christopher Findlay is Executive Dean of the Faculty of the Professions at the University of Adelaide and was previously Head of the School of Economics there.

Prasanna Gai is a Professor of Economics at the University of Auckland and former Senior Advisor to the Bank of England.

Anton H. Gunawan is currently Chief Economist of Bank Danamon Indonesia (since 2008), after spending 8 years as an Economist with Citibank Indonesia.

Achmad Maulana is currently a Researcher at the Center for Economics and Development Studies of the Padjadjaran University, Bandung, Indonesia.

Kazuki Onji is a Lecture at Crawford School of Economics and Government at the Australian National University.

Friska Parulian is a Strategic and Policy Review Economist at the International Monetary Fund (IMF).

Victor Pontines is a Research Fellow with the Asian Development Bank Institute (ADBI) in Tokyo, Japan and is currently on leave from the Flinders Business School, Flinders University. Recently he was attached as a Senior

Economist for the South East Asian Central Banks (SEACEN) Research and Training Centre in Kuala Lumpur, Malaysia.

Reza Y. Siregar is Senior Economist of ASEAN+3 Macroeconomic Research Office (AMRO) in Singapore. He has assumed a number of professional posts, both at academic, multilateral and research institutions.

Shandre M. Thangavelu is an Associate Professor at the Department of Economics, National University of Singapore and is a Research Associate at the Institute of Policy Studies, Singapore.

Garry Twite is an Associate Professor in Finance at McCombs School of Business, the University of Texas at Austin.

1 Introduction

Shandre M. Thangavelu[1]
Department of Economics, National University of Singapore

Aekapol Chongvilaivan[2]
Institute of Southeast Asian Studies

Are there any linkages between financial shocks and real activities in the economy? Do shocks in the financial markets translate to real activities in the domestic economy? There is little empirical evidence to link financial activities to real activities, such as consumption, investment and welfare of the economy. The purpose of this book is critically to evaluate these questions in the Asian context, which has very little empirical literature.

The current global financial crisis (GFC) indicates that nominal external shocks could persist in the domestic economy, thereby affecting real activities in the economy. The linkages created through trade and global linkages through banks and financial markets tend to increase the persistence within and across countries. Thus, the key challenges to smoothing out economic shocks and business cycles are to understand the relationship between financial and real effects on the regional and domestic economy. This book consists of key studies that examine the relationship between financial markets and real activities in the region. In particular, the studies explore and identify the key factors that affect trade and regional integration in the Asian region.

The first part of this study begins with chapters that address the measurement of regional integration compared with the engagement with the global economy and how this influences the aggregate behaviour of the economies. The second part turns to the corporate sector. Using data on firms, the type of finance used by firms, its impact on their performance, and ownership-structure influence over productivity growth are discussed. Based on the findings, we present several policy recommendations and future research agendas for further economic integration in East Asia. The third part turns to a consideration of the financial sector and the efficiency and performance of banking in the region. This allows a discussion of whether, in the current crisis, the banking sector is an important channel for financial shock to transmit into real behaviour.

Chapter 2, by Cavoli, measures the bilateral real and financial integration for the Association of Southeast Asian Nations (ASEAN), plus the three countries of China, Korea and Japan. Based on macro-level data, several different measures of integration that incorporate real and financial dimensions are constructed. Using a multivariate approach, the chapter is able to investigate the individual measures that drive the overall level of regional integration.

The chapter attempts to address the following questions: Which countries are 'closest' to each other in terms of economic integration? Do different measures of integration produce different results in relation to these clusters or groups? The results of the chapter have several policy implications in terms of trade and financial-sector liberalization in Asia.

The study by Pontines and Parulian in Chapter 3 examines the factors that drive business-cycle synchronization (BCS) in the Asia-Pacific region. The chapter incorporates three main factors that figure prominently in the literature, namely, trade intensity, similarity of industrial structure and financial integration, with the emphasis on the impact of financial integration on BCS. The evidence is mostly for OECD or industrial countries, and little empirical work has been done in this part of the world. This chapter contributes to the literature in a number of ways. First, it uses quantity-based indicators of financial integration to ensure robustness in the results. Second, it exploits the availability for a number of years of survey-based data on portfolio investment from the Coordinated Portfolio Investment Survey gathered by the International Monetary Fund (IMF). Finally, we examine the impact of trade and financial linkages on BCS across a broad cross-section of Asian and Pacific countries.

Using a dynamic, panel-based, generalized method of moments (GMM) approach in order to control for biases associated with simultaneity and unobserved country-pair specific effects, the results agree with theoretical predictions from the benchmark international business-cycle models – greater financial integration leads to divergent BCS. This strongly suggests that, once such biases are accounted for, the prediction by theory regarding the inverse relationship between financial integration and BCS becomes evident, whereas the contrasting evidence of a positive relationship between financial integration and BCS found in previous empirical literature is overturned.

The chapter by Corbett and Maulana studies the degree of consumption risk sharing between East Asian countries. Using three easily measured variables – growth in aggregate output, change in net factor income and change in national saving – this chapter identifies the degree of consumption risk sharing between countries in East Asia using Penn World Table data for nine countries in East Asia. The results of the empirical analysis provide evidence that about 22 per cent of shocks to gross domestic product (GDP) are smoothed through the credit market channel, whereas the significance of the capital market is very marginal. Furthermore, they also found that around 75 per cent of shocks to GDP remain unsmoothed among the selected East Asian countries. Investment intensity calculation reiterates the observation that East Asian countries have not sufficiently utilized the consumption risk-sharing mechanism yet. Given these results, they argue that countries in the region may benefit from having an integrated financial system that could be used to increase consumption risk sharing.

Corbett and Twite examine the pattern of corporate financing choices in listed firms in the East Asian region. In particular, the chapter analyses the main drivers of debt, equity and maturity choices, and examines the effect of financing choices on the growth of firms' investment in tangible assets. The chapter contributes by creating a large database of financial data from the balance sheets of listed companies in East Asia and by considering the combined effects of firm factors, industry characteristics and country features in explaining firms' financial choices. The chapter also introduces a measure of financial openness into country characteristics to allow policy lessons to be drawn about financial opening. Their results indicate that East Asian firms have a distinctive financial pattern, depending heavily on external equity finance, and their choice of financial structure is determined by their own characteristics, their industry affiliation and their country characteristics. The growth of investment in tangible assets, however, is driven only by country characteristics, such as legal, institutional and financial market structures. They also suggest further extensions to derive the effect of more detailed, country-level policy variables and the interactions between financial market structures and policies to develop concrete policy advice.

The chapter by Thangavelu, Findlay and Chongvilaivan empirically investigates the effects of foreign ownership, financial constraints and other firm characteristics, using a micro panel of firms in Vietnam from 2002 to 2008. Taking into account the unobserved productivity shocks, unobserved firm heterogeneity and endogeneity of variables, among other relevant econometric issues, through the semi-parametric framework of Levinsohn and Petrin (2003), the empirical results indicate that firms with higher foreign ownership tend to exhibit higher total factor productivity (TFP). Financial constraints (e.g. low liquidity and limited access to external credit) appear to be a major threat to the productive performance of firms in the manufacturing industries in Vietnam. In particular, financial constraints appear to have a negative impact on a firm's productivity performance. The evidence also points to the presence of scale efficiency and the importance of high-tech- and human-capital accumulations for productivity enhancement.

The chapter by Onji, Gai and Corbett focuses on the lending sector channel of financial transmission. The fundamental question posed by the chapter is whether bank behaviour exaggerated the shock from the rest of the world in the GFC. Evidently, the global fall in demand for industrial products manufactured in East Asia was behind the declines in exports from Asia. Conventional wisdom also suggests that the financial sector in East Asia withstood the GFC relatively well (Pomerleano, 2009). The shock to the real sector is probably the main factor behind the decline, but, given the well-established body of literature linking financial shocks and loan supplies (e.g. Peek and Rosengren, 1997), one would suspect that the output decline in Asia after the Lehman Brother shock of September 2009 might have been amplified by the transmission of financial shocks into the real sector, even with a relatively healthy financial sector.

This chapter explores two possible channels: (1) direct holding of Lehman stock, and (2) reliance on the money market as a source of funding. Overall, the results indicate that the lending channel would have amplified the GFC shock in Asia, but to a limited degree. Understanding the regional diversity in the transmission channel of financial crisis is important in identifying the potential policy needs of the banking sector in East Asia.

The chapter by Thangavelu and Findlay studies the determinants of banks' efficiency in the South-East Asian countries of Indonesia, Malaysia, the Philippines, Singapore, Thailand and Vietnam. The study, which covers nearly 600 banks from 1994 to 2008, adopts the two-stage least square fixed-effects (FE2SLS) and two-stage least square random-effects estimators (RE2SLS) to address individual bank heterogeneity and endogeneity issues related to bank efficiency. It focuses on three key areas: (1) bank-specific activities such as off-balance-sheet activities of banks; (2) financial liberalization through foreign participation and ownership; and (3) impact of bank regulation and supervision. The results in the chapter indicate that off-balance-sheet activities tend to reduce bank efficiency. Foreign participation and ownership in the financial markets tend to increase bank efficiency. The results in the chapter indicate that bank regulation and supervision will be crucial to improve the efficiency of the banks and stability in the financial markets in South-East Asia.

The objective of the study by Siregar is to examine the role of trade financing in explaining recent slowdowns of export activities in Indonesia, Korea and Thailand. In general, the findings confirm the vital role of trade credit in shaping the export flows of these three economies during the past two decades. Nonetheless, the impacts of trade financing on export demand differ from one country to another. In particular, the experiences of the three countries appear to suggest that the more developed a country's financial sector, the more significant the role of trade financing is likely to be. As expected, the adverse consequences of falling trade credit for export performance were amplified during the financial crisis. This last finding highlights the importance of crisis contagion channels from the financial sector to the real sector of an economy.

The chapter by Siregar and Gunawan examines the impact of the GFC on the Indonesian export sector. Given the minimal empirical study of these important questions, this study examines the link between export credits and export performance. Despite the relatively strong economic landscape, Indonesia's export sector suffered a more severe decline during the recent GFC than in the 1997 Asian financial crisis. Has the Indonesian export sector been too dependent on export credit during the past two decades? In particular, did export financing contribute to the boom and bust of the two major export groups, namely manufacturing and minerals? Did the economic and financial crisis amplify the role of export credit in sustaining exports? Furthermore, is working capital more critical than investment capital in explaining the performance of Indonesia's exports?

With the availability of time series export credit data from the third quarter 1993 to the first quarter 2009 from Bank Indonesia, the study is in a unique position to look more comprehensively into the role of export financing to explain the performance of the export sector. The test results found robust evidence that export credit contributed to the boom and bust of the export sector in Indonesia. However, the results also suggest that the size of the contribution is modest at the most. The significance of export credit has indeed magnified during the crisis. Furthermore, it is short-term financing, not investment capital, that has been detrimental to the performance of the export sector in Indonesia. Similar conclusions are reported when we examine the two largest export groups in the country.

Two traditional determinants of export demand remain the most significant contributing factors, namely income and price factors. The slump of the economies of its major trading partners weakened demand for Indonesia's exports. Finally, the country's exports have been highly sensitive to the uncertainties and volatilities in the price of major commodities in the world market.

There are several policy implications arising from the studies. There are substantial gains from further financial integration in the region. Greater openness and more integrated financial markets allow the region to smooth out consumption and income fluctuations. However, greater openness also increases the transmission of shocks from the rest of the world to the region. The studies also highlight that well-regulated, risk-managed financial markets are able to diversify the risk and contain the external shocks in the region.

The studies also highlight that the degree of integration will depend on the quality of the institutions in the region. There is great diversity in the quality of the institutions, and this affects the ability of the region to smooth out and diversify the shocks from the rest of the world. Thus, priority should be paid to creating better institutional quality in the region. Regional and trade cooperation will be crucial to create and deepen institutional quality and coordination in the region.

Several chapters in the book have identified the linkages between financial markets and real activities in the region. The linkages are also stronger and significant in open economies that rely on external markets for growth. Understanding of the linkages between financial markets and real activities will be very important to manage external shocks and to mitigate their effects on real activities in the domestic economy. Identifying the linkages and developing appropriate policy will be crucial to sustain economic growth in the region.

Acknowledgements

We would like to thank Economic Research Institute for ASEAN and East Asia (ERIA) for its financial support for this project. The papers were presented at the ERIA Workshop Programme, 'Linkages between Real and Financial Aspects of Economic Integration in East Asia', Singapore, 28 February 2010.

Notes

1 Corresponding author: Department of Economics, National University of Singapore, AS2 Arts Link 1, Singapore 117570. Tel: +65–6516–6835; email address: ecssmt@nus.edu.sg.
2 Institute of Southeast Asian Studies (ISEAS), 30 Heng Mui Keng Terrace, Singapore 119614. Tel: +65–6870–4509; email address: aekapol@iseas.edu.sg.

References

Levinsohn, J. and Petrin, A. (2003) 'Estimating production functions using inputs to control for unobservables', *The Review of Economic Studies*, 70: 317–41.
Peek, J. and Rosengren, E.S. (1997) 'The international transmission of financial shocks: the case of Japan', *American Economic Review*, 87(4): 495–505.
Pomerleano, M. (2009) 'What is the impact of the global financial crisis on the banking system in East Asia?', ADBI Working Paper Series, no. 146.

2 Regional economic integration among ASEAN, China, Japan and Korea

A simple multivariate examination

Tony Cavoli
School of Commerce and Centre for Asian Business, University of South Australia

Introduction

A commonly asked question in the area of international trade and finance is: What is the extent of economic integration in East and South-East Asia? The reasons for this question are multifarious. For instance, there is increasing evidence that real and financial integration (as subsets of 'economic' integration) are closely connected; it is plausible to consider a situation where trade integration is associated with more synchronous business cycles, together producing spillovers that facilitate the prospects for monetary integration (see Frankel and Rose, 1998). Monetary integration itself is rooted in the preconditions pertaining to integration and is well documented in the optimal currency area (OCA) literature. Furthermore, some political economy considerations can be either the cause or the effect of greater real and financial integration.

This chapter seeks to employ various measures of bilateral real and financial integration for the ASEAN Plus3 countries[1] for two reasons. First, no single measure of real or financial integration sufficiently captures all of the salient characteristics of the extent of integration between the economies in East and South-East Asia. Second, no single measure is able to pinpoint the particular aspects of integration that drive the overall degree of closeness between individual economies and economies within particular regional groups.

Measuring the extent of integration through individual metrics is not new and is only one of many methods employed to measure the degree of real and financial integration (see Cavoli and Rajan, 2009, and, for a recent treatment, Kim and Lee, 2008). Real integration measures include BCS (see Imbs, 2006) and trade openness, as well as relative purchasing power parity (PPP) (see Alba and Papell, 2007; Barumshah *et al.*, 2007; Kim *et al.*, 2009; and Liew *et al.*, 2009, for recent contributions to measuring PPP). On the other hand, financial-integration measures can be divided into arbitrage conditions such as uncovered interest parity (UIP) (see Chinn, 2006; Goh *et al.*, 2006; Alper *et al.* 2009), asset market correlations (see Chi *et al.*, 2006), quantity measures using flows data (Lane and Milesi-Ferretti, 2001), macroeconomic measures such as savings/investment correlations and consumption correlations (Kim and Lee, 2008) and many more.

Attempts have been made to find a multivariate measure of integration. Takagi and Hirose (2004) and de Brouwer (1999) have employed techniques to combine various measures of financial integration and reduce them to one measure. Chinn and Ito (2008) have also created an index of capital mobility. The advantages of these techniques are: first, they capture the breadth of available measures of integration for the sample of country pairs considered – information is simply not lost by virtue of the non-employment of a measure – and, second, the index and all the information contained within can be assessed over time.

This chapter also seeks to calculate the extent of 'overall' integration in the region. The objective here is to employ data that are readily available and to construct several measures of integration that incorporate the real and financial dimensions. By employing our multivariate approach to this problem, we are able to investigate which individual measure drives the overall level of integration. Although each measure may not be perfect and the list of measures adopted here may not be exhaustive, there is much value in gaining information about the stylized facts of integration in Asia and providing insights into the nature of integration in the region, as this information and these insights have significant implications for policies of trade and finance liberalization. This chapter also intends to measure the extent of integration between a country and a set of other countries in the cluster or region. The questions we seek to answer here are: Which countries are 'closest' to each other in terms of economic integration? Do different measures of integration produce different results in relation to these clusters or groups?

By examining different measures, we hope to provide a broad perspective of real and financial integration in the Asian region – a perspective that is currently lacking in the literature owing to an extensive focus by researchers on refining individual measures rather than examining their interactions. The information we gather that can inform policies include: insights into the suitability of a number of political instruments of integration (trade agreements vs investment accords, removal of controls over FDI flows vs portfolio vs bank flows, and so on), as well as information on whether the 'closeness' of the region justifies the setting up of OCAs and a possible monetary union in Asia. This chapter is structured as follows: the next section outlines the data sources, defines each of the measures of integration employed in this study and sets out the methodology under which integration is calculated. The third section presents the results for bilateral levels of integration, as well as each country's level of integration with regional groups. It also presents two methods for deriving an overall integration metric. Section 4 gives the conclusion.

Data and methodology

We employ four measures in this study. Two measures are essentially quantity based – business-cycle correlations and trade openness – and the other two are price based, namely deviations from relative PPP and deviations from UIP. As these measures are simple, easily comprehensible and (in the case of the parity conditions) underpinned by economic intuition about agent behaviour, they lend themselves appropriately as ways to ascertain the degree of integration between countries and regions. We briefly describe each measure below.

The first is a measure of BCS measured by the correlations of GDP growth between country i and country/region j[2] and is given by Equation (2.1):

$$BCS(ij) = \rho_{GDPi,GDPj} \tag{2.1}$$

where $GDPi$ is the annual growth rate of GDP for country i. $BCS(ij)$ is calculated from twelve monthly observations. A higher correlation implies greater integration, suggesting that the particular pair of countries react in the same way to common shocks. The OCA literature has emphasized the importance of high BCS in signalling the plausibility of a regional zone of fixed exchange rates.

The second measure is the deviation from relative PPP (RPPD) between country i and country/region j. This is given by:

$$RPPD(ij) = ABS(\Delta e_t^{d/f} + \pi_t^f - \pi_t^d) \tag{2.2}$$

where e_t is the nominal exchange rate at time t and $\pi_t^f(\pi_t^d)$ refers to the foreign (domestic) inflation rate at time t. A smaller value implies greater integration, as the law of one price with respect to goods prices is more likely to hold.

Trade openness or intensity (TI) between country i and country/region j is given by:

$$TI(ij) = T_{ij}/T_{ALL} \tag{2.3}$$

where T_{ij} is the trade (exports plus imports) between country i and j, and T_{ALL} is all trade recorded for each country pair within the sample examined (not double counted). A higher value means greater integration, as it implies that trade between the country/region pair examined occupies a greater share of total trade in the region.

The last measure, deviations from uncovered (money market rates) interest parity (UID) between country i and country/region j, is measured by:

$$UID(ij) = ABS(i_t^d - i_t^f - \Delta e_{t+1}{}^{d/f}) \tag{2.4}$$

where i_t^d *and* i_t^f refer to domestic and foreign interest rates, respectively. A lower value implies greater integration between two countries or regions, as the law of one price with respect to financial assets is more likely to apply.

The objective is to use data that are readily and publicly available, so as to show the ease with which the overall measures can be calculated. The main data source is the international integration statistics database of the Asian Development Bank's (ADB) Asia Recovery Integration Center.[3] The data used to calculate the UID and RPPD measures are from the IMF's *International Financial Statistics*. This sample consists of data from 2000–9, and measures are bilateral in order to assess integration between country pairs as well as between countries and predetermined groups. The groups that one might initially consider would be ASEAN-5 – Indonesia, Malaysia, the Philippines, Singapore and Thailand; the more recent members, the so-called New ASEAN – Brunei, Cambodia, Lao PDR, Myanmar and Vietnam; and the larger regional economies, known as Plus3 – China, Japan and Korea. The availability of data is such that all countries in the sample are represented in the four measures: BCS, RPPD, UID and TI. Seven measures are presented for the ASEAN-5 and the Plus3 nations, indicating that the more established nations in terms of development are able to report more comprehensively on integration.

We use the measures as follows. For instance, if we want to measure the extent of Indonesia's integration with Malaysia, we estimate the measures individually between the two countries. If we want to measure the extent of Indonesia's integration with a regional group such as the Plus3, we calculate the measures individually between Indonesia and each country in the Plus3 and then average them. Hence, Indonesia's level of integration with the Plus3, measured using UID, equals the average of the UID between Indonesia and China plus the UID between Indonesia and Japan plus the UID between Indonesia and Korea. To derive the level of integration between a particular country and the region of which it is a member, the country is left out of the regional group.

Once we have analysed the individual measures of integration, we can create a measure of 'overall' integration. We do this in two ways. First, we impose cumulative normal distributions on all of the measures such that they map on to the same distribution. The normalized individual measures are then summed to create an overall measure.[4] The second method is to reduce the raw individual measures of integration to a single measure by employing principal components analysis. Given the data considerations outlined above, two composite measures of integration are presented for the normalized metric and the principle components score, one using the four individual measures for the whole sample, and the other using all seven measures for the ASEAN-5 and Plus3 sample. The next section presents the results.

Results

Bilateral integration and regional groupings

This section is divided broadly into two parts. The first examines the extent (or level) of bilateral integration by calculating the level of integration under each individual measure. The second part examines how each country is integrated into a number of regional groupings.

Bilateral integration measures by type

Table 2.1 presents the extent of bilateral integration for each measure with potentially interesting results highlighted. From Table 2.1a, we can see that the level of BCS is high for Malaysia/Philippines and for Singapore/Thailand.

Table 2.1a Business-cycle synchronization

	BR	*CA*	*PRC*	*ID*	*JP*	*KR*	*LAO*	*MA*	*MY*	*PH*	*SG*	*TH*	*VT*
BR													
CA	−0.08												
PRC	−0.16	0.62											
ID	−0.60	0.41	0.78										
JP	0.23	0.66	0.38	0.33									
KR	0.51	−0.06	0.01	0.07	0.71								
LAO	−0.11	0.38	0.79	0.77	0.21	−0.04							
MA	−0.14	0.40	0.57	0.60	0.85	0.64	0.78						
MY	−0.11	0.42	−0.03	0.33	0.66	−0.01	0.17	0.63					
PH	−0.10	0.48	0.59	0.65	0.86	0.61	0.60	0.94	0.49				
SG	0.06	0.64	0.55	0.61	0.84	0.63	0.58	0.88	0.63	0.95			
TH	0.33	0.33	0.32	0.25	0.89	0.58	0.32	0.91	0.68	0.82	0.75		
VT	0.05	0.89	0.74	0.47	0.83	0.40	0.56	0.78	0.13	0.76	0.76	0.74	

Source: Author's calculations

Table 2.1b RPPD deviations

	BR	*CA*	*PRC*	*ID*	*JP*	*KR*	*LAO*	*MA*	*MY*	*PH*	*SG*	*TH*	*VT*
BR													
CA	0.092												
CH	0.132	0.417											
ID	0.332	0.007	0.798										
JP	0.236	0.321	0.251	0.313									
KR	0.366	0.021	0.558	0.207	0.105								
LA	0.285	0.179	0.462	0.139	0.675	0.263							
MA	0.124	0.11	0.304	0.107	0.205	0.069	0.271						
MY	1.685	1.382	0.275	1.504	1.677	1.699	1.278	1.512					
PH	0.014	0.091	0.485	0.084	0.229	0.123	0.287	0.023	1.515				
SG	0.035	0.131	0.255	0.123	0.189	0.084	0.305	0.015	1.524	0.039			
TH	0.029	0.062	0.272	0.054	0.258	0.118	0.223	0.049	1.512	0.029	0.069		
VT	0.131	0.074	0.513	0.126	0.317	0.345	0.198	0.171	1.345	0.135	0.177	0.122	

Source: Author's calculations

The BCS for Japan/Philippines and Japan/Thailand are also high. The RPPDs in Table 2.1b also revealed a high level of integration (low RPPD) for pairings involving Malaysia and the Philippines. The same is found for the UIDs in Table 2.1d.

We observe that, for the quantity-based measure, TI, higher levels of integration occur in the larger economies of Japan, China and Korea, possibly

Table 2.1c Trade intensity (per cent)

	BR	*CA*	*PRC*	*ID*	*JP*	*KR*	*LAO*	*MA*	*MY*	*PH*	*SG*	*TH*	*VT*
BR													
CA	0.016												
PRC	0.035	0.041											
ID	0.119	0.012	1.880										
JP	0.320	0.015	23.079	3.738									
KR	0.113	0.014	12.762	1.425	9.073								
LAO	0.000	0.017	0.023	0.000	0.005	0.005							
MA	0.054	0.010	3.343	0.962	4.116	1.434	0.002						
MY	0.000	–0.002	0.188	0.020	0.047	0.037	0.000	0.046					
PH	0.002	0.002	1.447	0.201	2.155	0.697	0.000	0.584	0.001				
SG	0.077	0.069	3.258	1.513	4.300	1.312	0.076	3.161	0.216	0.707			
TH	0.049	0.070	2.650	0.747	4.911	0.832	0.151	1.623	0.314	0.457	0.832		
VT	0.000	0.050	1.181	0.185	1.090	0.614	0.029	0.306	0.007	0.128	0.640	0.403	

Source: Author's calculations

Table 2.1d UID deviations

	BR	*CA*	*PRC*	*ID*	*JP*	*KR*	*LAO*	*MA*	*MY*	*PH*	*SG*	*TH*	*VT*
BR													
CA	0.149												
PRC	0.299	0.279											
ID	0.108	0.233	0.046										
JP	0.073	0.092	0.347	0.326									
KR	0.111	0.044	0.181	0.188	0.166								
LAO	1.326	1.545	1.247	1.159	1.703	1.238							
MA	0.084	0.147	0.136	0.06	0.155	0.114	1.3						
MY	0.699	0.766	0.484	0.603	0.848	0.795	0.678	0.647					
PH	0.599	0.319	0.04	0.086	0.412	0.275	1.149	0.193	0.448				
SG	0.086	0.092	0.162	0.14	0.185	0.018	1.333	0.039	0.685	0.227			
TH	0.196	0.144	0.163	0.138	0.184	0.018	1.387	0.035	0.676	0.224	0.001		
VT	0.131	0.007	0.117	0.011	0.204	0.222	1.401	0.015	0.593	0.163	0.082	0.091	

Source: Author's calculations

emphasizing the importance of size for trade flows. We can see this effect most emphatically in the case of TI in Table 2.1c for the Japan–China, Japan–Korea and China–Korea pairings.

Figure 2.1a presents the extent of integration (by each measure) of each country with a pre-determined grouping of countries. The results here confirm the patterns mentioned above; that Malaysia, Singapore and Thailand are among

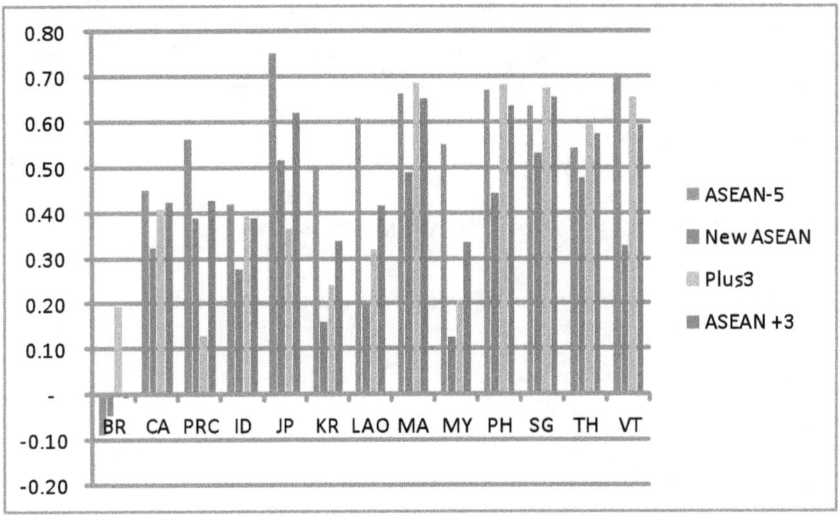

Figure 2.1a Regional integration by type: Business-cycle correlation (per cent)

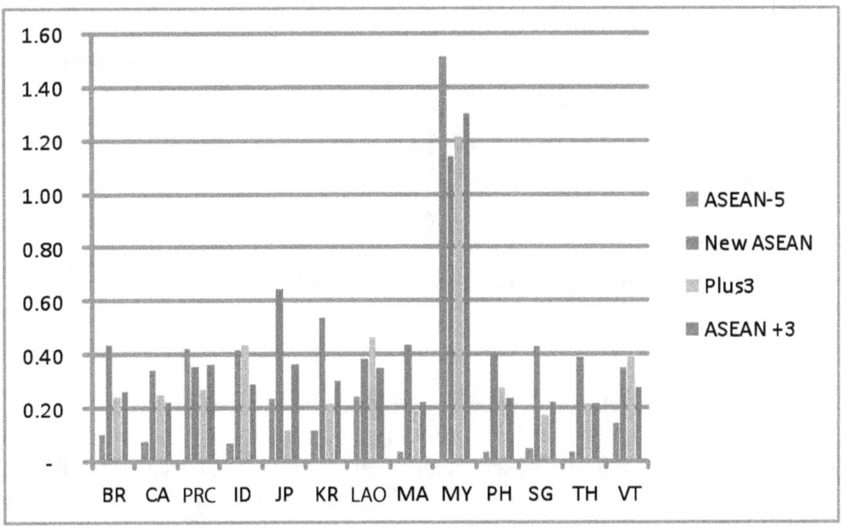

Figure 2.1b Regional integration by type: RPPD deviations

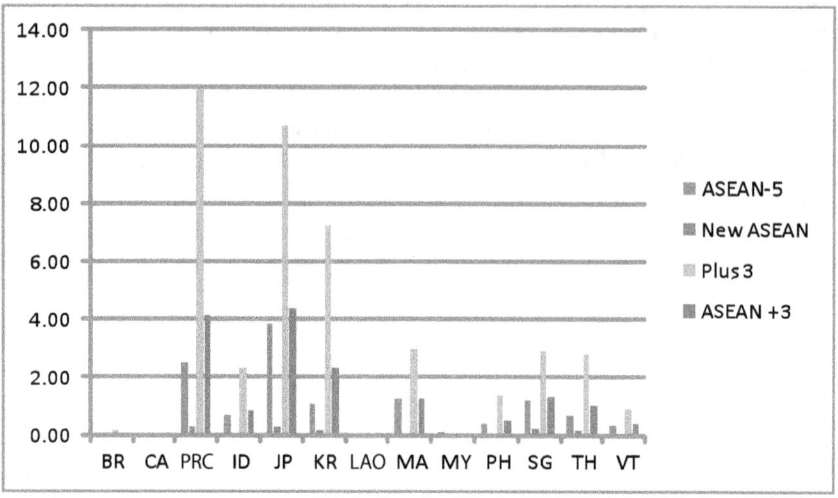

Figure 2.1c Regional integration by type: Trade intensity (per cent)

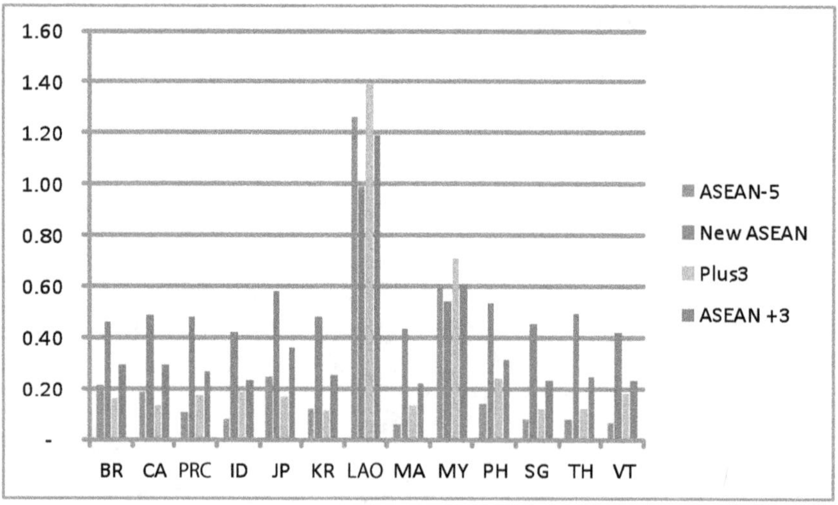

Figure 2.1d Regional integration by type: UID deviations

the most integrated when one observes the price-based measures (RPPD, UID) as given in Figures 2.1b and 2.1d, while the larger regional economies exhibit higher integration when one observes the quantity measure TI, as given in Figure 2.1c. Furthermore, across all measures, Figure 2.1 (a–d) shows that the new ASEAN nations are among the least integrated generally, both in terms of the extent of integration with each other and with the other groupings in the sample.

Normalized overall measure of integration

Using the next set of results, we attempt to use all of the available measures to return an overall measure of integration that captures both real and financial dimensions. This helps us to pinpoint the individual measure driving the overall level of integration and, in doing so, address the question of the possible sources of integration between countries in the region. Each measure of integration against the defined regional groupings has been normalized to a value between 0 and 1, where 0 = least integrated and 1 = most integrated. The UID and RPPD measures were inverted such that a larger value now implies more integration. Each value is then simply summed to present an overall measure of integration for each country against the regional groupings. The benefit of this exercise is that it removes any issue of the scaling of individual measures, as each metric is scaled from 0 to 1. As such, we can examine where each, individual measure is in a cumulative normal distribution, thus facilitating comparisons.

Figure 2.2 presents the results for overall integration where four measures are used. By construction, each normalized individual measure of integration shows the position it assumes in the distribution. As such, the larger the segment in each column graph relating to a particular measure, the more that measure contributes to the total.

Generally speaking, we observe that no one individual measure dominates the total measure, although the equity market correlation and BCS are quite influential for the original ASEAN nations, and the effect of UID seems to be generally greater than that of RPPD. From Figure 2.2, it can be seen that Singapore and Japan remain the most integrated economies in the sample, and this result occurs irrespective of which groupings these countries are measured against. We also see two interesting results in Figure 2.2. First, Malaysia's level of overall integration is higher under this measure, possibly indicating the importance of BCS, RPPD, UID and TI for that country. Second, for the New ASEAN nations, it can be seen that Vietnam and Cambodia are the most integrated, but these levels are significantly lower than those for the ASEAN-5 and Plus3 countries.

Principle components analysis

We compute the principal components of the estimated (Spearman rank-order) correlation matrix of our series of measures, and display our results in Table 2.2 and Figure 2.3. Principal components analysis models the variance structure of a set of observed variables using linear combinations of the variables. It is essentially an optimization algorithm that selects the optimal weights in a linear combination such that the variance of the linear combination is maximized (see Johnson and Wichern, 1992, for more information). These linear combinations or components can be used in subsequent analysis, and the combination coefficients or loadings can be used in interpreting the components. Principal components analysis was used to act as a robustness test for the above measures of (normalized) integration and to augment them, as they are not subject to any formal statistical testing.

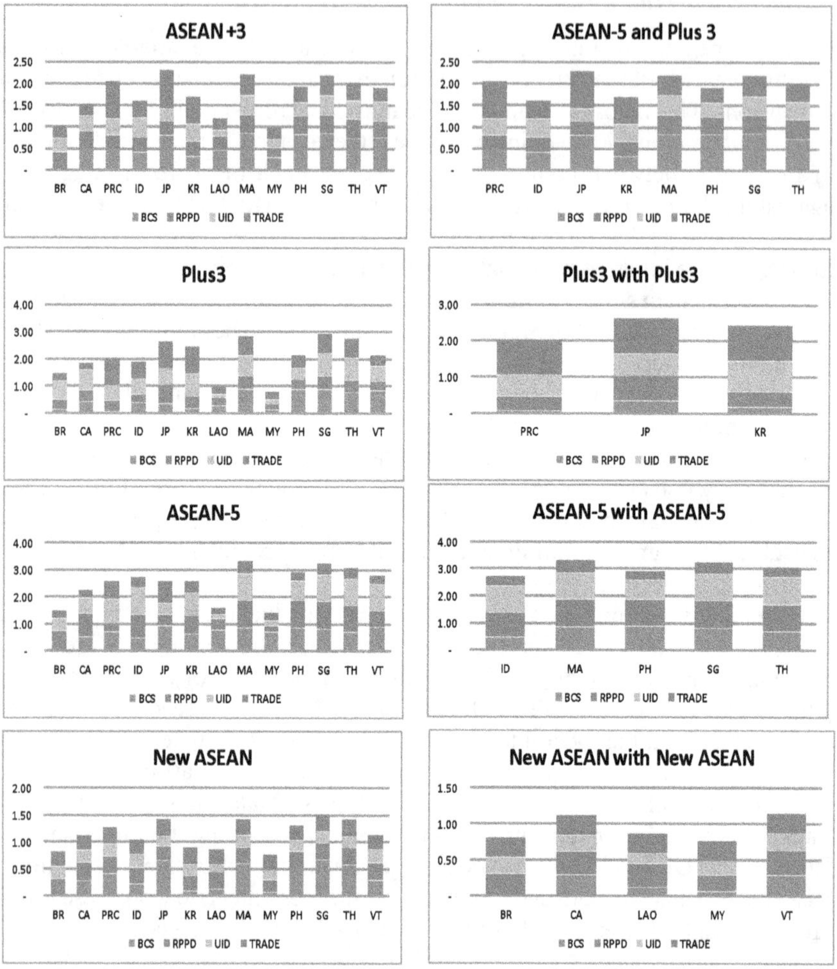

Figure 2.2 Overall integration

Source: Author's calculations

The first panel of Table 2.2 shows that the first principal component explains 48 per cent of the total variation in the data. The second panel shows that each variable is (reasonably) similarly weighted in the first component, but the component shows some differences between the price measures UID and RPPD and the others in explaining the variation in the second component.

Figure 2.3 shows the level of overall integration of each nation against country groupings. As with the normalized results, a larger number implies higher integration. An obvious result is that the Plus3 nations are much less integrated than the ASEAN-5 countries and, surprisingly, much less integrated than suggested in the earlier tests, particularly the normalized measures.

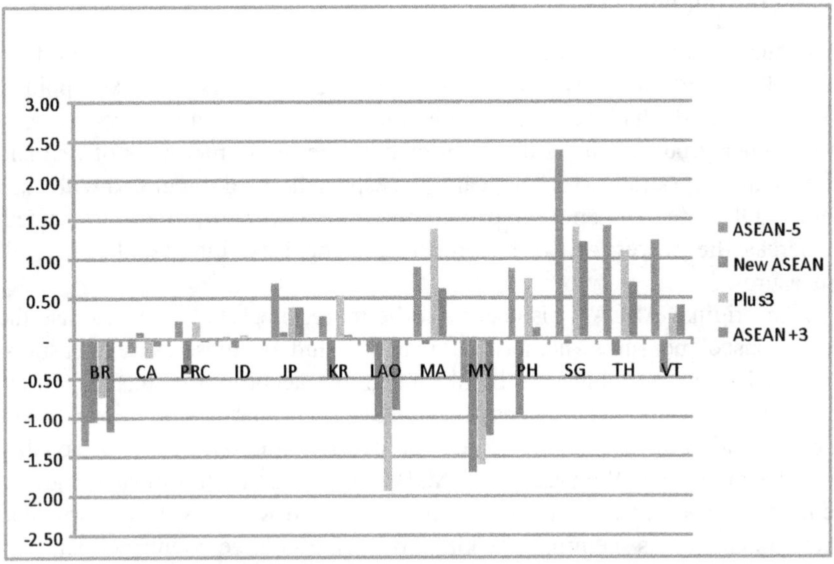

Figure 2.3 Overall integration using principal components score (BCS, UID, RPPD, trade)

Source: Author's calculations

Table 2.2 Principal components analysis (using BCS, UID, RPPD, trade)

Eigenvalues: (sum = 4, average = 1)					
Number	*Value*	*Difference*	*Proportion*	*Cum value*	*Cum prop*
1.00	1.95	0.95	0.49	1.95	0.49
2.00	1.00	0.33	0.25	2.95	0.74
3.00	0.67	0.28	0.17	3.61	0.90
4.00	0.39	—	0.10	4.00	1.00
Eigenvectors (loadings):					
Variable	*PC 1*	*PC 2*	*PC 3*	*PC 4*	
BCS	0.43	0.58	0.65	–0.25	
RPPD	0.44	–0.65	0.45	0.43	
TR	0.54	0.39	–0.49	0.56	
UID	0.58	–0.30	–0.37	–0.66	

Source: Author's calculations

Concluding remarks

Our analysis of the extent of real versus financial market integration finds that, overall, the original ASEAN nations – Indonesia, Malaysia, the Philippines, Singapore and Thailand – seem to be more integrated with the rest of Asia than other groups. This is the case for both the broad measures of real and financial integration, which appear to be especially well integrated with each other. Of these, Singapore and Malaysia appear to be the most connected, whereas the newer ASEAN members are the least integrated across all measures.

The original ASEAN also seems to be more integrated when we use the price-based measures, namely UID, RPPD and business-cycle measures. Japan, Korea and China are highly integrated according to the real (trade intensity) measure that is ostensibly quantity based. The principal components scores and the normalized scores for overall integration are reasonably consistent, in that Singapore and Malaysia emerge as the most integrated countries. The scores differ for China, Japan and Korea, with the principal component scores seemingly picking up more of a large country effect.

What are the policy implications of this analysis? The first is that the measures of integration appear to be more consistently spread for the original ASEAN members, whereas the Plus3 countries seem to be integrated more outside its group and mainly through trade integration. As such, it might be argued that liberalization policies may be more flexibly applied to more facets of integration in the original ASEAN than other groups. That said, the ASEAN-5 nations appear to have more financial than real integration – suggesting the possible success of policies for financial integration. Finally, the results suggest that the ASEAN-5 is the most integrated group and is thus the most suitable for further integration in an OCA.

Notes

1 This chapter draws on work by the author as part of the project entitled 'Achieving sustainable growth in Asia' for the ERIA.
2 'S' for synchronicity.
3 See: http://aric.adb.org/ (accessed 8 June 2012).
4 One can take averages rather than sums, but, for the purposes of creating a comparison between measures, the effect is much the same.

References

Alba, J.D. and Papell, D.H. (2007) 'Purchasing power parity and country characteristics: evidence from panel data tests', *Journal of Development Economics*, 83: 240–51.

Alper, C.E., Ardic, O.P. and Fendoglu, S. (2009) 'The economics of uncovered interest parity condition for emerging markets: a survey', *Journal of Economic Surveys*, 23(1): 115–38.

Barumshah, A.Z., Chan, T.-H. and Fountas, S. (2007) 'Re-examining purchasing power parity for East Asian countries: 1976–2002', *Applied Financial Economics*, 18(1): 75–85.

Cavoli, T. and Rajan, R.S. (2009) *Exchange Rate Regimes and Macroeconomic Management in Asia*, Hong Kong: Hong Kong University Press.

Chi, J., Li, K. and Toung, M.R. (2006) 'Financial integration in East Asian equity markets', *Pacific Economic Review*, 11: 513–26.

Chinn, M.D. (2006) 'The (partial) rehabilitation of interest rate parity in the floating rate era: longer horizons, alternative expectations, and emerging markets', *Journal of International Money and Finance*, 25: 7–21.

Chinn, M.D. and Ito, H. (2008) 'A new measure of financial openness', *Journal of Comparative Policy Analysis*, 10(3): 309–22.

de Brouwer, G. (1999) *Financial Integration in East Asia*, Cambridge: Cambridge University Press.

Frankel, J. and Rose, A. (1998) 'The endogeneity of optimum currency area criteria', *Economic Journal*, 108: 1009–25.

Goh, K.G., Lim, G.C. and Olekalns, N. (2006) 'Deviations for uncovered interest parity in Malaysia', *Applied Financial Economics*, 16: 745–59.

Imbs, J. (2006) 'The real effects of financial integration', *Journal of International Economics*, 68: 296–324.

Johnson, R.A. and Wichern, D.W. (1992) *Applied Multivariate Statistical Analysis* (3rd Edition), Upper Saddle River, New Jersey: Prentice Hall.

Kim, B.-H., Kim, H.-K. and Oh, K.-Y. (2009) 'The purchasing power parity of Southeast Asian countries: a time-varying coefficient approach', *Economic Modelling*, 26: 96–106.

Kim, S. and Lee, J.-W. (2008) 'Real and financial integration in East Asia', ADB Working Paper on Regional Economic Integration, no. 17.

Lane, P.R. and Milesi-Ferretti, G.M. (2001) 'The external wealth of nations: measures of foreign assets and liabilities for industrial and developing countries', *Journal of International Economics*, 55: 263–94.

Liew, V.K.-S., Lee, H.-A. and Lim, K.-P. (2009) 'Purchasing power parity in Asian economies: further evidence from rank tests for cointegration', *Applied Economic Letters*, 16: 51–4.

Takagi, S. and Hirose, K. (2004) 'A multivariate approach to financially integrated economies', in *Exchange Rate Regimes in East Asia*, eds M. Kawai and G. De Brouwer, New York: Routledge.

3 The nexus between business-cycle synchronization and financial integration in the Asia-Pacific region

Victor Pontines
Flinders Business School, Flinders University

Friska Parulian
Strategic Review and Policy Department, International Monetary Fund[1]

Introduction

The dramatic global economic downturn that accompanied the global economic crisis of 2007–9 has been emphatically ascribed to the strong growth of openness in trade and finance and was facilitated by the significant improvements in transportation and communication in past decades. The impression has been that globalization is an unavoidable force that makes sovereign nations and countries become increasingly 'borderless', or operate in sync as a single global market. This can lead countries to be tied together in various phases of the economic cycles over time. It is not difficult for one to think that greater trade and financial linkages would lead to tighter business cycles, instead of their being divergent or asynchronous. A perfunctory inspection of the data would indeed suggest so (Lane and Milesi-Ferretti, 2004, 2007).

However, theoretical predictions suggest that trade and financial linkages can influence BCS either way. For example, standard international-business-cycle theories predict that greater financial integration should lead to a lower degree of BCS, whereas models of financial contagion, such as Allen and Gale's (2000), show how international financial integration can lead to financial panic and thus to synchronized business cycles. Although the question is therefore an empirical one, the current empirical literature does not provide much direction, as it fails to find a robust and systematic relationship. Pure cross-sectional studies, for instance, find a significantly positive relationship between financial integration and BCS, e.g. Imbs (2004, 2006). However, recent studies using panel data show a strong negative effect, e.g. Cerqueira and Martins (2009) and Kalemli-Ozcan *et al.* (2009), and thus are in conformity with the basic ideas of standard international-business-cycle theories.

This chapter contributes to the empirical literature in a number of ways. First, we take the pragmatic approach of using quantity-based indicators of financial integration to ensure robustness in our results. This is important, as the lack of mandatory reporting of actual bilateral information on foreign direct investment (FDI) and portfolio investment data, which limits many previous studies (including ours), makes this a sensible and logical strategy.[2] Second, in view of the data limitation just mentioned, we exploit the availability for a number of years of survey-based data on portfolio investment from the Coordinated Portfolio Investment Survey (CPIS) gathered by the IMF. To the best of our knowledge, no study employs this dataset to ascertain the direction of the BCS–finance link in a panel context. Third, as we are using panel data, we adopt a panel-based GMM approach in our estimation. We believe that this technique gives us two important advantages as compared with previous approaches, namely controlling for biases associated with simultaneity and unobserved country-pair-specific effects. Finally, we examine the impact of trade and financial linkages on BCS across a broad cross-section of Asian and Pacific countries. The evidence is mostly for OECD or industrial countries, and little empirical work has been done in this part of the world. Previous empirical works by Park and Shin (2009) and Shin and Sohn (2006) find either a negligible or an insignificant effect of financial integration on BCS.[3]

Our results agree with the benchmark standard international-business-cycle models. This strongly suggests that controlling for biases associated with simultaneity, let alone unobserved country-pair heterogeneity, using a panel-based (instrumental-variable) IV estimator is crucial in unravelling the contrasting evidence found in the empirical literature. In a pure cross-sectional IV regression, any unobserved, time-invariant, country-pair-specific effects would be part of the error term, leading to biased estimates of the coefficients. As such, previous studies that examine the direction of the BCS–finance link using pure cross-sectional data are afflicted by this problem. Once biases associated with simultaneity and unobserved country-pair-specific factors are accounted for, the theoretical prediction regarding the inverse relationship between financial linkages and BCS becomes apparent in the results.

The rest of the chapter is structured as follows. The next section reviews the literature on the relationship between financial integration and BCS. The third section describes the data and the measures used for each of the variables, followed by a section describing the estimation strategy, one presenting the empirical results and the conclusion.

Literature background

Financial integration has been argued to affect BCS, but whether it should lead to tighter or synchronized business cycles is unclear. Standard international macro theories predict that greater financial integration should lead to a lower degree of BCS. As shown by Backus *et al.* (1992) and Baxter and Crucini (1995), in a two-country general equilibrium model with complete financial markets, a country hit by a positive productivity shock receives capital from the other country, resulting in a negative output correlation between the two. Similarly, Backus *et al.* (1994) document that complete markets result in negatively correlated GDP, because an economy hit by a positive technology shock will attract capital flows away from the no-shock economy.

However, surprisingly, the empirical evidence is still mixed as to the relationship between financial integration and business-cycle correlation. In a pure cross-sectional context, studies find a significantly positive relationship between financial integration and BCS. Using a system of simultaneous equations, Imbs (2004) finds evidence that economic regions with strong financial links are significantly more synchronized. Employing the same approach but using the 2001 CPIS gathered by the IMF, Imbs (2006) finds similar results. Kose *et al.* (2003), using a cross-country sample of seventy-six countries – twenty-one industrial and fifty-five developing – find evidence that financially open developing economies have synchronized cycles with the core rich G7 countries over the period 1960–99. Finally, Kose *et al.* (2008a) and Kose *et al.* (2008b) find the same results with a dynamic latent factor model.

A notable exception that documents a negative relationship between financial integration and BCS in a pure cross-section context is by Garcia-Herrero and Ruiz (2008). Using actual bilateral financial flows from Spain, these authors estimate a system of simultaneous equations and find that greater financial integration leads to divergent BCS.

Although one can reconcile these studies that find a positive relationship between financial integration and BCS based on models of financial contagion, such as Allen and Gale's (2000), which show how international financial integration can lead to financial panic and thus to synchronized business cycles, these studies conflict with the benchmark international-business-cycle models discussed above.

Although some cross-country studies consistently find a positive effect of financial integration on BCS, some recent studies using panel data show a robust negative effect and thus are in conformity with the basic ideas of standard theories. For instance, using panel three-stage least squares estimation for fifteen OECD countries, from 1984 to 2003, Xing and Abbott (2007) find that economic regions with strong financial links are significantly less synchronized. Using GMM methods for twenty OECD countries, from 1970 to 2002, Cerqueira and Martins (2009) also find a negative and significant effect of financial integration on BCS. Using data for eight Asian countries – ASEAN-5 (Indonesia, Malaysia, the Philippines, Singapore and Thailand), plus three additional members in East Asia (China, Japan and Korea) – Lee and Azali (2010) also find a similar, significantly negative effect. Finally, Kalemli-Ozcan *et al.* (2009), using a rich panel-data structure on banks' international bilateral exposure over the past three decades, across twenty developed countries, show that once country-pair and time-fixed effects are controlled for, a higher degree of cross-border financial integration leads to less synchronized, more divergent business cycles.

Data and measurement

In order to examine empirically the effect of financial linkages, as well as the effect of two other channels – trade linkages and similarity in industrial structure – on BCS, we estimate the following equation:

$$\rho_{ij,t} = \alpha_0 + \alpha_1 \rho_{ij,t-1} + \beta_1 T_{ij,t} + \beta_2 S_{ij,t} + \beta_3 F_{ij,t} + \upsilon_{ij,t} \tag{3.1}$$

where *i, j* represents country pair *i* and *j*; $\rho_{ij,t}$ denotes the business-cycle correlation or synchronization (BCS) between countries *i* and *j*; $\rho_{ij,t-1}$ is the lagged BCS between countries *i* and *j*; $T_{ij,t}$ is a measure of bilateral trade intensity; $S_{ij,t}$ is an index of the similarity of the industrial structure between countries *i* and *j*; and $F_{ij,t}$ is a measure of financial integration between countries *i* and *j*. In Equation (3.1), we assume that $\rho_{ij,t}$ contains the following two effects: (a) the unobserved time-invariant, country-pair-specific effect, $\eta_{ij,}$, and (b) a stochastic error term $\varepsilon_{ij,t}$, varying across time and cross-section.

We adopt a panel approach over the period 1980–2007. To acquire a meaningful measure of business-cycle correlation, as well as to purge any possible cyclical effects on the variables, the twenty-eight years have been split into sub-periods of four years each.[4] Our strategy of investigation assumes that countries in the Asia-Pacific region integrate within the region as well as with two major economic blocs – the United States and the EU-14. The EU bloc includes Austria, Belgium, Denmark, Finland, France, Germany, Greece, Ireland, Italy, the Netherlands, Portugal, Spain, Sweden and the United Kingdom. The Asia-Pacific bloc comprises China, Hong Kong, India, Indonesia, Japan, Korea, Malaysia, the Philippines, Singapore, Taiwan, Thailand, Australia and New Zealand.

The business-cycle correlations refer to the Pearson correlation of the cyclical component of annual real GDP, expressed in US dollars, between countries *i* and *j* over the relevant sub-periods. The cyclical components of GDP are computed in two ways after taking the natural logarithms of real GDP: using (a) the Hodrick–Prescott (HP) filter and (b) the Baxter–King (BK) band-pass filter.[5]

Two different measures of bilateral trade intensity will be considered. The first is a standard measure used in many recent studies, for instance, Clark and van Wincoop (2001), Frankel and Rose (1997, 1998) and Imbs (2004), among others, and is calculated as:

$$T^1_{i,j} = \frac{1}{T} \sum_t \frac{X_{ij,t} + M_{ij,t}}{Y_{i,t} + Y_{j,t}} \tag{3.2}$$

where $X_{ij,t}$ denotes total merchandise exports from country *i* to country *j* in year *t*, $M_{ij,t}$ denotes imports to *i* from *j*, and Y_i denotes nominal GDP in country *i*. An alternative measure, proposed by Clark and van Wincoop (2001), based on the model in Deardoff (1998) and employed by Imbs (2004, 2006), among others, can be constructed as:

$$T^2_{i,j} = \frac{1}{2}\frac{1}{T}\sum_t \frac{(X_{ij,t} + M_{ij,t})Y^W_t}{Y_{i,t} \times Y_{j,t}} \tag{3.3}$$

where Y^W_t is world GDP. T^2 differs from T^1 in that it is independent of country size and depends only on trade barriers. In the empirics, we take the natural logarithm of both measures of bilateral trade intensity. We interpret that the *higher* the values of T^1 and T^2, the greater the trade intensity between countries i and j. In terms of Equation (3.1), the sign of β_l can be positive or negative, as theory predicts that closer bilateral trade could result in synchronized (positive) or asynchronous (negative) business cycles.

There are no standard measures of similarity in industrial structures (Imbs, 2004). We use two measures of similarity in industrial structures for comparability with existing research. The first, a measure akin to a Herfindahl index of concentration, is employed in Clark and van Wincoop (2001), Imbs (2004, 2006) and Krugman (1991), among others, and is measured as:

$$S^1_{i,j} = \frac{1}{T}\sum_t \sum_n^N \left| S_{ni} - S_{nj} \right| \tag{3.4}$$

where S_{ni} and S_{nj} denote the GDP shares for industry n in countries i and j, respectively. If two countries had identical industrial structures, that is, the industry shares in GDP were the same for countries i and j, then the index would be zero. On the other hand, when two countries have completely disjointed or different industrial structures, the index reaches a maximum value of two. Therefore, *lower* values of S^1 imply more similarity in industrial structure between countries i and j.

Our second measure of similarity of industrial structure, suggested by Shea (1996) and used by Baxter and Kouparitsas (2005) is the correlation of industry shares:

$$S^2_{i,j} = \frac{1}{T}\sum_t \frac{\sum_n^N S_{ni} S_{nj}}{\sqrt{\sum_n^N S^2_{ni}}\sqrt{\sum_n^N S^2_{nj}}} \tag{3.5}$$

If $S_{ni} = S_{nj}$, that is, GDP shares of each industry are the same in countries i and j, S^2 is equal to one. In other words, *lower* values of S^2 imply less similarity in industrial structure between countries i and j. We also take the natural logarithms of both measures of similarity of industrial structure in our empirics. Theory clearly predicts that similar production patterns between countries should lead to synchronized business cycles, and, as such, the sign of β_2 changes depending on the measure used for similarity of industrial structure in Equation (3.1). That is, S^1 implies $\beta_2 < 0$, whereas S^2 implies $\beta_2 > 0$.

Bilateral financial integration can be difficult to measure effectively. On this basis, our measures of financial integration encompass a number of quantity-based measures to ensure robustness. Our quantity-based measure of financial integration is constructed in three ways. The first measure uses the recently updated dataset of Lane and Milesi-Ferretti (2007) and, following Cerqueira and Martins (2009), is calculated as the average of the sum of stocks of assets and liabilities of FDI and portfolio investment between countries *i* and *j*, scaled by nominal GDP:[6]

$$F^1_{ij,t} = \frac{1}{T}\sum_t \left(\frac{A_{i,t} + L_{i,t}}{Y_{i,t}} + \frac{A_{j,t} + L_{j,t}}{Y_{j,t}} \right) \tag{3.6}$$

where $A_{i,t}$ and $L_{i,t}$ are the total assets and liabilities of country *i*, at time *t*. We can interpret F^1 as a measure of the extent of openness between pairs of countries to global financial markets, and as such we think of *higher* values of F^1 when pairs of countries are more financially integrated with world financial markets. An alternative measure of financial openness, which builds on the IMF's Annual Report on Exchange Arrangements and Exchange Restrictions (AREAER) and is based on information on controls on financial flows, is the index-based measure recently put together by Chinn and Ito (2008). To construct a bilateral measure, the average of the sum of the indices between countries *i* and *j* is calculated as:

$$F^2_{ij,t} = \frac{1}{T}\sum_t (ITO_{i,t} + ITO_{j,t}) \tag{3.7}$$

where $ITO_{i,t}$ and $ITO_{j,t}$ denote the Chinn–Ito indices for countries *i* and *j*, respectively. Likewise, F^2 takes higher values when pairs of countries have officially lower restrictions on financial flows.

Finally, one of this chapter's contributions is to use, in a panel context, the CPIS gathered by the IMF that provides direct observations on bilateral asset holdings from 2001 until 2007.[7] At the outset, however, one should also recognize that the data have their own limitations. Problems of under-reporting (Lane and Milesi-Ferretti, 2004), non-inclusion of FDI and the absence of some countries in the collection in view of the non-mandatory nature of the reporting are some of the concerns that plague this dataset (Imbs, 2006).[8] Nonetheless, given our awareness of the problems inherent in the dataset, which are born out of the lack of data sources based on mandatory reporting of bilateral information on FDI and portfolio investment, our third quantity-based measure of financial integration is computed, as in Garcia-Herrero and Ruiz (2008):

$$F^3_{ij,t} = \frac{I_{ij,t} + I_{ji,t}}{Y_{i,t} + Y_{j,t}} \tag{3.8}$$

where $I_{ij,t}$ represents financial flows from country i to country j at time t. Similar to F^1 and F^2, F^3 takes higher values when pairs of countries are more financially integrated.

As discussed in the section on the literature background, above, standard international-business-cycle theories show that greater financial integration leads to divergent business cycles, and, as such, the sign of β_3 changes, depending also on the measure used for financial integration in Equation (3.1). That is, F^1, F^2 and F^3 all imply $\beta_3 < 0$.[9]

Some stylized trends

As a preliminary step, this section presents a graphical evolution of our measures of BCS, as well as the measures of financial integration that we employ later in our analysis. We begin by examining the stylized trends in our BCS measures over the period considered in our analysis.

Figure 3.1 presents the BCS between the Asia-Pacific economies and the EU-14. The figure has two graphs, one for each of the de-trending techniques used – the HP filter and the BK band-pass filter. Each graph contains time-series plots of the average BCS for all possible pairs of Asian and EU-14 countries at a point in time. The average BCS level varies over time between –0.5 and 0.5, but there are no obvious trends. The Asian financial crisis of 1997–8 made the business cycle asynchronous between these two regions, as well as during the mid 2000s. However, by the end of the period of interest, there is a divergence in outcome on whether Asian business cycles became more (HP filter) or less (BK filter) correlated with the EU-14 countries.

Figure 3.2 is an analogue that considers the BCS of the Asia-Pacific economies to the United States. In the aftermath of the steep decline in BCS levels around the time of the Asian financial crisis, BCS levels typically hovered around 0.4 or so in the 2000s. However, as portrayed in the figure, there is a tendency for business cycles across the Asia-Pacific countries and the United States in 2007 to be less correlated.

Finally, Figure 3.3 is an analogue that considers the intra-Asia-Pacific countries' BCS levels over time. The single most striking observation from Figure 3.3 is the marked contrast in average BCS levels in this figure as compared, in particular, with the average BCS levels presented in Figure 3.2. This suggests a shrinking relationship between the business cycles of the Asia-Pacific countries and those of the major countries outside, most especially the United States, whereas, at the intra-regional level, decoupling does not seem to be a phenomenon over time.

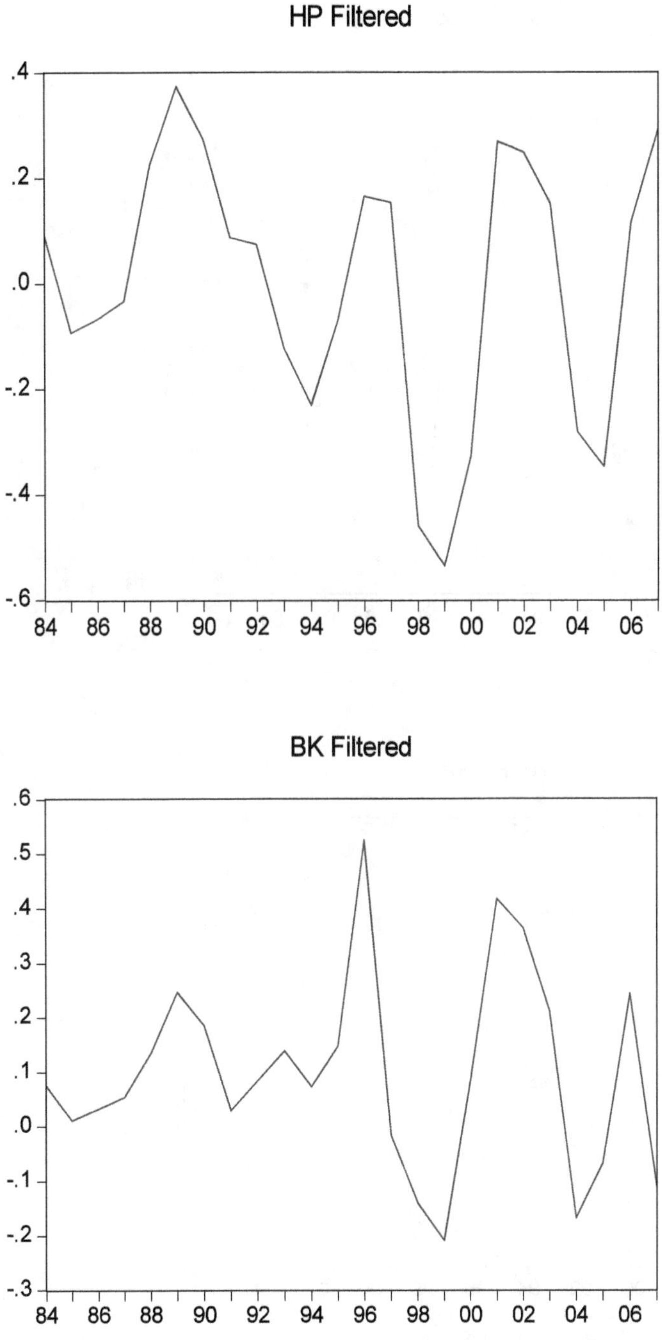

Figure 3.1 Asia–EU business-cycle correlation across time

Note: The correlation is estimated with a four-year rolling window
Source: Authors' calculations

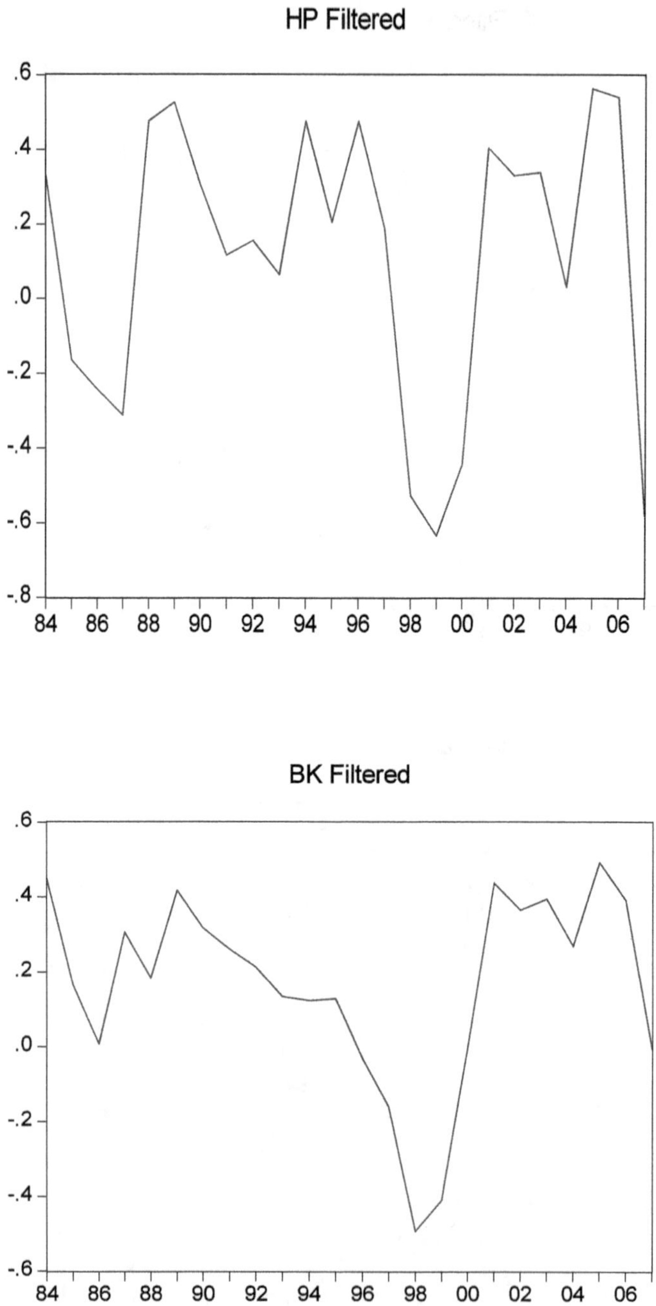

Figure 3.2 Asia–US business-cycle correlation across time

Note: The correlation is estimated with a four-year rolling window
Source: Authors' calculations

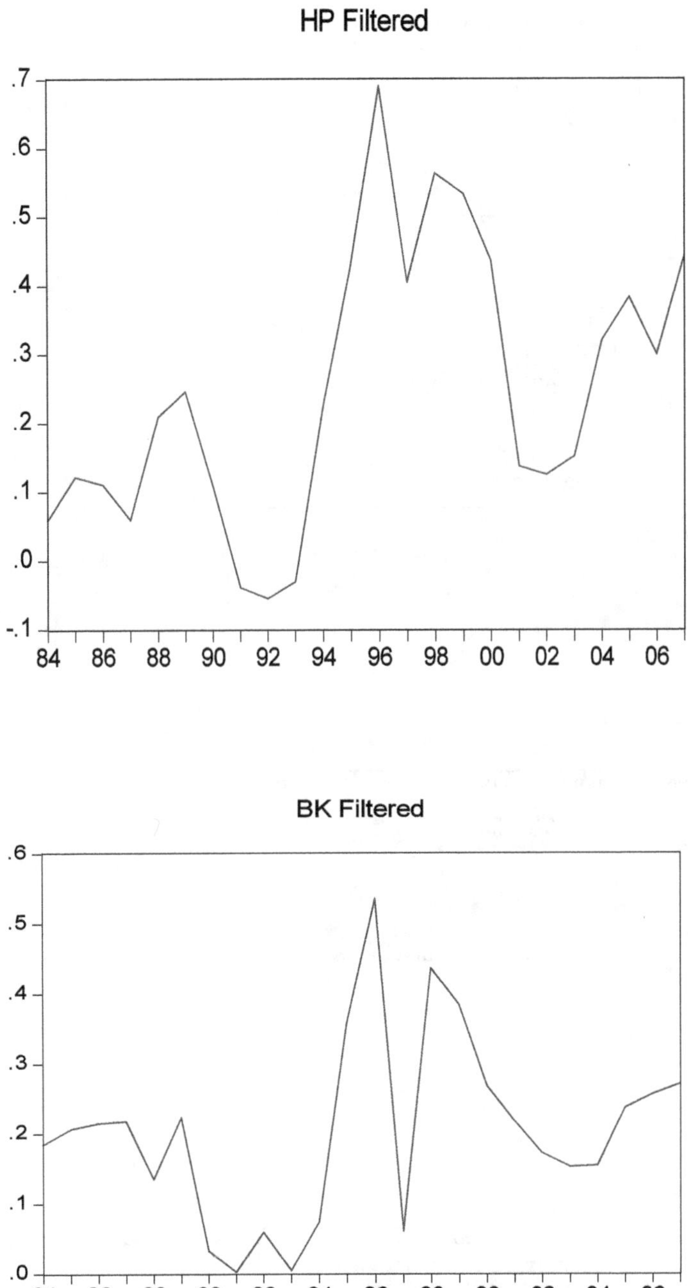

Figure 3.3 Intra-Asia-Pacific business-cycle correlation across time

Note: The correlation is estimated with a four-year rolling window
Source: Authors' calculations

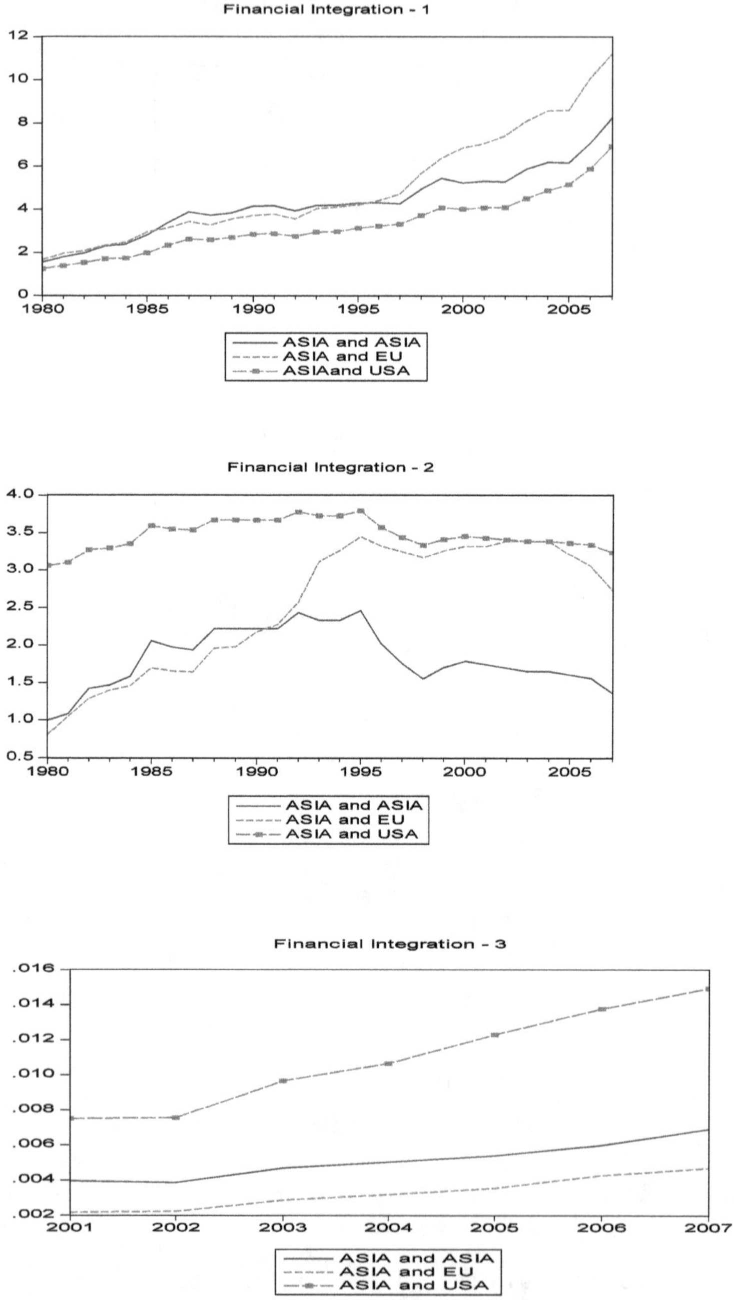

Figure 3.4 Financial integration over time (quantity-based)

Note: The correlation is estimated with a four-year rolling window
Source: Authors' calculations

Obviously, the above analysis has its limitations and thus should be taken as indicative only of whether business cycles in the Asia-Pacific economies are moving asynchronously or are 'decoupled' over time with the two major economic blocs considered in the analysis. For one, the analysis is unconditional – no other factors have been taken into account as possibly affecting BCS. This will be the focus of our attention in the subsequent sections, but, before that, we take a brief look at the trends of our financial integration measures over time.

Figure 3.4 gives a graphical depiction of the evolution over time of our quantity-based measures of bilateral financial integration.[10] Figure 3.4 has three graphs, one for each of our bilateral financial-integration measures (F^1, F^2 and F^3). Each graph contains time-series plots of the cross-country-pair average of the relevant financial integration measure. Figure 3.4 clearly shows that, according to our first measure of financial integration, Asia's integration with world financial markets has increased considerably over the past three decades. Indeed, a more detailed inspection of this particular plot of F^1 indicates that the dramatic rise occurred around the middle of the 1990s. Whereas there is a clear and persistent upward trend in F^1, there is a reversal in Asia's openness to financial flows at some time in the mid 1990s according to our second bilateral measure (F^2). From this point until the end of the period considered, our second measure seems to fluctuate around an approximately constant mean, which intuitively suggests that Asia has not made much further progress in reducing formal restrictions on financial flows in recent years. With regards to our last quantity measure of bilateral financial integration (F^3), consistent with Kim and Lee (2008), its evolution portrays Asia's increasing, though limited, intra-regional financial integration as it falls behind that of its integration with the United States.

Methodology

Dynamic panel GMM technique[11]

In a pure cross-sectional regression, any unobserved time-invariant, country-pair-specific effects would be part of the error term, leading to a biased estimate of the coefficients. Previous studies of the direction of the BCS–finance link using pure cross-sectional data are afflicted by this problem. A panel context, however, allows us to control for these unobserved time-invariant, country-pair-specific effects, and, as a result, the problem of biased coefficient estimates is either reduced or eliminated. This is important, as there is growing evidence in the literature that cultural biases and differences, for instance, have a substantial impact on a variety of financial flows – portfolio and direct investment (Ekinci *et al.*, 2008; Guiso *et al.*, 2009), as well as on foreign bank lending (Mian, 2006; Giannetti and Yafeh, 2008). In addition, the GMM estimator does not require any particular distributions of the error term. This veers away from the complicated inference introduced by using a

Pearson correlation coefficient (bounded at –1 and 1) to measure BCS, as the error term is unlikely to be normally distributed.

In order to estimate our model, Equation (3.1), consistently and efficiently, we use a GMM estimator for dynamic panel data models that was introduced by Holtz-Eakin *et al.* (1990) and Arellano and Bond (1991), and was further developed in a series of papers, including Arellano and Bover (1995) and Blundell and Bond (1998). This estimator encompasses a regression equation in both differences and levels, each one with its specific set of IVs. Consider the following regression equation for BCS:

$$y_{ij,t} = \alpha y_{ij,t-1} + \beta X_{ij,t} + \eta_{ij} + \varepsilon_{ij,t} \tag{3.9}$$

where y is the business-cycle correlation measure; X represents the set of explanatory variables, apart from the lagged business-cycle correlation measure; η is an unobserved, time-invariant, country-pair-specific effect; ε is the error term; and the subscripts i, j and t represent country pairs and time period, respectively.

We eliminate country-pair-specific effects (η_{ij}) by taking first differences of Equation (3.9):

$$y_{ij,t} - y_{ij,t-1} = \alpha(y_{ij,t-1} - y_{ij,t-2}) + \beta(X_{ij,t} - X_{ij,t-1}) + (\varepsilon_{ij,t} - \varepsilon_{ij,t-1}) \tag{3.10}$$

The use of own suitable lagged levels of $y_{ij,t}$ as instruments is required to deal with the problem that, by differencing the lagged dependent variable, $(y_{ij,t-1} - y_{ij,t-2})$ is correlated with the error term, $\varepsilon_{ij,t} - \varepsilon_{ij,t-1}$. The same strategy is applied to form instruments for other explanatory variables that are allowed to be endogenous in the sense that they can be affected by current and past realizations of business-cycle correlations. This feature enables us to avoid simultaneity bias due to the endogeneity of our financial-linkages variables. Strictly speaking, under the assumption that (a) the explanatory variables, X, are weakly exogenous (no correlation with future realizations of the error term), and (b) the error term, ε, is not serially correlated, the dynamic panel GMM estimator exploits the following moment conditions:

$$E[y_{ij,t-s} \cdot (\varepsilon_{ij,t} - \varepsilon_{ij,t-1})] = 0 \quad \text{for } s \geqslant 2;\ t = 3, \ldots, T \tag{3.11}$$

$$E[X_{ij,t-s} \cdot (\varepsilon_{ij,t} - \varepsilon_{ij,t-1})] = 0 \quad \text{for } s \geqslant 2;\ t = 3, \ldots, T \tag{3.12}$$

The resulting GMM estimator based on these conditions is known as the difference-GMM estimator. There is, however, an issue with the difference-GMM estimator. If lagged dependent variables and explanatory variables are persistent over time, the lagged levels probably represent weak instruments for the first-differenced variables. This causes finite sample bias and low accuracy, which leads to the need to complement the regression in first differences with a regression in levels. The instruments for the regression in first differences are the same as above. The instruments for the regression in levels, in turn, are the lagged differences of the same corresponding variables, under the assumption that, although there may be correlation between the levels of the right-hand-side variables and the country-pair-specific effect in Equation (3.11), none exists between the differences of these variables and the country-pair-specific effect.

The additional moment conditions for the regression in levels are:

$$E[y_{ij,t-s} - y_{ij,t-s-1}) \cdot (\eta_{ij} + \varepsilon_{ij,t})] = 0 \quad \text{for } s = 1 \tag{3.13}$$

$$E[X_{ij,t-s} - X_{ij,t-s-1}) \cdot (\eta_{ij} + \varepsilon_{ij,t})] = 0 \quad \text{for } s = 1 \tag{3.14}$$

The consistency of the GMM estimator depends on whether lagged values of the explanatory variables are valid instruments in the regression. To address this issue, we consider two specification tests: the first is the Hansen test of over-identifying restrictions, which tests the overall validity of the instruments. Failure to reject the null hypothesis supports the model. The second test examines the hypothesis that the error term is not serially correlated. We test whether the differenced error term, that is, the residual of the regression in differences, is second-order serially correlated.[12] If the test fails to reject the null hypothesis of absence of second-order serial correlation, we conclude that the original error term is serially uncorrelated and use the corresponding moment conditions.

Estimation results

Table 3.1 presents the dynamic panel GMM estimation results using business-cycle correlation or synchronization as the dependent variable. The table has six columns. The first column refers to the explanatory variables used in the estimation of a particular specification of the dynamic panel GMM. The second to fourth columns contain the coefficient estimates of the explanatory variables, that is, measures of trade, similarity of industrial structure, and financial, respectively, along with the p-values in square brackets; estimates that are significantly different from zero at the 0.10, 0.05 and 0.01 level are marked by one, two and three asterisks, respectively. The last two columns contain the specification tests' results. The table also contains two panels. The upper panel contains the results obtained using the HP filter; the lower panel contains the estimates obtained using the BK band-pass filter. Each panel has two sets of results, and each set is delineated based on the measure of financial integration (*F*) used as the explanatory variable in the GMM estimation. In turn, each set contains four rows of results that pertain to all possible permutations of *F* with the other explanatory variables *T* (bilateral trade) and similarity of industrial structure (*S*).

Table 3.1 Dynamic panel GMM estimations of business-cycle synchronizations (crisis years included)

Variables	*Trade* ($T_{ij,t}$)	*Specialization* ($S_{ij,t}$)	*Finance* ($F_{ij,t}$)	*Hansen test (p-value)*	*AB test for AR(2) (p-value)*
Hodrick–Prescott de-trended					
T^1, S^1, F^1	1.153 [0.00]***	–0.448 [0.04]**	–0.446 [0.01]**	0.38	0.29
T^2, S^1, F^1	0.448 [0.01]**	0.633 [0.01]**	–0.443 [0.00]***	0.78	0.26
T^1, S^2, F^1	0.654 [0.00]***	1.27 [0.03]**	–0.415 [0.00]***	0.61	0.08
T^2, S^2, F^1	0.534 [0.01]**	–1.85 [0.03]**	–0.494 [0.00]***	0.87	0.17
T^1, S^1, F^2	0.448 [0.00]***	–0.439 [0.00]***	–0.109 [0.00]***	0.14	0.66
T^2, S^1, F^2	1.516 [0.05]**	2.361 [0.12]	–0.902 [0.03]**	0.78	0.84
T^1, S^2, F^2	0.609 [0.00]***	2.780 [0.00]***	–0.139 [0.00]***	0.81	0.76
T^2, S^2, F^2	0.349 [0.02]**	2.68 [0.00]***	–0.458 [0.00]***	0.35	0.40
Baxter–King de-trended					
T^1, S^1, F^1	0.307 [0.01]**	–0.311 [0.00]***	–0.302 [0.00]***	0.92	0.63
T^2, S^1, F^1	0.228 [0.00]***	–0.287 [0.00]***	–0.208 [0.00]***	0.75	0.51
T^1, S^2, F^1	0.282 [0.01]**	1.571 [0.00]***	–0.280 [0.00]***	0.86	0.56
T^2, S^2, F^1	0.226 [0.00]***	1.491 [0.00]***	–0.195 [0.00]***	0.71	0.51
T^1, S^1, F^2	0.003 [0.98]	–0.223 [0.30]	–0.081 [0.01]**	0.87	0.25
T^2, S^1, F^2	0.037 [0.02]**	–0.189 [0.28]	–0.052 [0.00]***	0.53	0.12
T^1, S^2, F^2	0.071 [0.51]	0.620 [0.21]	–0.094 [0.01]**	0.96	0.31
T^2, S^2, F^2	0.040 [0.02]**	0.453 [0.25]	–0.058 [0.00]***	0.48	0.08

Notes: Numbers in square brackets are p-values. Significance levels: *10%, **5%, ***1%. The GMM estimations include lags of the dependent variable as well as time-dummies. AB is the Arellano-Bond test of the presence of autocorrelation.
Source: Authors' calculations

We begin by examining the specification test results. The Hansen test of over-identifying restrictions in all cases does not reject the null hypothesis that the instruments are not correlated with the error process. In addition, tests of serial correlation fail to reject the null hypothesis that the error term, expressed in first differences, is not second-order serially correlated in all cases. This supports using lags of the explanatory variables as instruments.[13]

The estimates of the impact of bilateral trade intensity on BCS are strongly positive (more trade between two countries induces higher BCS). Of the sixteen coefficients (= 2 de-trending techniques × 2 measures of bilateral trade linkages × 2 measures of similarity of industrial structure × 2 measures of financial integration),[14] eight are significant at the 5 per cent level, and six at the 1 per cent level. Of these statistically significant coefficients, these coefficients range from 0.04 to 1.516 (using T^2 as one of the regressors in the GMM estimation), and this means that an increase in bilateral trade intensity by one standard deviation implies that BCS starting from its mean would increase from 0.024 (= 1.547 * 0.016) to 0.254 (= 0.04 * 6.35). On average, this represents moving the correlation of output by about 22 per cent of one standard deviation, quite an economically significant effect.

Concerning similarity of industrial structure, most estimated coefficients are significant, although, once we control for endogeneity, some of the estimated coefficients have incorrect signs (we should expect that $S^1 < 0$, $S^2 > 0$; more similar countries have higher BCS). Of the sixteen coefficients, thirteen have correct signs; of these thirteen coefficients, four are significant at the 5 per cent level, and seven at the 1 per cent level.

Finally, we found in our estimation results that the higher the financial linkages between countries (higher F^1 and F^2), the less synchronization there is of business cycles. This finding is strikingly consistent across all estimated coefficients, all of which are statistically significant at conventional significance levels. These estimated coefficients range from –0.902 to –0.052 (both using F^2 as one of the regressors). This means that an increase by one standard deviation of our relevant measure of financial linkages implies that BCS starting from its mean would be reduced from 0.786 to 0.045 (using F^2 as one of the regressors). In turn, this represents moving the correlation of output from 20 per cent to 60 per cent of one standard deviation, again quite an economically significant effect.

Table 3.2 is also an analogue to Table 3.1 that considers our final indicator of financial integration (which is also our third quantity-based indicator of financial integration) using the 2001–7 CPIS data.[15] Although four of the eight estimated coefficients of the indicators for financial and bilateral trade linkages, respectively, are statistically indistinguishable from zero, this additional sensitivity test does not undermine the initial findings: both specification tests are fulfilled; a slightly weaker, although consistent, result indicates that more trade between two countries induces higher BCS; there are some indications that more similar countries have higher BCS; and, finally, increased financial linkages between countries leads to divergent BCS.

Table 3.2 Dynamic panel GMM estimations of business-cycle synchronizations (using CPIS data)

Variables	*Trade* ($T_{ij,t}$)	*Specialization* ($S_{ij,t}$)	*Finance* ($F_{ij,t}$)	*Hansen test (p-value)*	*AB test for AR(2) (p-value)*
Hodrick–Prescott de-trended					
T^1, S^1, F^3	0.051 [0.04]**	–0.042 [0.17]	–0.050 [0.09]*	0.53	0.31
T^2, S^1, F^3	0.089 [0.05]*	–0.058 [0.29]	–0.058 [0.27]	0.77	0.28
T^1, S^2, F^3	0.010 [0.81]	0.552 [0.09]*	–0.054 [0.05]**	0.86	0.32
T^2, S^2, F^3	0.062 [0.09]*	0.128 [0.73]	–0.019 [0.66]	0.30	0.23
Baxter–King de-trended					
T^1, S^1, F^3	1.141 [0.03]**	–0.427 [0.01]***	–0.348 [0.03]**	0.23	0.20
T^2, S^1, F^3	1.066 [0.52]	–7.641 [0.02]**	–0.339 [0.09]*	0.41	0.36
T^1, S^2, F^3	1.722 [0.30]	–1.089 [0.94]	–0.581 [0.05]*	0.24	0.83
T^2, S^2, F^3	0.063 [0.93]	–5.743 [0.62]	–0.458 [0.04]**	0.16	0.34

Notes: Numbers in square brackets are p-values. Significance levels: *10%, **5%, ***1%. The GMM estimations include lags of the dependent variable as well as time-dummies. AB is the Arellano–Bond test of the presence of autocorrelation.

Source: Authors' calculations

Conclusion

This chapter examines empirically the effect of three factors, namely financial and trade linkages, as well as similarity of industrial structure, on BCS in the Asia-Pacific region. We adopt a panel approach and employ dynamic panel GMM estimation in order to unpack endogeneity problems, as well as to control for country-pair-specific, unobservable time-invariant factors. Our modelling strategy assumes that the Asia-Pacific countries integrate, not just within the region, but also with major countries outside the region. As also documented in the chapter, this strategy conforms to the stylized fact that Asia's integration within itself and with countries outside the region has increased considerably over the past three decades. Furthermore, as opposed to previous studies, our measures of financial integration encompass both quantity- and price-based indicators to ensure robustness in our results. The main results are as follows: there are some indications that more similar countries have higher BCS; we find consistent support for the evidence that shows that more trade between two countries induces higher BCS; and increased financial linkages between countries lead to divergent BCS.

Although the first two findings are in line with Imbs (2004, 2006), the third is contrary to his and other studies that use pure cross-sectional data to examine the direction of the finance–BCS link. Our third finding conforms to the basic ideas of benchmark international-business-cycle models. What perhaps drives the conflicting evidence found by pure cross-sectional studies and that of the theoretical benchmarks is that, apart from being able to control for simultaneity, one also needs to account for the role of country-pair-specific, unobservable time-invariant factors. Similar to our approach, which used panel IV techniques, recent studies such as Cerqueira and Martins (2009) and Kalemli-Ozcan *et al.* (2009) have controlled for such influences. These works are now considered to be fundamental and basic in any study that tries to ascertain the link between BCS and finance. Once biases associated with simultaneity and unobserved country-pair-specific factors are accounted for, the prediction by theory regarding the inverse relationship between financial linkages and BCS becomes apparent in the results.

The implications of the above results for Asian policy-making are important and far-reaching. Given that Asia's integration within itself and with countries outside the region has advanced steadily in recent years, the finding of an inverse relationship between bilateral financial linkages and BCS might indicate that financial integration makes it easier for these countries to transfer financial assets, which should help Asian countries diversify against country-specific risks, and thus enable their decoupling (Garcia-Herrero and Ruiz, 2008; Flood *et al.*, 2009). This is consistent with the basic argument underlying the theory of international risk sharing, as further financial integration offers better opportunities for risk diversification.

In view of the benefits of increasing financial integration by affording better risk-sharing opportunities, the importance in actuality of developing and strengthening capital markets through which agents can diversify their portfolio via cross-border ownership of assets is essential and cannot be overemphasized. Moving forward, reforms aimed at improving the capability of agents to adjust the size of their asset portfolio (savings rate), e.g. pension-fund schemes, in response to shocks, as well as to being more receptive of cross-border mergers and acquisitions can further enhance risk-sharing opportunities between countries (Kalemli-Ozcan *et al.*, 2004).

On the other hand, it is alleged that the downside of greater financial integration is that it can pose risks to financial stability. This claim takes on ever-increasing traction and prominence in discussions, especially in light of the recent painful experience with the GFC, which tends to demonstrate the role that financial linkages play in the transmission of shocks between economies. However, despite concerns in policy circles, it appears that the jury is still out on whether greater financial integration increases the likelihood of crises. For instance, in a recent study, Fecht *et al.* (2008) show that the availability of better risk-sharing mechanisms tends to offset the risk of spillover or transmission of shocks, and thus financial integration leads to an improvement in welfare, as specialization benefits are magnified and realized.[16] Furthermore, a few studies argue that greater integration poses no risk to financial stability on its own, but, when too rapid a liberalization of financial markets interacts, for instance, with certain distortions in the economy, such as weak and lax supervisory regulations as well as problems of credibility and enforcements of contracts, these distortions become magnified, and financial-instability problems arise (Fecht *et al.*, 2008).[17]

Nonetheless, as financial integration deepens and international capital flows become more intense, the enduring and considerable challenge for policymakers is to be able to counterbalance the benefits and alleged risk of greater financial integration. This trade-off will vary across economies, as it will be a function of the level of financial-market development of individual countries in the region. Thus, the appropriate policy approach to enable countries to reap the benefits of the opportunities that come with further financial integration, e.g. international risk sharing, and at the same time contain the alleged inherent risk of greater financial integration, will likely differ across countries in the region (Bank for International Settlements (BIS), 2009).

Notes

1 This chapter was prepared and completed by the second author during her stint with the ERIA.
2 Exceptions to this limitation are Kalemli-Ozcan *et al.* (2009), who use BIS proprietary data on OECD countries, and Garcia-Herrero and Ruiz (2008), who use a novel dataset on bilateral flows between Spain and a large number of countries taken from the Spanish balance of payments.
3 An exception is by Lee and Azali (2010), who look at a smaller subsection of countries than those we examine in this chapter and who emphasize OCA criteria.
4 These sub-periods are: 1980–3, 1984–7, 1988–91, 1992–5, 1996–9, 2000–3 and 2004–7.

5 We do not broach the literature on the appropriate measure of synchronizations of business cycles, noting only that most studies employ simple bilateral correlation coefficients in order to measure the strength and direction of the association between the cyclical components of the annual real GDP of two countries.
6 Also using the Lane and Milesi-Ferretti dataset, Imbs (2004) constructs his own, alternative measure of bilateral financial integration using the difference between the stocks of assets and liabilities (net foreign asset) between countries i and j.
7 Imbs (2006) uses the 2001 CPIS survey data, which effectively makes it a pure cross-sectional study.
8 For instance, two of the thirteen Asia-Pacific countries that are examined in this chapter, namely China and Taiwan, are both absent from the collection.
9 Obviously, in relation to cross-country empirical studies that find a positive relationship between financial integration and BCS, the sign of β_3 is the reverse of the above, so that $\beta_3 > 0$ for F^1, F^2 and F^3.
10 Notice that the time-scale axis for the graph containing the F^3 measure is not in sync with the other two measures. Recall from our previous discussion that the F^3 measure is constructed using the CPIS data, which are only available for 1997 and then from 2001 to 2007.
11 The discussion that follows draws in part on Calderon and Chong (2001), Chong and Gradstein (2007) and Levine *et al.* (2000).
12 Second-order serial correlation of the differenced residual indicates that the original error term is serially correlated and follows a moving-average process at least of order one.
13 In addition, apart from using 'internal' instruments, i.e. lags of the explanatory variables, we also included the pair-wise sum of the recently updated exchange rate regime classification of Reinhart *et al.* (2010), the pair-wise sum of GDP per capita and the absolute value of differences in GDP per capita as 'external' instruments in the GMM estimations.
14 Note that there are three measures of financial integration used in this chapter. The results using the third measure are presented in a separate table.
15 In order to create the measure of BCS, i.e. the correlation between cyclical output in countries i and j, we follow Rose (2009) by using twenty quarterly observations (five years) proceeding through time τ.
16 See also Bonfiglioli and Mendicino (2004) and Glick *et al.* (2006). For contrasting evidence, see, for instance, Demirguc-Kunt and Detragiache (2001) and Hartmann *et al.* (2005).
17 See, for instance, Ishii and Habermeier (2002).

References

Allen, F. and Gale, D. (2000) 'Financial contagion', *Journal of Political Economy*, 108: 1–33.

Arellano, M. and Bond, S. (1991) 'Some tests of specification for panel data: Monte-Carlo evidence and an application to employment equations', *Review of Economic Studies*, 58: 277–97.

Arellano, M. and Bover, O. (1995) 'Another look at the instrumental-variable estimation of error component models', *Journal of Econometrics*, 68: 29–52.

Backus, D., Kehoe, P. and Kydland, F. (1992) 'International real business cycles', *Journal of Political Economy*, 100(4): 745–75.

Backus, D., Kydland, F. and Kehoe, P. (1994) 'Dynamics of the trade balance and the terms of trade: the J-curve?', *American Economic Review*, 84: 84–103.

Bank for International Settlements (BIS) (2009) 'The international financial crisis: timeline, impact and policy responses in Asia and the Pacific', PBC–BIS Shanghai Conference Proceedings (forthcoming).

Baxter, M. and Crucini, M. (1995) 'Business cycles and the asset structure of foreign trade', *International Economic Review*, 36: 821–54.

Baxter, M. and Kouparitsas, M. (2005) 'Determinants of business cycle co-movement: a robust analysis', *Journal of Monetary Economics*, 51(1): 113–57.

Blundell, R. and Bond, S. (1998) 'Initial conditions and moments restrictions in dynamic panel data models', *Journal of Econometrics*, 87: 115–43.

Bonfiglioli, A. and Mendicino, C. (2004) 'Financial liberalization, banking crises, and growth', SSE/EFI Working Paper Series in Economics and Finance no. 567.

Bordo, M. and Heibling, T. (2003) 'Have national business cycles become more synchronized', NBER Working Paper 10130.

Calderon, C. and Chong, A. (2001) 'External sector and income inequality in interdependent economies using a dynamic panel data approach', *Economics Letters*, 71: 225–31.

Cerqueira, P. and Martins, R. (2009) 'Measuring the determinants of business cycle synchronization using a panel approach', *Economics Letters*, 102: 106–8.

Chinn, M. and Ito, H. (2008) 'A new measure of financial openness', *Journal of Comparative Policy Analysis*, 10(3): 307–20.

Chong, A. and Gradstein, M. (2007) 'Inequality and institutions', *Review of Economics and Statistics*, 89(3): 454–65.

Clark, T. and van Wincoop, E. (2001) 'Borders and business cycles', *Journal of International Economics*, 55: 59–85.

Deardoff, A. (1998) 'Determinants of bilateral trade: does gravity work in a neo-classical world?', in *The Regionalization of the World Economy*, ed. Jeffrey Frankel, Chicago: The University of Chicago Press.

Demirguc-Kunt, A. and Detragiache, E. (2001) 'Financial liberalization and financial fragility', in *Financial Liberalization: How Far, How Fast?*, eds G. Caprio, P. Honohan and J. Stiglitz, Cambridge: Cambridge University Press.

Ekinci, M., Kalemli-Ozcan, S. and Sörensen, B. (2008) 'Financial integration within EU countries: the role of institutions, confidence and trust', NBER Working Paper 13440.

Fecht, F., Gruner, H.P. and Hartmann, P. (2008) 'Financial integration, specialization and systemic risk', Deutsche Bundesbank Discussion Paper Series no. 1: Economic Studies no. 23/2008.

Flood, R., Marion, N. and Matsumoto, A. (2009) 'International risk sharing during the globalization era', IMF Working Paper, 09/209.

Frankel, J. and Rose, A. (1997) 'Is EMU more justifiable ex post than ex ante?', *European Economic Review*, 41: 753–60.

Frankel, J. and Rose, A. (1998) 'The endogeneity of the optimum currency area criteria', *Economic Journal*, 108: 1009–25.

Garcia Herrero, A. and Ruiz, J. (2008) 'Do trade and financial links foster business cycle synchronization in a small open economy', *Moneda y Credito*, 226(1): 187–226.

Giannetti, M. and Yafeh, Y. (2008) 'Do cultural differences between contracting parties matter? Evidence from syndicated bank loans', ECGI Finance Working Paper no. 224.

Glick, R., Guo, X. and Hutchison, M. (2006) 'Currency crises, capital-account liberalization, and selection bias', *Review of Economics and Statistics*, 88: 698–714.

Guiso, L., Sapienza, P. and Zingales, L. (2009) 'Cultural biases in economic exchange?', *Quarterly Journal of Economics*, 124(3): 1095–131.

Hartmann, P., Straetmans, S. and de Vries, C. (2005) 'Banking system stability: a cross-Atlantic perspective', NBER Working Paper no. 11698.

Heathcote, J. and Perri, F. (2002) 'Financial autarky and international business cycles', *Journal of Monetary Economics*, 49: 601–27.

Heathcote, J. and Perri, F. (2003) 'Why has the U.S. economy become less correlated with the rest of the world?', *American Economic Review (Papers and Proceedings)*, 93: 63–9.

Heathcote, J. and Perri, F. (2004) 'Financial globalization and real regionalization', *Journal of Economic Theory*, 119: 207–43.

Holtz-Eakin, D., Newey, W. and Rosen, H. (1990) 'Estimating vector auto-regressions with panel data', *Econometrica*, 56: 1371–95.

Imbs, J. (2004) 'Trade, specialization and synchronization', *Review of Economics and Statistics*, 86(3): 723–34.

Imbs, J. (2006) 'The real effects of financial integration', *Journal of International Economics*, 68(2): 296–324.

Inklaar, R., Jong-A-Pin, R. and de Haan, J. (2008) 'Trade and business cycle synchronization in OECD countries – a re-examination', *European Economic Review*, 52: 646–66.

Ishii, S. and Habermeier, K. (2002) 'Capital account liberalization and financial sector stability', IMF Occasional Paper, no. 211.

Jansen, W. and Stokman, A. (2004) 'Foreign direct investment and international business cycle co-movement', Working Paper Series 401, European Central Bank.

Kalemli-Ozcan, S., Sörensen, B. and Yosha, O. (2004) 'Asymmetric shocks and risk sharing in a monetary union: updated evidence and policy implications for Europe', CPER Discussion Paper DP4463, London.

Kalemli-Ozcan, S., Papaioannou, E. and Peydro, J. (2009) 'Financial integration and business cycle synchronization', NBER Working Paper 14887, NBER, Cambridge, MA.

Kim, S. and Lee, J. (2008) 'Real and financial integration in East Asia', ADB Working Paper Series on Regional Economic Integration no. 17.

Kose, M., Prasad, E. and Terrones, M. (2003) 'How does globalization affect the synchronization of business cycles', *The American Economic Review (Papers and Proceedings)*, 93: 57–62.

Kose, M., Otrock, C. and Prasad, E. (2008a) 'Global business cycles: convergence or decoupling', IZA Working Paper 93.

Kose, M., Otrock, C. and Whiteman, C. (2008b) 'Understanding the evolution of world business cycles', *Journal of International Economics*, 75(1): 110–30.

Krugman, P. (1991) *Geography and Trade*, Cambridge: MIT Press.

Lane, P. and Milesi-Ferretti, G.M. (2004) 'International investment patterns', IIIS Discussion Paper 24.

Lane, P. and Milesi-Ferretti, G.M. (2007) 'The external wealth of nations mark II: revised and extended estimates of foreign assets and liabilities, 1970–2004', *Journal of International Economics*, 73: 223–50.

Lee, G. and Azali, M. (2010) 'The endogeneity of the optimum currency area criteria in East Asia', *Economic Modelling*, 27(1): 165–70.

Levine, R., Loayza, N. and Beck, T. (2000) 'Financial intermediation and growth', *Journal of Monetary Economics*, 46: 31–77.

Mian, A. (2006) 'Distance constraints: the limits of foreign lending in poor economies', *Journal of Finance*, 61(6): 1465–505.

Obstfeld, M. (1994) 'Risk-taking, global diversification, and growth', *American Economic Review*, 84(5): 1310–29.

Park, Y.C. and Shin, K. (2009) 'Economic integration and changes in the business cycle in East Asia: is the region decoupling from the rest of the world?', *Asian Economic Papers*, 8(1): 107–40.

Reinhart, C., Rogoff, K. and Ilzetzki, E. (2010) 'Exchange rate arrangements entering the 21st century: which anchors will hold?', mimeo.

Rose, A. (2009) 'Understanding business cycle synchronization: is inflation targeting paving the way to Asian monetary union?', mimeo; see: http://faculty.haas.berkeley.edu/arose/ADBPaper.pdf (accessed 8 June 2012).

Schiavo, S. (2008) 'Financial integration, GDP correlation and the endogeneity of optimum currency areas', *Economica*, 75: 168–89.

Shea, J. (1996) 'Co-movements in cities', *Carnegie Rochester Conference Series on Public Policy*, 44: 169–206.

Shin, K. and Sohn, C.H. (2006) 'Trade and financial integration in East Asia: effects on co-movements', *The World Economy*, 29(12): 1649–66.

Xing, T. and Abbott, A. (2007) 'The effects of trade, specialisation and financial integration for business cycle synchronisation', Discussion Paper, Bath University; see: www.etsg.org/ETSG2007/papers/xing.pdf (accessed 8 June 2012).

4 Consumption risk sharing and its implications for financial integration

The case of nine East Asian countries[1,2]

Jenny Corbett
Australia–Japan Research Centre, Crawford School, Australian National University

Achmad Maulana
ANU/CEDS Padjadjaran University

Introduction

The case for financial integration in East Asia has been of interest for some policymakers in the region. They argue that financial integration could bolster the region's economic growth and reduce its exposure to global shocks (Corbett, 2010).[3]

Corbett (2010) argues that one of the benefits of financial integration is that consumers or citizens in the region could improve their ability to achieve consumption smoothing, while another possible benefit is the welfare improvement for countries. On the other hand, financial integration also creates some costs for the participating countries, and other disadvantages include exposing the domestic market to external shocks and the higher possibility of financial contagion.

As noted above, consumption smoothing is one of the benefits of financial integration. This condition, however, can be achieved when consumers can insure their income against various shocks in the economy. In the regional setting, it means that a country can hold other countries' assets and sell these assets at a later date when the country experiences a negative shock, in order to minimize its effects. This phenomenon is identified in the literature as consumption risk sharing. When there is a high degree of consumption risk sharing, countries share their country-specific output shocks via several mechanisms. Two of the most common are capital- and credit-market channels. In the first channel, members share their individual shocks through cross-ownership of productive assets between countries, facilitated by the developed capital market. In the second channel, countries smooth their consumption via lending and borrowing activities in the international credit market. Any shocks to GDP that are not dampened by these two channels are classified as 'unsmoothed'.

Moving to the literature review on consumption risk sharing, two studies using the same framework to estimate the degree of risk sharing are examined. These studies are Kim *et al.* (2006), who estimate the degree of consumption risk sharing in the East Asian region, and Asdrubali *et al.* (1996), who estimate the interstate consumption risk sharing in the United States.

Kim *et al.* (2006) use a data series from the Penn World Table (PWT) between 1971 and 2000 to estimate the degree of consumption risk sharing. They analyse the channels of consumption risk sharing among ten East Asian countries: Indonesia, Malaysia, the Philippines, Thailand, Singapore, Korea, Taiwan, China, Hong Kong and Japan. Kim *et al.* (2006) find that only 20 per cent of the shocks to GDP are smoothed within the region. Among these 20 per cent, the credit market is the most important mechanism that dominates the capital market in absorbing the shocks. In addition, the authors also calculate the potential welfare gain that each country could attain if they had complete risk sharing. They concluded that the East Asian region was yet to achieve the desired level of consumption risk sharing necessary for the formation of a common currency area, compared with OECD countries.

Meanwhile, Asdrubali *et al.* (1996) use regional data from 1963 to 1990 in the United States, an example of successful monetary union, to estimate the risk-sharing channels. They identify three main channels for risk sharing between states in the United States: the capital market, the credit market and fiscal transfer channels. Asdrubali *et al.* find that 25 per cent of shocks to state output are not smoothed. They also find that, unlike in the analysis by Kim *et al.* (2006), the capital market is the more important channel for consumption risk sharing between states. This channel is used particularly by states that experience persistent shocks to their output. Even though their findings showed that perfect insurance is not achieved, they argue that states in the United States have achieved a considerable level of risk sharing.

The main objective of this chapter is to estimate the existing degree of consumption risk sharing in East Asian countries. To this end, we estimate the extent, on average, of each channel of consumption risk sharing in nine East Asian countries. We use a different framework to identify how consumption risk sharing actually takes place within the region.

The chapter is structured as follows: after the introduction comes a section discussing the conceptual framework that we employ to achieve our objectives. The next section clarifies the methodologies. The fourth section contains the description and some summary statistics of the data. The fifth section discusses the results, followed by the concluding section.

Conceptual frameworks

From standard macroeconomic theory, we know that, at the optimum, the consumer cannot gain from a feasible shift of consumption between periods.

Under certain conditions, it implies that agents will act to smooth their consumption between different periods. Moreover, a 'deeper' financial system has been associated with consumers' improved ability to achieve consumption smoothing (Corbett, 2010). Based on these arguments, we presume that there exists a close connection between consumption smoothing and a sound financial system.

As mentioned in the introduction, there are two mechanisms through which risk sharing can occur among countries. The first mechanism is the capital market. Through capital markets, citizens or the government of a country can own claims to output produced in other countries. This implies that the consumption of a particular country depends on the world income rather than its own individual income. To illustrate, suppose there is a Malaysian mutual fund that invests all of its wealth by buying other countries' assets. So, we expect that the revenue of the firm will be closely related to the movements of other countries' incomes. This implies that the Malaysian firm will be insulated from some of the negative shocks that occur in the Malaysian economy, because it is insured through ownership of other countries' assets. This form of risk sharing is also known as income insurance. The extent to which income insurance is used can be captured by the difference between a country's aggregate output, as measured by GDP, and its aggregate income, as measured by gross national product (GNP).

The second mechanism is through credit markets. Through credit markets, citizens or the government of a country can smooth consumption by borrowing and lending internationally or within their own country. This form of risk sharing is also known as consumption insurance. This form of consumption smoothing is directed by the agent's intertemporal decisions. For a given level of international borrowing and lending, the aggregate amount of saving in a country must be reflected in the country's investment level, as measured by the difference between aggregate income (GNP) and total consumption (Cons).

It was previously stated that financial integration would lead to welfare improvements. Following Corbett (2010), these improvements stem from the increase in tax revenue for the domestic government and the possibility of economies of scale. She further argues that countries with low levels of consumption risk sharing have the most to gain from financial integration. On the macro policy side, financial integration may lead to greater scrutiny of monetary and fiscal policy.

Methodologies

To achieve our main objectives, we use two different approaches. These approaches are the estimation of a risk-sharing model and the calculation of investment intensity. The first part of this section discusses the framework of the risk-sharing model, which uses the modified variance decomposition technique. This technique allows us to quantify the proportion of shocks to GDP that are smoothed through international factor income flows, saving behaviour, and the amount of shocks that are not smoothed. In addition to the first approach, we use the results from the investment intensity index to approximate how the risk sharing actually takes place in East Asian countries. The second part of this section is devoted to explaining the index. In the third part, we discuss the estimation strategy used to estimate the risk-sharing model.

Decomposing cross-sectional variance in aggregate output

Asdrubali *et al.* (1996) modified variance decomposition techniques to break down the channels of risk sharing. They rule out any heterogeneity that may arise at the country levels, for example, citizenship and type of government. This framework also assumes that GDP is exogenous.[4]

We start with the following identity:

$$GDP^i = (GDP^i/GNP^i)\,(GDP^i/Cons^i) \tag{4.1}$$

where i is an index of countries.

In order to obtain a simple measure from (4.1), we take logs and differences on both sides:

$$\Delta\log(GDP^i) = \Delta\log(GDP^i) - \Delta\log(GNP^i) + \Delta\log(GNP^i) - \Delta\log(Cons^i) + \Delta\log(Cons^i) \tag{4.2}$$

Multiplying both sides by $\Delta\log(GDP^i)$ and taking expectations, we obtain the following decomposition of cross-sectional variance in GDP:

$$\mathrm{Var}\{\Delta\log(GDP^i)\} = \mathrm{cov}\{\Delta\log(GDP^i); \Delta\log(GDP^i) - \Delta\log(GNP^i)\} \tag{4.3}$$
$$+ \mathrm{cov}\{\Delta\log(GDP^i); \Delta\log(GNP^i) - \Delta\log(Cons^i)\}$$
$$+ \mathrm{cov}\{\Delta\log(GDP^i); \Delta\log(Cons^i)\}$$

Divide both sides by the $\mathrm{var}\{\Delta\log(GDP^i)\}$ to get:

$$1 = \mathrm{cov}\{\Delta\log(GDP^i); \Delta\log(GDP^i) - \Delta\log(GNP^i)\}/\mathrm{var}\{\Delta\log(GDP^i)\} \tag{4.4}$$
$$+ \mathrm{cov}\{\Delta\log(GDP^i); \Delta\log(GNP^i) - \Delta\log(Cons^i)\}/\mathrm{var}\{\Delta\log(GDP^i)\}$$
$$\mathrm{cov}\{\Delta\log(GDP^i); \Delta\log(Cons^i))\}/\mathrm{var}\{\Delta\log(GDP^i)\}$$

Note that the first term on the right-hand side of (4.4) is the ordinary least square (OLS) formula of the slope in the bivariate regression between $\Delta\log(GDP^i) - \Delta\log(GNP^i)$ on $\Delta\log(GDP^i)$; the second term is the slope in bivariate regression between $\Delta\log(GNP^i) - \Delta\log(Cons^i)$ on $\Delta\log(GDP^i)$; and the last term is the slope of the OLS formula for the regression between

$\Delta\log(Cons^i)$ and $\Delta\log(GDP^i)$. We define βk, βc and βu as the corresponding parameters from the OLS regression and rewrite (4.4) to get:

$$1 = \beta k + \beta c + \beta u \qquad (4.5)$$

Investment intensity index

The investment intensity index is given by:

$$\frac{A_{ij}}{A_i} \Big/ \frac{L_j}{L_w} \qquad (4.6)$$

where A_{ij} is the asset holding by country i in country j; A_i is the total foreign asset holding by country i; L_j is the total of assets held by foreigners in country j; and L_w is the global total of foreign assets.

Corbett (2010) asserts that intensity indices can indicate whether bilateral holdings of assets are large or small in terms of the investing country's total holdings of foreign assets and the recipient country's size in the world. The indices parallel the idea of intensity indices used in international trade and indicate whether the asset holding by a particular country in another country is a large share of the investor country's holdings relative to the size of the host country. For example, if country i holds 10 per cent of its total overseas assets in country j, and country j accounts for 10 per cent of the world's foreign-held assets, then the intensity of i's holdings in j would be one. Numbers larger than one indicate that holdings by j in i are disproportionately large relative to i's role as a host to foreign portfolio investment.

Estimation of the risk-sharing model

In the preceding section, we have shown how the framework developed by Asdrubali *et al.* (1996) could be used to quantify the extent of risk sharing via the various channels, and how it corresponds to the slope of the OLS regression. Thus, we can estimate the following system of equations (where all variables are in constant per capita):

$$\Delta\log(GDP^i) - \Delta\log(GNP^i) = d_{k,t} + \beta_k\Delta\log(GDP^i) + e^i_{k,t} \qquad (4.7)$$

$$\Delta\log(GNP^i) - \Delta\log(Cons^i) = d_{c,t} + \beta_c\Delta\log(GDP^i) + e^i_{c,t}$$

$$\Delta\log(Cons^i) = d_{u,t} + \beta_u\Delta\log(GDP^i) + e^i_{u,t}$$

where $d_{k,t}$, $d_{c,t}$ and $d_{u,t}$ are time-fixed effects. The time-fixed effects capture year-specific impacts on the growth rate, specifically the aggregate output of nine East Asian countries. So, the β coefficients could be interpreted as the weighted average of year-by-year cross-sectional regressions.[5]

Next, we discuss the connection between the conceptual frameworks that we developed earlier and the sign and magnitude of the parameters in (4.5), which is equivalent to (4.7) (Sørensen and Yosha, 1998). If the region has full risk sharing, then $\text{cov}\{\Delta\log(GDP^i),\Delta\log(Cons^i)\} = 0$, and hence $\beta u = 0$. However, if risk sharing is not achieved, the consumption level in country i changes positively with individual shocks to country i's output, and we have $\beta u > 0$. Sørensen and Yosha (1998) claim that, if we run a regression of consumption on output using cross-sectional data and we also control for fluctuations in regional consumption, we have a test of full risk sharing. Their view was indirectly echoed by Asdrubali *et al.* (1996), Kim *et al.* (2006) and Yehoue (2005), who used the same approach to quantify the channels of risk sharing.

If full risk sharing is achieved via international capital market channels, then

$$\text{cov}\{\Delta\log(GNP^i),\Delta\log(GDP^i)\} = 0$$

and, hence,

$$\text{cov}\{\Delta\log(GDP^i),\Delta\log(GDP^i) - \Delta\log(GNP^i)\} = \text{var}\{\Delta\log(GDP^i)\}$$

implying that $\beta k = 1$.[6]

Suppose that full risk sharing is not achieved via the international capital-market channel, but is achieved through the combination of this channel and the credit-market channel. This causes the condition (4.5) to become $1 = \beta k + \beta c$.

In any case, coefficient βu represents the share of shocks to GDP that remains unsmoothed, and coefficients βk and βc represent the shares of shocks to GDP that are dampened by the change in net factor income and the change in national savings. We expect βu, which shows the extent of the unsmoothed part, to be positive if a full risk-sharing mechanism is not achieved. On the other hand, we do not expect any particular sign for βk and βc. This is because we leave open the possibility of dis-smoothing in our observations.

Importantly, βc does not measure which countries smooth consumption optimally via saving. It measures the marginal share of shocks to GDP smoothed via savings (Sørensen and Yosha, 1998). Nor does $\beta u > 0$ indicate that, given the uninsured shocks to income, consumption is not intertemporally smoothed optimally. On the other hand, it measures the amount of deviation of regional consumption patterns from the full risk-sharing allocation.

Now we will define each of the variables in the above system. As seen, we have an identical regressor for all of the equations, which is the growth in GDP. Given the fact that the constant represents time-fixed effects, change in the covariate captures the change in aggregate output outside year-specific components on the regional growth of GDP. In other words, a change in the growth rate of GDP represents shocks to GDP. The next variable, $\Delta\log(GDP^i) - \Delta\log(GNP^i)$, represents the change in the net factor income of a country.

$\Delta\log(GNP-) - \Delta\log(Cons^i)$ captures the difference between growth in aggregate income and aggregate consumption and can be used to proxy national savings. The last term is $\Delta\log(Cons^i)$, which measures growth in total consumption.

In short, using the above system, we can measure how shocks to GDP affect the other three variables: net factor income payment, total consumption and national savings. As we have a panel data estimation with time-fixed effects, our estimator yields consistent estimates, even if there are unobserved regional shocks that affect all countries (e.g. Wooldridge, 2002, 2008).

The model in (4.7) consists of three linear regressions for some N countries that expand for T periods.[7] Our objective is to find an appropriate estimator that could take into account such a degree of complexity. We call (4.7) a seemingly unrelated regression (SUR) system (Wooldridge, 2002). We assume that the error terms of each equation have desirable properties: zero mean, constant variance and no serial correlation. However, we will test whether the error in one equation correlates with other errors in different equations, but in the same country. We employ the Breusch–Pagan test (BP test) for error independence to check. It turns out that the conclusion from this test will determine our optimal estimator for (4.7). If the BP test concludes that the errors are independent, then we use OLS as our estimator for the system. On the other hand, if the errors between equations are not independent, then the optimal estimate for the βs is the generalized least square (GLS) estimator or the feasible GLS (FGLS) in an operationalized version. Cameron and Trivedi (2008) state that there exists a more robust estimator than FGLS to estimate a system like (4.7), which is the iterated FGLS (IFGLS).[8]

Wooldridge (2002) discussed the cases in which the OLS estimator and FGLS yield identical results for the SUR system. Case one: OLS and FGLS are identical when the errors are independent; in other words, we do not observe any correlation between equations for a specific country. Case two: both estimators are identical when the regressors of each equation in the systems are identical. Obviously, the specification in (4.7) falls into the latter case, as we have $\Delta\log(GDPi)$ as the regressors for each equation. Another benefit of using FGLS is the fact that we could do joint hypothesis testing of the βs across equations. Using OLS, we can only do hypothesis testing in each equation separately. In addition to that, OLS assumes that the variance matrix of the vector of error is non-singular. System (4.7) clearly does not satisfy the singularity condition, owing to the additive constraint in (4.5).

To overcome the singularity issue in our SUR system, we use a reparameterization 'trick', as explained in Wooldridge (2002). In this trick, we exploit condition (4.5), $\beta u = 1 - \beta k - \beta c$, and substitute it into one of the equations, which is βu (4.7). In so doing, we can estimate all of the equations jointly. The result is as follows:

$$\Delta\log(Cons^i) = d_{u,t} + (1 - \beta k - \beta c)\Delta\log(GDP^i) + e^i_{u,t} \tag{4.8}$$

With some rearrangement, this becomes:

$$\Delta\log(Cons^i) - \Delta\log(GDP^i) = d_{u,t} + (\beta k + \beta c)\Delta\log(GDP^i) + e^i_{u,t} \qquad (4.9)$$

We replace the last equation in (4.7) with (4.9).

Data descriptions and summary statistics

Data

This chapter utilizes Penn World Table version 6.2 (hereafter PWTv62), collected from the Centre for International Comparisons of Production, Income and Prices at the University of Pennysylvania (Heston *et al.*, 2006). This version of PWT used the data in thirty OECD countries as a benchmark and 2002 as the base year. The compiler utilized several different methodologies to make sure all the series could be used in an international comparison study. This study focuses on nine East Asian countries: Indonesia, Malaysia, Singapore, Thailand, the Philippines, Korea, Japan, China and Hong Kong. We cover the period from 1971 to 2003.

The first variable is real GDP. This variable acts as a proxy for aggregate output. For consistency, the PWT compiler produced the GDP series by employing some aggregation techniques that have taken into account price and currency differences between countries.

The second variable is total consumption. PWT compilers did not provide these data directly, but provided estimates for the ratios of consumptions by the private and government sectors to real GDP. We used this measure to calculate total consumption by multiplying the share of each of those components of real GDP and adding them together.

We encountered the same problem as before for the GNP data. However, PWT compilers provided the ratio of GNP to GDP. Using this, we were able to estimate the GNP figure. The collectors of PWT data extracted the ratio of GNP to GDP from World Bank and UN archives. As the PWT compilers did not provide the ratio of GNP to GDP for Taiwan, and we could not find the source of Taiwan GNP data as used in Kim *et al.* (2006), we decided to drop Taiwan from our sample. We exploited the CPIS published by the IMF to calculate the investment intensity index. This dataset is a unique tool for capturing the world totals and the geographical distribution of the holdings of portfolio assets. Hence, by analysing these data, we could infer some pattern in capital flows between countries and provide some intuition on how the risk sharing actually takes place between countries. We only used the total of portfolio investment assets, without further disaggregating it into more detailed types of asset. We used only two years of data: 2001 and 2007.

Summary statistics

Table 4.1 compares the summary statistics for several variables in three different periods. The first variable to compare is the average economic growth, as measured by growth in GDP per capita. On average, nine East Asian countries had 9.2 per cent growth in their economy before 1997, which was the year of the Asian financial crisis, and it remained above 7 per cent for years after 1997. These numbers look impressive and confirm, to some extent, the tale of the Asian miracle in East Asia. The relatively insignificant difference in the GDP growth pre- and post-crisis indicates that the crisis only affected some of the countries in East Asia. On the other hand, the crisis caused an increase in volatility of the economy of nine East Asian countries, as measured by its standard deviation. The volatility of growth of output increased from 4.7 per cent in the pre-crisis period to 5.2 per cent in periods that include the crisis. The patterns were similar to the other three variables, except for the change in net factor income, which remained unchanged.

Table 4.1 shows that the growth of consumption is lower than the growth of output and income in all three different periods. This is a rough indicator of the saving process in these countries. Table 4.1 also suggests that the credit market is one channel that was dominant in absorbing the shocks to GDP. This last claim needs further justification, and, in the following section, we try to evaluate it using the proposed econometric framework.

Now we move on to describe the geographic breakdown of total portfolio investment assets. In 2001, most of the East Asian countries held significant amounts of US assets. For example, Indonesia investors invested approximately US$248 million in the US market. The figure was even higher for other countries, such as Japan, Korea, Hong Kong, the Philippines and Thailand. Only Singapore held a balanced portfolio asset: the amount of money invested in the US market was roughly equal to the amount of money invested in East Asian markets.

Table 4.2 also explains the pattern in which foreign countries hold domestic assets. Taking Malaysia as an example, almost US$6 million of their assets were held by Singaporeans, whereas Hong Kong and Japanese investors only held about US$4.9 million of Malaysian assets in 2001. Likewise, Singaporean investors held a significant amount of Japanese assets. These two examples show that Singaporeans were actively holding East Asian countries' assets.

Table 4.1 Summary statistics for several variables

	1971–2003		*1971–2000*		*1971–96*	
Variable	*Mean*	*Std dev.*	*Mean*	*Std dev.*	*Mean*	*Std dev.*
$\Delta\log(GDP)$	0.079	0.052	0.083	0.052	0.092	0.047
$\Delta\log(GNP)$	0.079	0.053	0.083	0.052	0.091	0.047
$\Delta\log(Cons)$	0.078	0.047	0.081	0.048	0.088	0.041
$\Delta\log(GDP^i) - \log(GNP)$	0.000	0.012	0.000	0.012	0.000	0.012
$\Delta\log(GNP^i) - \log(Cons)$	0.002	0.031	0.002	0.03	0.003	0.03

Source: PWTv62

Table 4.2 Geographic breakdown of total portfolio investment assets, 2001 (US$ million)

Recipients	*Investor*									
	East Asia								*Non-East Asia*	
	HK	*IND*	*JPN*	*KOR*	*MAL*	*PHI*	*SGP*	*THL*	*AUS*	*US*
Australia	18,575.00	54.90	19,179.60	52.42	21.67	9.98	7,743.11	9.00	—	55,182.65
China, PR	8,416.00	0.03	1,669.24	157.42	7.97	–	1,446.99	4.00	—	3,003.88
Hong Kong SAR of China	–	107.43	6,116.28	406.24	75.14	25.03	4,746.66	125.00	2,185.37	32,047.17
Indonesia	–	–	157.63	75.10	51.34	3.00	867.12	15.00	14.30	1,840.82
Japan	9,248.00	3.17	–	176.33	22.26	5.47	10,550.10	1.00	4,615.31	197,839.43
Korea, Republic of	5,100.00	0.08	5,834.95	–	11.13	6.54	3,215.82	–	429.41	34,474.50
Malaysia	2,421.00	2.11	2,538.18	452.41	–	8.96	6,886.15	–	56.17	4,258.11
Philippines	1,239.00	–	1,559.87	109.94	101.82	–	1,181.42	1.00	8.17	4,015.21
Singapore	2,685.00	39.82	2,132.59	152.24	471.16	61.64	–	106.00	778.67	22,817.61
Thailand	1,147.00	0.01	1,037.92	179.31	35.98	0.80	2,361.14	–	21.45	2,698.28
United States	39,253.00	248.95	490,200.13	3,763.86	208.33	1,844.21	18,011.01	292.00	44,446.20	—

Source: CIPS, IMF

Table 4.3 Geographic breakdown of total portfolio investment assets, 2007 (US$ million)

Recipients	*Investor*									
	East Asia								*Non-East Asia*	
	HK	*IND*	*JPN*	*KOR*	*MAL*	*PHI*	*SGP*	*THL*	*AUS*	*US*
Australia	42,436.00	15.97	65,931.22	2,948.54	363.22	359.74	24,119.34	4,157.05	—	222,570.00
China, PR	165,710.00	0.05	15,500.71	11,054.59	106.46	53.13	10,554.24	48.61	—	97,240.00
Hong Kong SAR of China	—	62.15	18,351.22	29,723.93	1,902.31	155.12	19,991.40	152.32	6,063.64	121,276.00
Indonesia	761.00	—	1,433.22	742.03	323.30	48.60	9,332.22	20.36	305.92	18,349.00
Japan	20,826.00	20.36	—	4,881.48	219.87	83.24	8,417.08	63.00	25,003.94	582,342.00
Korea, Republic of	20,233.00	5.37	13,762.89	—	961.14	169.71	20,276.93	525.55	3,905.49	139,555.00
Malaysia	5,875.00	4.00	3,228.55	934.11	—	271.91	25,537.63	48.11	523.67	25,209.00
Philippines	1,104.00	2.28	1,952.49	103.02	80.75	—	1,870.97	3.43	—	14,461.00
Singapore	8,774.00	87.99	11,314.22	1,579.39	2,250.72	500.79	—	565.70	2,766.46	64,710.00
Thailand	1,593.00	23.39	1,771.37	429.66	128.84	35.15	4,495.27	—	—	16,842.00
United States	70,387.00	262.21	813,311.39	52,745.76	1,408.14	2,368.53	40,188.80	1,362.28	182,311.35	—

Source: CIPS, IMF

Table 4.4 Unit root test results

Variables	*AUS*	*CHN*	*HK*	*IDN*	*JPN*	*KOR*	*MAL*	*PHI*	*SGP*	*THA*	*US*
$\Delta \log(GDP)$	Yes	No	No	No	No	No	No	Yes	No	No	No
$\Delta \log(GNP)$	No	Yes	Yes	Yes	Yes	No	No	No	No	Yes	Yes
$\Delta \log(GDP^i) - \log(GNP)$	No	No	No	No	No	No	No	No	No	No	No
$\Delta \log(GNP^i) - \log(Cons)$	No	No	No	No	No	No	No	No	No	No	No

Source: Authors' calculation

Although this measure is weak, we could infer that Singaporeans had been using the risk-sharing mechanism with countries in the region to maximize their welfare.

In 2007, the pattern of total portfolio investment assets differed significantly. Most East Asian countries' investors still invested their money in developed capital markets, such as the United States, Hong Kong and Japan. Using the Philippines as an example, the amount of money of that Filipinos invested in the US market was approximately US$2 billion. This number was higher than the amount that they invested in East Asian countries. On the other hand, Singaporeans invested their money in the same way that they did in 2001, making balanced investments between the East Asian markets and the US market.

In 2007, we found that China had attracted more funds than in 2001. Almost all the countries that we observed in East Asia, excluding Indonesia and Malaysia, started to hold Chinese assets in a significant manner. Aside from China, Hong Kong assets also attracted many investors from the region. The fact that Hong Kong has a more developed financial system could explain this finding. In the meantime, most East Asian investors were investing a relatively large sum in the US market. So, we could infer that these investors were using the US market as means to smooth their consumption by holding US assets.

Results and discussions

Risk-sharing model

In this section, we examine the degree of risk sharing at the aggregate level and within the various groupings of East Asian countries. By doing so, we have a simple sensitivity analysis of consumption risk sharing in East Asian countries. The last part of this section discusses the effect of including the United States in consumption risk sharing in several different periods. We use Kim *et al.*'s (2006) grouping of East Asian countries. These groups are as follows: The first group is ASEAN-5, which consists of Indonesia, Malaysia, the Philippines, Singapore and Thailand. The next group is North-East Asia

(NEA), comprising China, Korea and Japan. The last one consists of developed countries – Korea, Japan, Hong Kong and Singapore.

We use PWTv62 as the basis of our analysis of risk sharing in nine East Asian countries from this point forward. This is because PWTv61 only covers the data until the year 2000. Given our research question and the fact that there are some improvements in the PWTv62 data, we decided to use PWTv62 as the basis for our analysis.

We present the results of the unit root test for all variables in Table 4.4. Following the procedures in Wooldridge (2008) to check for unit roots, we found unit roots in some of the series in some countries. This finding weakly indicates that our study is subject to spurious regression.

In the preceding section, we explained that the estimator we use depends on the independence of the errors between equations. We follow procedures, as suggested by Cameron and Trivedi (2008), to perform the BP test for independence of the errors. First, we estimate system (4.7) using the SUR estimator, borrowing a trick from Wooldridge (2002) to estimate the consumption risk-sharing pattern in nine East Asian countries for the period 1971–2003. Then we calculate the corresponding BP statistic.

We present the estimate of system (4.7) for the period 1971–2003 for the aggregate nine East Asian countries. The numbers in parentheses below each estimate are standard errors. We also attach the value of the BP statistic for this system.

$$\Delta\log(GDP^i) - \Delta\log(GNP^i) = -0.0019 + 0.0235\Delta\log(GDP^i) + e^i_{k,t} \quad (4.10)$$
$$(0.00138) \ (0.0138)$$

$$\Delta\log(GNP^i) - \Delta\log(Cons^i) = -0.0164 + 0.2245\Delta\log(GDP^i) + e^i_{c,t}$$
$$(0.00322) \ (0.0321)$$

$$\Delta\log(Cons^i) = 0.0184 + 0.7519\Delta\log(GDP^i) + e^i_{u,t}$$
$$(0.00293) \ (0.0292)$$

BP statistic = 283.557; p-value (0.000).

Based on the conclusion of the BP statistic, we find enough evidence to reject the null hypothesis of no correlation between equations in this SUR system. This result justifies the decision to use the SUR estimator to estimate system (4.7).

Short interpretations of the estimation result of (4.10) are as follows. Only 2.3 per cent of shocks to the GDP of nine East Asian countries in the period 1971–2003 was due to the change in net factor income payments. This number, however, is statistically not different from zero. This suggests that the role of the international capital market in consumption risk sharing is far from optimal. From the second equation in (4.10), we find that 22.45 per cent of shocks to GDP were smoothed via saving-related activities, and this number is statistically significantly different from zero. Therefore, we observe a relatively significant role of the international credit-market channel in absorbing shocks to the GDP of nine East Asian countries. In the last equation, we identify that the amount of deviation of East Asian regional consumption patterns from full risk-sharing allocation is about 75.19 per cent, and we have enough evidence that this number is different from zero. This number can also be interpreted as the amount of shocks to the GDP that remain unsmoothed.

Table 4.5 reports the estimation results of the risk-sharing pattern in several groups of countries in East Asia. Columns 5 and 6 present the BP and F statistics. The F statistic that we present in Table 4.5 is used to test the null hypothesis of the insignificance of the capital- and credit-market channels in absorbing shocks to the GDP. From the p-value, we have enough evidence to reject the hypothesis that the capital and credit markets are not significant in absorbing shocks to GDP. Based on the p-value of the BP statistic, we find that, within the countries, errors between equations are correlated, and this conclusion again supports the use of the SUR estimator to estimate (4.7) for various groupings. The conclusion of these tests is consistent for all subgroups.

For the ASEAN-5 countries, the percentage of shocks to GDP that were smoothed through lending and borrowing activities is about 26 per cent. Surprisingly, this figure is not significantly different from that in developed countries. The importance of the international credit market in ASEAN-5 from 1971 to 2003 was similar to that of the EC8[9] countries from 1981 to 1990. Our own calculations for nine East Asian countries for the period 1981–90 showed that the marginal amount of shocks to GDP absorbed by saving behaviour was approximately 28 per cent, compared with Kim *et al.*'s (2006) finding of 23 per cent for the same period. From this comparison, we see that the risk-sharing pattern of East Asian countries was the same as that of the European countries during the 1980s (Sørensen and Yosha, 1998). For other

Table 4.5 Risk-sharing pattern in various subgroups for 1971–2003

Subgroups	*Capital market*	*Credit market*	*Unsmoothed*	*BP stat*	*F stat*
ASEAN-5	2.8	25.50	71.7	157.409	27.16
	(2.0)	(4.2)	(3.8)	(0.00)	(0.00)
NEA	0.10	23.56	74.54	104.614	11.10
	(1.9)	(5.7)	(5.9)	(0.00)	(0.00)
ASEAN-5 + NEA	2.07	24.81	73.12	252.470	39.13
	(1.49)	(3.38)	(3.06)	(0.00)	(0.00)
Developed	2.09	25.97	71.94	146.769	26.60
	(2.07)	(4.94)	(4.2)	(0.00)	(0.00)

Notes: Standard errors in parentheses. The numbers below the BP statistic and F statistic are p-values.
Source: PWTv62

groups, such as ASEAN-5 plus the NEA and the NEA alone, the role of the credit market is about 24 per cent on average, similar to our finding in the preceding paragraph on the aggregate risk-sharing pattern in East Asian countries.

Moving to the capital-market channel, we can see that there is a substantial difference between the role of the capital market in NEA countries versus that in the other three groups. The capital-market channel in NEA accounts for only 0.1 per cent, and this figure is lower than what the other groups of countries have achieved. Similar to previous findings, we conclude that the percentage of smoothing being carried out by the change in net factor income is statistically not different from zero. Our findings on this matter are echoed by Kim *et al.* (2006) and can be explained to some extent by the China factor. Before 2001, the year that China was accepted as a full member of the World Trade Organization (WTO), some people argued that China could be classified as a closed economy (Unit, 2003), and this indirectly asserts that exchange of productive assets between China and the other countries is likely to be insignificant. Assuming that this situation persisted until 2000, a year before the WTO accepted China's membership, it is likely that this condition affected the capital-market channel in NEA countries.

One result that remains puzzling is the finding on the fraction of shocks being smoothed between ASEAN-5 and the developed countries. Our calculations show that the former outperforms the latter group, and this is not consistent with the findings in most studies of consumption risk-sharing patterns. These studies find that the fraction of shocks to GDP that are being smoothed is higher in developed countries (Yehoue, 2005; Kim *et al.*, 2006). One possible explanation for the puzzle is our decision to exclude Taiwan from our analysis. In addition to this, the fact that the countries in the ASEAN-5 group began their economic cooperation in early 1970 could be another explanation. This formal cooperation between the ASEAN-5 countries is marked by the formation of the ASEAN in 1967, with a goal to promote economic cooperation between member countries.

After examining the pattern of risk sharing between groups of countries, we now investigate whether the same pattern is observed in three different periods, including the United States. We consider the following three periods: 1971–2003, 1971–2000 and 1971–96. Table 4.5 displays the comparison of the risk-sharing channel. In short, introducing the United States into the framework does not alter the overall pattern of consumption risk sharing that we found in the previous sections. For example, in the period 1971–96, we see that the cross-country factor income flow amounted to only 3 per cent. This number is not statistically significantly different from zero. Therefore, the pattern of consumption risk sharing when the United States is included is relatively similar to the pattern of consumption risk sharing across the nine East Asian countries. Hence, the presence of the United States does not provide much help to East Asian countries to smooth their GDP shocks via the common channels.

So far, we have several different analyses of the risk-sharing pattern in nine East Asian countries: an aggregate risk-sharing pattern for nine East Asian countries; a risk-sharing pattern between different groups of countries; a risk-sharing pattern in different time periods; and a risk-sharing pattern that includes the United States (see Tables 4.6–4.8).

Table 4.6 Sensitivity analysis of risk-sharing channels

Channel	*Periods*	*Kim* et al. *(2006)*	*System (7)*	*System (7)*
Capital market	1971–2000	0.6	0.4	1.6
		(0.8)	(1.0)	(1.4)
	1971–96	2.1	2.2	3.4
		(0.9)	(1.2)	(1.7)
	1991–2000	–2.4	–2.7	0.7
		(1.2)	(2.1)	(3.9)
Capital market	1971–2000	19.4	23.0	21.5
		(3.9)	(3.5)	(3.4)
	1971–96	18.9	28.0	28.0
		(4.2)	(4.2)	(4.0)
	1991–2000	11.6	18.0	9.9
		(6.0)	(5.9)	(6.5)
Unsmoothed	1971–2000	79.6	76.6	76.9
		(4.0)	(3.5)	(3.2)
	1971–96	78.7	69.8	68.6
		(4.2)	(4.1)	(3.7)
	1991–2000	92.1	84.7	89.4
		(6.1)	(5.5)	(5.2)
Source		PWT	PWTv61	PWTv62
Estimator		SUR	SUR	SUR
Number of countries		10	9	9

Note: The numbers below the BP statistic and F statistic are p-values.
Source: Authors' calculation

Table 4.7 Consumption smoothing and risk sharing (per cent): East Asian countries and the US

Periods	*Capital market*	*Credit market*	*Unsmoothed*	*BP stat*
1971–2003	2.43	22.17	75.40	348.287
	(1.22)	(2.87)	(1.77)	(0.00)
1971–2000	1.74	21.13	77.13	313.728
	(1.22)	(5.7)	(5.9)	(0.00)
1971–96	3.13	26.79	70.08	275.824
	(1.46)	(3.52)	(3.22)	(0.00)

Note: Standard errors in parentheses. The numbers below the BP statistic and F statistic are p-values.
Source: PWTv62

Table 4.8 Estimate of country variations, 1971–2003

Countries	*Capital market*	*Credit market*	*Unsmoothed*
Benchmark: all countries excluding Japan			
China	–0.55	22.66	97.43
Hong Kong	4.44	3.04	91.2
Indonesia	1.96	4.36	78.63
Korea	–0.61	19.4	64.73
Malaysia	1.88	35.91	77.03
Philippines	4.01	21.1	62.67
Singapore	4.89	33.33	56.72
Thailand	–0.64	38.2	75.96

Source: Authors' calculation

It is immediately apparent from the three results that the contribution of the international capital market to consumption risk sharing is insignificant. This finding is consistent with Kim *et al.* (2006) and Sørensen and Yosha (1998), who find the same pattern in European and OECD countries. The insignificance of this channel may suggest the existence of a 'home-bias puzzle' in the region (French and Poterba, 1991). The home-bias puzzle is a situation in which a citizen in one country prefers to invest his or her money in his or her own domestic capital market rather than in the capital market of another country. As argued by Obstfeld and Rogoff (1996), one reason that this can happen in East Asian countries is the absence of a supranational legal authority whose main task is to enforce contracts between countries. In addition to the home-bias puzzle, which may be caused by the lack of a supranational legal authority, the absence of common capital markets in East Asia could play some role in explaining the finding that countries in East Asia are not smoothing their income shocks via the international capital market.

In addition to the above analysis, we estimate the risk-sharing channels in a way to find variations in country levels. We used a different strategy to estimate the country variation. First, we selected countries to be benchmark countries. In relation to that, we used all countries except Japan in our observations. Then, we defined a dummy variable for each country and interacted this dummy with the growth rate of output. In the next process, we estimated system (4.7) by including these two new variables. To illustrate, to estimate China's country variation, we estimate system (4.7), including a dummy variable for China and the interaction of this dummy with the growth rate of output. It can be seen in Table 4.8 that around 97 per cent of the total shocks to GDP in China were unsmoothed. In general, the pattern of risk sharing in each country does not differ much from the aggregation analysis that most of the shocks are still unsmoothed. However, our result does not hold when the risk-sharing model (4.7) was estimated separately, using quarterly data for each country (see Table 4.9).

Table 4.9 Estimate of risk-sharing channels using quarterly data

Country	*Capital market*	*Credit market*	*Unsmoothed*	*Period*	*Conclusion*
Japan	–0.00169	–0.0055	1.007*	1969:1–2009:3	Uninsured
Indonesia	–0.011	1.09*	–0.087	1997:1–2009:3	Fully insured
Malaysia	0.0865	0.0167	0.8967*	2000:1–2008:4	90% unsmoothed
Thailand	–0.161*	1.001*	0.15*	1993:1–2009:3	Fully insured
Korea	0.011*	1.02*	–0.341	1969:1–2009:2	Fully insured
Hong Kong	0.109	0.625*	0.264*	1999:1–2009:2	73% insured
Philippines	0.01	0.07	0.91*	1981:1–2006:3	90% unsmoothed

* Statistically significant
Source: IFS, IMF

Intensity index result calculation

As explained in the previous section, we use investment intensity indices as a means to identify the relative engagement of countries in East Asia with their neighbours. Our goal is to identify which countries have started the risk-sharing behaviour. One must bear in mind that our approach is far from ideal, as the index only shows the trade in investment portfolios between countries, and nothing more.

Table 4.10 establishes that, in 2001, there were two countries that had relatively high engagement with the other East Asian countries, as shown by the two intensity indices, which have a value of more than one, both as investors and recipients of funds. In contrast to Singapore and Malaysia, investors in countries such as Indonesia and the Philippines decided to hold assets from countries with more developed financial markets, such as Hong Kong and the United States. This finding, of course, is not surprising and even confirms our previous suspicions about the home-bias puzzle in East Asian countries. However, the presence of a deep financial system can overcome the tendencies for investors to invest in the domestic market, as shown in the case of Indonesia and the Philippines in 2001.

In 2007, the pattern of exchange of assets was different. Developing countries such as Indonesia, for example, were starting to reallocate their funds from the US market to the financial markets of neighbouring countries. In 2001, Indonesia's intensity index as an investor in the US market was approximately 1.42, whereas, in 2007, the figure dropped to 0.65, as shown in Table 4.11. Table 4.11 also reveals Japan's lack of portfolio investment in the developing countries. Japanese investors only hold a significant amount of US and Australian assets.

Table 4.10 Intensity index of total portfolio investment assets, 2001 (US$ million)

Recipients	*Investor*									
	East Asia								*Non-East Asia*	
	HK	*IND*	*JPN*	*KOR*	*MAL*	*PHI*	*SGP*	*THL*	*AUS*	*US*
Australia	6.76	5.73	1.11	0.49	0.71	0.35	5.50	0.82	—	1.79
China, PR	25.68	0.02	0.81	12.29	2.19	—	8.63	3.04	—	0.82
Hong Kong SAR of China	—	19.69	0.62	6.65	4.33	1.54	5.93	19.92	3.62	1.83
Indonesia	—	—	0.28	21.42	51.61	3.22	18.88	41.66	0.41	1.83
Japan	1.05	0.10	—	0.51	0.23	0.06	2.35	0.03	1.36	2.01
Korea, Republic of	4.11	0.02	0.75	—	0.81	0.51	5.06	—	0.90	2.48
Malaysia	6.63	1.66	1.11	31.69	—	2.36	36.82	—	0.40	1.04
Philippines	6.02	—	1.21	13.67	44.62	—	11.21	1.21	0.10	1.74
Singapore	3.27	13.92	0.41	4.75	51.82	7.24	—	32.21	2.46	2.48
Thailand	5.90	0.01	0.85	23.62	16.70	0.40	23.74	—	0.29	1.24
United States	0.78	1.42	1.56	1.92	0.37	3.54	0.70	1.45	2.30	—

Source: CIPS, IMF

Table 4.11 Intensity index of total portfolio investment assets, 2007 (US$ million)

Recipients	*Investor*									
	East Asia							*Non-East Asia*		
	HK	*IND*	*JPN*	*KOR*	*MAL*	*PHI*	*SGP*	*THL*	*AUS*	*US*
Australia	2.99	0.41	1.43	1.02	1.54	3.02	4.07	15.50	—	1.70
China, PR	20.26	0.00	0.58	6.63	0.78	0.78	3.09	0.31	—	1.29
Hong Kong SAR of China	—	3.28	0.82	21.06	16.53	2.67	6.91	1.17	1.76	1.90
Indonesia	0.66	—	0.39	3.18	16.98	5.06	19.50	0.94	0.54	1.73
Japan	0.72	0.26	—	0.82	0.45	0.34	0.69	0.11	1.73	2.17
Korea, Republic of	2.78	0.27	0.58	—	7.94	2.78	6.67	3.82	1.08	2.07
Malaysia	2.93	0.73	0.50	2.28	—	16.18	30.47	1.27	0.53	1.36
Philippines	1.39	1.05	0.76	0.64	6.14	—	5.66	0.23	—	1.98
Singapore	2.57	20.16	1.02	2.27	39.73	17.54	—	8.79	1.63	2.05
Thailand	1.58	8.46	0.54	2.09	7.67	4.15	10.65	—	—	1.80
United States	0.48	0.65	1.71	1.76	0.58	1.92	0.65	0.49	2.50	—

Source: CIPS, IMF

Concluding remarks

This chapter investigates the extent of consumption risk sharing in nine East Asian countries between 1971 and 2003 using PWT data. In addition, it evaluates the effect of including the United States in the observations. We have employed the variance decomposition technique developed by Asdrubali *et al.* (1996). We provide evidence that, for nine East Asian countries, about 22 per cent of shocks to GDP are smoothed via the credit-market channel, whereas factor income flows do not smooth income shocks. We further found that around 75 per cent of shocks to GDP remain unsmoothed. These findings are consistent across subgroups of countries. Moreover, the inclusion of the United States does not change the overall pattern that we found.

The general picture that arises is that capital- and credit-market channels in nine East Asian countries are not well integrated, owing to the low portion of change in net factor income and national savings adjustment. Our conclusion is supported by the investment intensity calculation. These two imply that there is substantial room for improvement in the design of market mechanisms for income and consumption risks. In this respect, policymakers in East Asian countries should give serious consideration to any attempt to increase financial integration in the region. If they are able to do so, the countries will experience welfare improvements via the increase in risk-sharing mechanisms between countries.

Despite the intuitive result, we found several weaknesses in terms of the methodology. First, we assumed that GDP was an exogenous series. To some extent, this assumption may not be realistic, as almost all studies using time-series data of macroeconomic variables conclude that GDP series are actually endogenous (e.g. Nelson and Plosser, 1982). Second, our approach of using the investment intensity index that was applied to CPIS data is far from ideal, because what is required in estimating how the risk sharing takes place in the region includes not only the size of transactions in portfolio assets exchanges, but also a matrix of exchange in cross-country assets.

Notes

1 Paper submitted to the ERIA.
2 Corresponding authors: jenny.corbett@anu.edu.au and achmad.maulana@fe.unpad.ac.id
3 For a complete discussion of the benefits and costs of financial integration in Asia, see Corbett (2010).
4 We test this assumption indirectly by testing whether two lags of growth in consumption could be strong instrument variables for growth in GDP. Based on our over-identifying restriction test, we found that these two variables are weak instruments for the growth rate in GDP.
5 Please consult Asdrubali *et al.* (1996) for a more careful argument of this statement.
6 This claim is based on footnote 19 of Sørensen and Yosha (1998).
7 The main references used for the discussion in this section are Greene (2003), Cameron and Trivedi (2008) and Wooldridge (2002).

8 It is beyond the scope of this study to proceed using this estimator.
9 Belgium, Denmark, France, Germany, Ireland, Italy, the Netherlands and the United Kingdom.

References

Asdrubali, P., Sørensen, B. and Yosha, O. (1996) 'Channels of interstate risk sharing: United States 1963–1990', *The Quarterly Journal of Economics*, 111(4): 1081–110.

Cameron, A. and Trivedi, P. (2008) *Microeconometrics Using Stata*, College Station, TX: Stata Press.

Corbett, J. (2010) 'Asian financial integration', in *Globalization and Economic Integration*, eds N. Gaston and A.M. Khalid, Cheltenham: Edward Elgar.

French, K. and Poterba, J. (1991) 'Investor diversification and international equity markets', *The American Economic Review*, 81(2): 222–6.

Greene, W. (2003) *Econometric Analysis*, Upper Saddle River, NJ: Prentice Hall.

Heston, A., Summers, R. and Aten, B. (2006) *Penn World Table version 6.2*, Center for International Comparisons of Production, Income and Prices at the University of Pennsylvania.

Kim, S., Kim, S.H. and Wang, Y. (2006) 'Financial integration and consumption risk sharing in East Asia', *Japan and the World Economy*, 18(2): 1431–57.

Nelson, C. and Plosser, C. (1982) 'Trends and random walks in macroeconomic time series: some evidence and implications', *Journal of Monetary Economics*, 10: 139–62.

Obstfeld, M. and Rogoff, K. (1996) *Foundations of International Macroeconomics*, Cambridge, MA: MIT Press.

Sørensen, B. and Yosha, O. (1998) 'International risk sharing and European monetary unification', *Journal of International Economics*, 45(2): 211–38.

Unit, E. (2003) *China Country Report*, Economist Intelligence Unit, London, United Kingdom, December.

Wooldridge, J. (2002) *Econometric Analysis of Cross Section and Panel Data*, Cambridge, MA: MIT Press.

Wooldridge, J. (2008) *Introductory Econometrics: A Modern Approach*, Mason, OH: South-Western Cengage Learning.

Yehoue, E. (2005) *International Risk Sharing and Currency Unions: The CFA Zones*, International Monetary Fund, Washington, DC: IMF Institute.

5 Capital structure of firms and real financial linkages in East Asia[1]

Jenny Corbett
Australia–Japan Research Centre, Crawford School, Australian National University

Garry Twite
School of Finance, Actuarial Studies and Applied Statistics, Australian National University

Introduction

Companies raise finance to undertake economic activities in a variety of ways. Some depend heavily on bank loans, while others use their own stores of funds, amassed from retained earnings, with little recourse to outside earnings. Although economic theory may try to develop a general explanation of how firms will finance themselves (or, as in Modigliani–Miller, argue that financial structure is irrelevant, so that there will be no presumption of a systematic pattern in company financing structures), data show that there are a variety of patterns for company finance, and that patterns vary over time and place. However, some systematic patterns can be discerned.

An attempt to uncover such patterns within the East Asian region is, in itself, of interest, because few, if any, studies do this. There are, furthermore, additional important policy questions that can be informed by such a study. The theme of this volume, the linkages between the real and financial sectors of the economy, requires an analysis of several links in a chain. On one side is the financial system itself, where it is important to understand the structure of banks and other financial institutions and how they are financed, what business model they use, and where their vulnerabilities and inefficiencies lie. Surrounding those institutions is a structure of financial (capital) markets that are themselves worthy of study, as failures, inefficiencies or absences of those markets also impact on the provision of finance.

Many studies of financial systems stop there, but, if we are interested in the link between the real behaviour of the economy and how it responds to financial pressures and shocks, then one important element of the black box between the real and financial sides of the economy is the structure of corporate financing. To use the example above, if there is a banking crisis, the firm that relies heavily on bank finance may behave differently from the firm that uses its own finance. In the absence of any crisis, when financial systems are working well, the firm that restricts itself to using only its own finance will probably not grow as rapidly as one that accesses other sources of funding. If we lack knowledge about the way the corporate sector is financed, it may be more difficult to understand how the economy will respond to changes in the financial system. Corbett (2009) surveys the large body of literature on corporate finance, which addresses both microeconomic questions (usually with a positive focus and little policy relevance) and macroeconomic questions (both positive and normative in the literature on growth and finance).

This chapter picks up the challenge identified by Corbett (2009) and analyses the drivers of corporate financing choices in East Asia, and it also gives a preliminary analysis of the effect of financing choices on firms' growth. Although the chapter uses standard analytical methods, it makes a number of new contributions, including the following:

- It creates a large database of financial data from the balance sheets of listed companies in East Asia. Few such databases have been compiled. The data cover the pre- and post-Asian crisis period, allowing a clear picture of the changes through time.
- It considers the combined effects of firm factors, industry characteristics and country features in explaining firms' financial choices and the growth of firms.
- It introduces a measure of financial openness into the country characteristics to allow policy lessons to be drawn about financial opening. Few, if any, studies that use microdata to explain the link between financial structure and growth pay attention to the openness or integration of countries' financial systems.

There is still much work to do to refine the results and to draw correct policy inferences from them. However, the work that has gone into creating this database and demonstrating the uses to which it can be put is a very significant step towards improving understanding of what will make a robust and efficient corporate financial structure in the region.

This chapter is structured as follows. The next section sets out the detailed research questions, and there follows a section describing the data. The fourth section gives a descriptive overview of the data, identifies some intriguing features that are distinctive of the East Asian region and highlights significant changes before and after the Asian crisis. The following section sets out the results from analysis of the drivers of the choice of financial structure (the use of debt versus other types of finance and the choice of debt maturity). The next section describes the results of analysis of the impact of finance on the growth of firms' investment in assets and identifies the key country characteristics that matter. The final section sets out conclusions and opportunities for future research.

The research questions

This chapter addresses a number of distinct but interrelated questions. We are first concerned to see what the structure of finance is like within the region, and whether we can explain the choice of debt, the choice of maturity, the use of trade credit and the extent to which earnings are retained. By using a fairly standard model, we are able to make some comparisons with the results of other samples of countries reported in other literature. These interests dictate two research questions: (1) what are the choices firms make about the extent of debt financing in the countries we are examining, and what determines it; and (2) what are the debt maturity choices of firms and their choices on the retention of earnings and the use of trade credit, and what determines them?

The second part of the chapter considers what effect financing choices have on the growth of investment in two categories of investment: fixed and current assets. This research agenda addresses the question of whether different financial structures (i.e. choice of financing or sources of funds) have an impact on the real behaviour of firms, as demonstrated by their investment decisions.

Data

We use firm-level data from the COMPUSTAT Global Database of Wharton Research Data Services from 1990 to 2009 (the data were collected in December 2009). We include data for Australia, China, Indonesia, India, Japan, Korea, Malaysia, New Zealand, the Philippines, Singapore and Thailand. We were unable to get data for Vietnam, Laos, Cambodia, Brunei Darussalam or Myanmar, and so these countries are not included in the analysis, but would be of considerable interest for future research.

Table 5.1 shows the sample size, which is considerable in total and for most countries. Some cleaning of the data was required, and we dropped companies

Table 5.1 Sample size

	Number of companies	*Total company years*
AUS	1,818	12,856
CHN	1,645	8,538
IDN	265	2,549
IND	1,392	6,217
JPN	3,201	39,803
KOR	917	5,234
MYS	967	9,089
NZL	139	1,077
PHL	151	1,429
SGP	658	5,243
THA	453	4,077
Total	11,606	96,112

Source: COMPUSTAT Global Database

that had negative retained earnings and zero or negative shareholders' equity. Because we are using listed company data, we are not able to draw conclusions about the whole corporate sector, and unlisted SMEs and non-listed firms such as family firms are not covered (see the discussion in Corbett, 2009). Definitions of our financial variables are given in Appendix 2.

Empirical puzzles

Figures 5.1 and 5.2 show patterns in the aggregate data on the use of debt finance in the region. The figures show both sample averages and period averages for individual countries, as there is a presumption that financing patterns differ across countries in both the use of external finance and the composition of that finance. The Appendix figures give the variation over time in the patterns for individual countries, but the discussion in the chapter is limited to the averages.

The figures show the sample averages, aggregate time pattern and country time patterns for the ratios of key financing variables: long-term debt as a share of total financing (LTD/TF); short-term debt as a share of total financing (STD/TF); trade credit as a share of total financing (TC/TF); retained earnings as a share of total financing (RE/TF); and common stock as a share of total financing (CS/TF). Total debt (used later in the regressions) is simply the sum of long-term and short-term debt. These figures therefore show the proportions of each type of finance in the total finance raised by firms.

The noticeable features in Figure 5.1 are the low equity finance ratios in Japan, Korea and India, shown by the ratio CS/TF. These countries also display higher ratios of total debt (LTD/TF and STD/TF) than of equity (stock market) finance, so that they conform to the conventional view of 'debt-financed' Asian economies. However, the other country data call this stereotype into question. Several countries in the region show much higher use of equity finance than of debt; thus, clearly, country differences matter.

Figure 5.2 illustrates two striking features of the financial structure of listed companies in the region. First, it has not been true that retained earnings have been the major source of finance in this region over this time period. Unlike the conventional wisdom reported in Corbett (2009), it appears that listed companies in East Asia and Australia/New Zealand rely heavily on outside sources of finance. The second feature is that, over time, the ratio of equity has risen dramatically as retained earnings have fallen. The trend is particularly noticeable after 2001, and the timing of other changes is also suggestive. The drop in retained earnings began somewhat before the onset of the Asian financial crisis, suggesting that firms were increasingly fragile. During the crisis, retained earnings dropped very steeply and, by 2001, had become negative in Australia and dropped to half their previous levels in the rest of the sample, on average. The individual country results in the Appendix show that, for many of the countries, retentions were negative for the years immediately after the Asian crisis. Even more striking is that, from that time on, the external finance

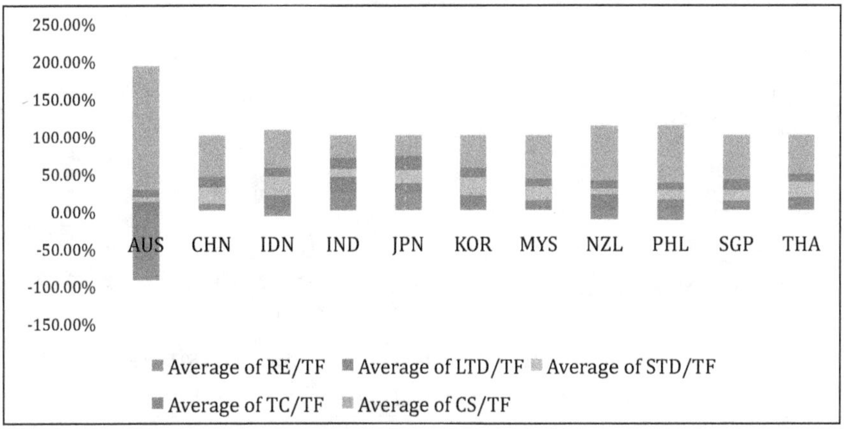

Figure 5.1a Full period (1990–2008) country averages

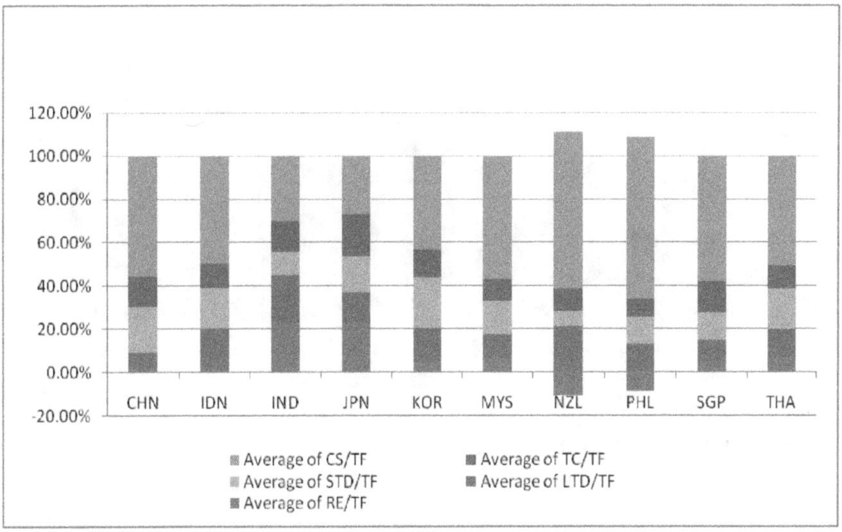

Figure 5.1b Financing structure (without Australia)

came in the form of equity finance rather than debt. It appears that there was financial fragility before the crisis, and that it took several years before companies were able to restructure to cover their growing losses. Once restructuring had been achieved, their access to stock market finance enabled them to use much higher proportions of equity finance than before the crisis. Whether this is a sign of financial health is a different matter: East Asian firms are now much more dependent on external (outside the company) finance than

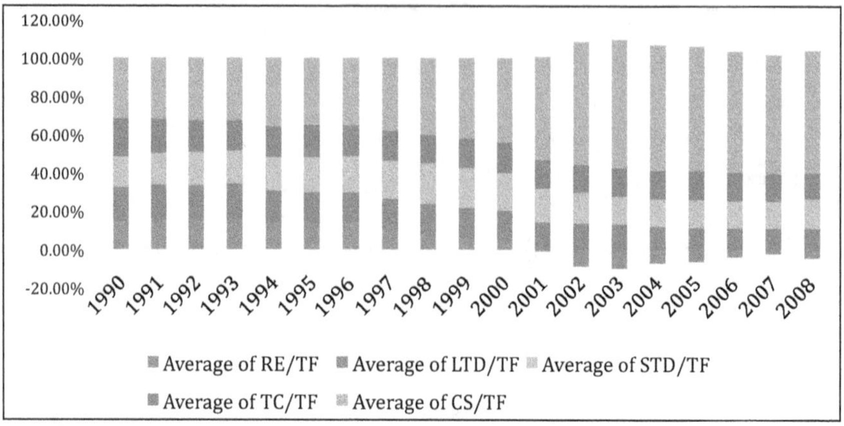

Figure 5.2a Financing structure annual averages (with Australia)

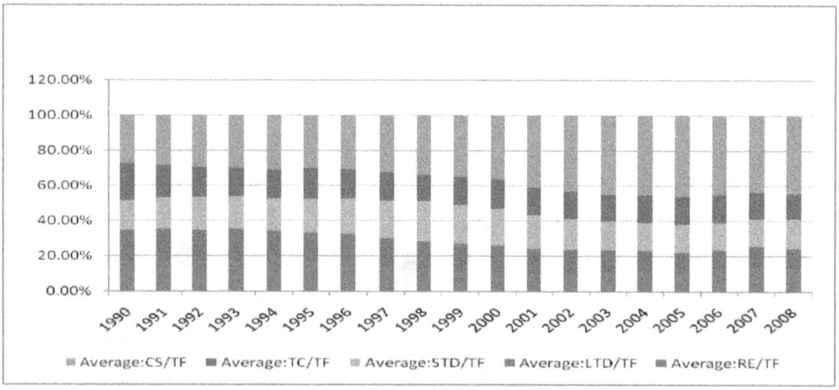

Figure 5.2b Financing structure (without Australia)
Source: COMPUSTAT Global Database

they were previously. We have no data on the origin of funding, and so we cannot distinguish how much is foreign, nor how much comes from other investors in the region compared with elsewhere.

Figures 5.3–5.5 reinforce the empirical puzzle in terms of the financial flow data. These data show the change in firms' financing structure and give a picture of the sources of funds used to finance business activities. Again, there is significant country variation. Rapidly growing countries show higher growth of financing sources than the slow growing ones of Japan, Korea and the Philippines. Another group of three, India, Japan and Korea, show quite different patterns from the rest of the group, with small amounts of new equity finance. All other countries show the significant use of stock market finance that

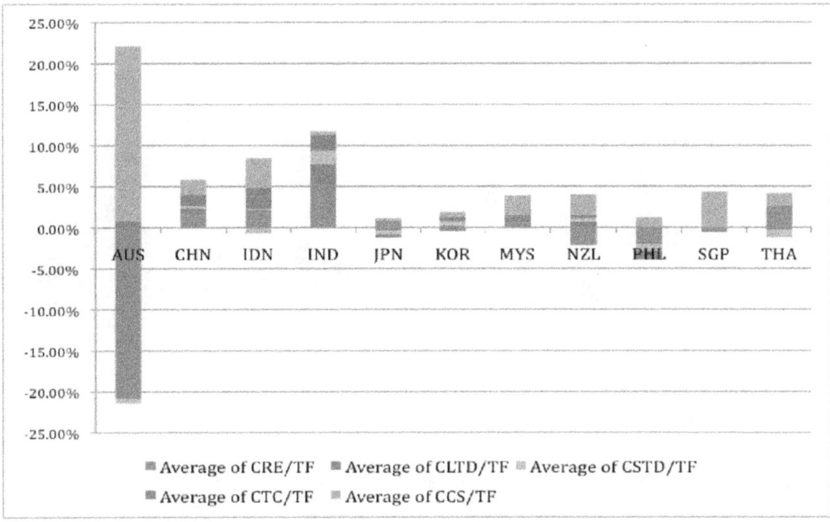

Figure 5.3 Average financing flows for sample period 1990–2008
Source: COMPUSTAT Global Database

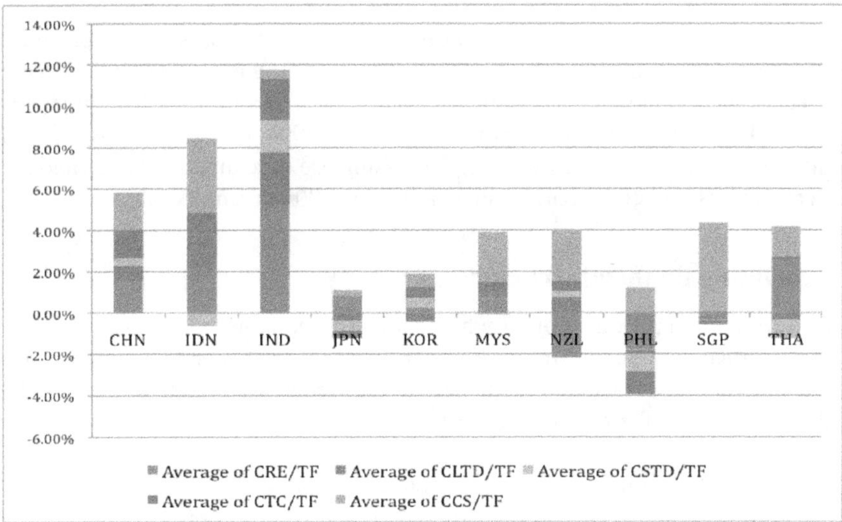

Figure 5.4 Average financing flows for sample period 1990–2008 (without Australia)
Source: COMPUSTAT Global Database

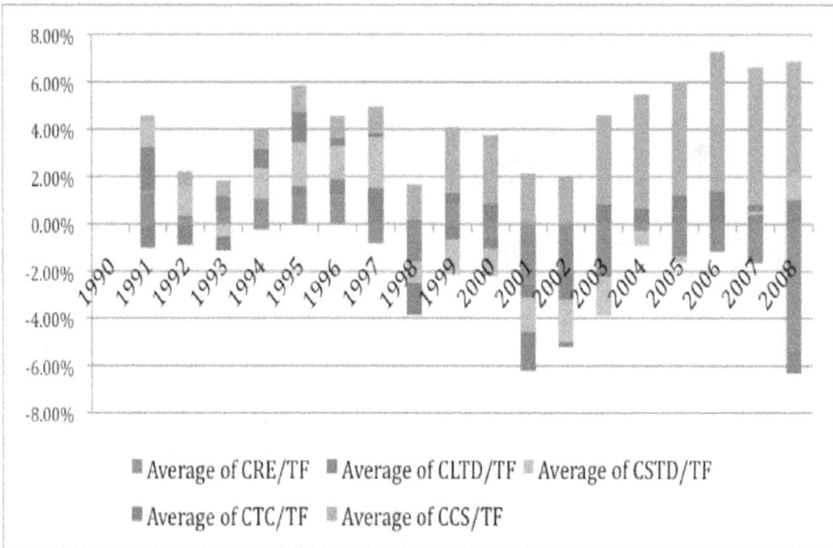

Figure 5.5 Average annual financing flows for all countries in sample, 1990–2008
Source: COMPUSTAT Global Database

is consistent with the position demonstrated above for the outstanding balances of different types of finance. Over time, Figure 5.5 again shows the dramatic effect of the Asian financial crisis on the sources of finance used by companies and the long period of restructuring from 1998 to 2004, where debt was reduced and equity financing increased. The decreasing use of retained earnings and the increasing use of stock market financing since 2004 is remarkable.

Explaining financial structure

We turn now to the question of which variables explain the observed patterns in the choice of financial structure. We run six regressions on the pooled cross-sections for all countries over the period. Each regression aims to explain the choice of one of the dependent variables:

1 total debt (excluding trade credit)/total assets (td_ta);
2 total debt (including trade credit)/total assets (td_tc_ta);
3 retained earnings/shareholder equity (re_shf);
4 long-term debt/total assets (ltd_ta);
5 short-term debt/total assets (std_ta);
6 trade credit/total assets (tc_ta).

In each case, we regress the financing-choice measure on a set of firm-level variables plus a set of industry dummies plus various country characteristics.

Firm-level variables

As further described in Appendix 2, the explanatory variables at the firm level are asset tangibility (fixed assets over total assets); profitability (net income over total assets); firm size (natural logarithm of total assets); the market-to-book ratio (market value of equity over book value of equity); and a dividend payment dummy (dummy equals one if the firm pays a dividend in a given year and zero otherwise).

The justification for this choice of variables is that they are close to the standard firm effects that have been found to be significant in many previous studies of financial structure. Asset tangibility indicates the availability of collateral with which firms can raise external finance, in particular debt. Profitability has been found to be a strong determinant of financial structure, and, in general, firms with high profitability tend to have lower debt ratios (and external finance generally), as they have more internal sources of finance and are not financially constrained. Where tax systems favour corporate income over personal, there is an incentive for firms to retain earnings. Pecking-order theories of finance, whether driven by information asymmetries or other causes, also suggest that retained profits will be used before other sources of finance. Firm size and the market-to-book ratio capture both the growth opportunities for firms and the observation that larger firms have greater access to external finance for a variety of reasons, from better disclosure to better governance. We expect that firms that pay a dividend have additional sources of financing (both internal and external) and are less financially constrained.

Country variables

The country variables cover several institutional features: the legal system (common law versus civil law dummy); a corruption index; a tax compliance variable; a business start-up cost index; a variable to capture the development of the banking system (bank deposits/GDP); and an indicator of whether the banking system is state owned. We also include variables for the stage of development of the economy (an indicator for the level of income) and for the degree of openness of the financial system. Finally, we include indicators showing the degree of development of the debt markets: an indicator of whether there is an explicit bankruptcy code and an index of the extent to which the tax system favours debt. It would be possible, in future work, to include indicators of the transparency of the accounting system and to break down the indicator of openness to look in more detail at the policy implications of different elements of capital-market liberalization. It would also be useful to consider further the structure on the lenders' side of the market, including the barriers to entry in banking and financial services that may restrict the financial choices open to firms.

The justification for these variable is as follows: (1) common-law systems are argued to provide better investor and property rights' protection, making external finance, particularly debt finance, less costly; (2) more corruption means less ability to protect property and to enforce non-defined contracts, giving an advantage to formally specified contracts and resulting in more debt and less investment; (3) higher tax compliance indicates a higher-quality system of regulation and property protection; (4) the fewer days required for contract enforcement, the more efficient the legal system is assumed to be, with the expectation that firms will have access to more debt (and that more investment will be carried out); (5) higher business start-up costs give more protection for entrenched businesses, allowing them to access more debt, although the overall investment impact is unclear. Turning to variables reflecting the level of development of the banking system and the debt markets, we have: (6) the larger the banking system, the more debt we expect firms to use, particularly short-term debt, which is the typical form of bank debt, and the higher we expect their investment to be; (7) where a deposit insurance scheme exists, we also expect more debt, because of the preferences of lenders, and in this case we expect more long-term debt, as banks with protection are more willing to lend long, even with short maturity deposits, and we would expect more investment. Where we have (8) state ownership of banks, we have possible conflicting effects, as state ownership may simply be associated with bigger and fewer banks, predisposed to more short-term debt. State banks may, however, also be more likely to engage in crony or related lending, resulting in more long-term debt to favoured clients, and thus the overall investment impact is unclear.

A second set of country variables indicates the level of development, openness and sophistication of the capital markets, as these all affect the availability of finance, which is, in turn, likely to affect firms' choice of finance. The index of openness is of particular interest in the context of the region's somewhat hesitant commitment to opening capital markets after the Asian crisis. Its theoretical effect is unclear. Although we would expect openness to lead to more investment growth, there is no obvious theoretical presumption about the impact on the choice of debt versus equity or retentions. It would be presumed to make more funds of both types available. The developed economy dummy would likely lead to more use of equity, as developed capital markets should have less asymmetric information and more disclosure (which we do not measure directly in this set of regressions). The effect on the growth of investment is unclear, as growth opportunities may be higher in developing economies rather than in mature, developed ones. The sophistication of the debt market is indicated by the bankruptcy code index, with the expectation that an explicit bankruptcy code (insolvency reorganization index) provides more protection of creditors, allowing use of more debt and more long-term debt. The tax-benefit-to-debt (Miller ratio) variable should have a straightforward effect, where a larger tax benefit to debt would result in more debt being used. We do not consider policy implications from this variable, and it is included here as a control to clarify the effects of other policy and institutional variables, but there would be possibilities for future research on tax effects.

Results

A simple exercise suggests that we should expect that all variables contribute to the explanation of financial structure, rather than any subset. Appendix 4 shows that regressions with all the variables have greater explanatory power than those with only subsets of the variables. This is a much less rigorous test than an approach using the general-to-specific method, or using Akaike information criteria (AIC) tests, but gives a rough idea of the effects of additional variables. The overall picture is consistent with the detailed results reported below. The strong message from both sets of results is that, in explaining financial-structure choices, all elements matter (namely, firm characteristics, industry affiliation and country characteristics).

In Appendix 1, Tables 5.a1.1–5.a1.6 give the results for the regressions, explaining the choice of each of the financial-structure variables.

Firm characteristics

Taking firm-characteristics effects first, the key results for the choice of debt are that higher tangible assets, size and market-to-book ratios are associated with higher levels of total debt. Financially constrained firms (dividend dummy) use less total debt.

Looking at debt maturity, we find that higher tangible assets, size and market-to-book ratios are associated with more long-term debt, and that financially constrained firms (dividend dummy) use less long-term debt. Larger size is also associated with more short-term debt (presumed to be bank debt), whereas financially constrained firms (dividend dummy) use less short-term debt.

Firms that choose higher levels of trade credit have lower levels of tangible assets (i.e. less collateral to offer for bank debt), larger size and higher market-to-book ratios. Although the latter may seem counter-intuitive, it is a feature of trade credit that flows are usually from smaller to larger firms; that is, small businesses are forced to offer credit terms to their larger customers.

We also find that more profitable firms and dividend-paying firms have higher levels of retained earnings.

These results are all broadly consistent with other studies, suggesting that, although firm characteristics matter for East Asian firms' choice of financial structure, there is nothing unusual about their effects. Firms in the region make financing choices in similar ways to firms elsewhere.

Industry-level results show that communications, entertainment, insurance, mining and services are associated with less total debt. Electricity, gas and sanitary services, banks and transport are associated with more long-term debt, while entertainment, insurance, mining and tobacco are associated with less long-term debt.

The automotive industry and banks are associated with more short-term debt, whereas chemical, communications, electronics, electricity, gas and sanitary services, entertainment, hotels, mining, newspaper, retail, services, tobacco and transport are associated with less short-term debt. Automotive, chemical, construction, food and beverages, manufacturing, metal fabrication, paper and pulp, retail, transport and wholesale use more trade credit. Insurance and mining are associated with higher levels of retained earnings.

For our purposes, we have not made any particular use of this information, and these variables function mainly as controls to ensure that industry effects are accounted for before we attribute significance to other variables. Other studies have used a variety of approaches to account for the fact that different countries have a different industrial mix, and this may impact on the way country variables affect financing (see, for example, Carlin and Mayer, 2003). This would be an interesting future question for research.

Country effects

In explaining the choice of total debt, the results indicate that being a common-law country, having higher corruption, a larger banking sector, higher levels of state ownership of banks and being a developed economy are associated with higher levels of total debt. These results are consistent with previous studies, although the sign on state ownership of banks was unclear in theory. Unexpectedly, the existence of an explicit bankruptcy code is associated with lower levels of total debt, although it was expected to provide better protection for debt holders and to facilitate the use of debt.

The ability to use more long-term debt is associated with common law, lower corruption and an open economy. The latter result is an interesting one to note for future research. Unexpectedly, the existence of an explicit bankruptcy code and higher tax compliance are associated with lower levels of long-term debt.

For the use of short-term debt (which is generally bank debt but is also less risky for lenders than long-term debt), we find that higher corruption, a closed economy, longer duration (less efficient) contract enforcement, being a developed economy, having higher levels of state ownership of banks and higher tax compliance are associated with higher levels of short-term debt. Common law is associated with lower levels of short-term debt, consistent with greater protection of debt holders' rights. The mix of results indicates that short-term debt is used both in developed countries with reasonable enforcement of obligations (as shown by tax compliance), where banks may be willing to provide loans, and in countries where uncertainty about debt holders' protection means that short-term, rather than long-term, debt has to be used.

Common law, lower corruption, less tax compliance, lower start-up costs, a larger banking sector and a more open economy are associated with higher levels of trade credit, suggesting that this is a form of finance that requires reasonably high levels of property-rights protection to be used (presumably because it is sometimes informal and would not be easy to pursue).

In explaining retentions (i.e. the proportion of equity coming from internal sources), higher corruption, higher tax compliance and higher levels of state ownership of banks are associated with higher levels of retained earnings.

Unexpectedly, a higher tax-benefit-to-debt ratio is associated with higher levels of retained earnings.

These results are still somewhat preliminary but demonstrate the potential for more detailed analysis of what improvements to financial systems would be associated with changes to the financing choices made by firms. In particular, the fact that financial openness has a significant impact warrants a much more detailed examination. The strong message that can be taken from the data is that country variables influence financing choices by firms, even after firm characteristics and industry effects have been taken into account. This is reassuring, as it is consistent with the results of other studies for large samples of developed and developing countries and it gives scope for policy variables of particular interest in the region to be examined. It also should allow an analysis of what may cause changes in the financial structure of firms that, as noted above, have been highly significant in the recent period.

Explaining the impact of sources of finance

Appendix Tables 5.a1.7 and 5.a1.8 give the results for regressions explaining the change in investment in tangible assets (property, plant and equipment) and in current assets.

As the focus of interest here is on how financing sources may impact on the investment activity of firms, we have included in our explanatory variables several measures of the sources of finance. Although our variable definitions (Appendix 2) express the sources of finance as a share of total finance, the regression results reported in Tables 5.a1.7 and 5.a1.8 were better when changes in the levels of finance were used (change is defined as t–t–1 for each variable).

The R-squared for these investment equations is low, but the results are broadly consistent with other studies, and so they may still be taken as informative. Essentially, the results confirm that financial-structure variables matter little for the amount of investment that firms carry out. Indeed, the only variables that have significant impact are country characteristics. These results remain puzzling in the finance literature, but they are consistently replicated in the literature across a number of different specifications of real activity by firms and with different samples of countries and firms. We may therefore conclude that East Asia is not different in this respect. This does not mean that there is nothing to be learned from these results. On the contrary, they give considerable (future) scope for considering which country characteristics matter, for focusing on particular policy and regulatory characteristics, and for further examining the interactions between country characteristics and firm and industry structure within countries. It would also be desirable to do more rigorous testing of which insignificant variables can be removed, and what the effect is on the remaining results (general-to-specific strategy).

Considering the detail of the results in Tables 5.a1.7 and 5.a1.8, it is clear that the sources of financing do not influence firms' fixed investment. For investment in current assets, there is some evidence that lower levels of short-term debt financing are associated with higher current-asset investment.

As expected, different industries have different investment behaviour. Electronics, electricity, gas and sanitary services, manufacturing, metal fabrication, paper and pulp and retail are associated with higher fixed-asset investment, whereas there is no industry effect on current-asset investment.

The interesting results are at the country level. The main significant effects are in this group of variables. In addition to the variables in earlier regressions, we add a shareholder rights index (where better protection is expected to make investors more able to enforce contracts and should lead to both the increased use of equity and higher investment) and a creditor rights index (where better protection should lead to more debt and more investment). Overall, lower corruption, lower start-up costs (i.e. less entrenched business), more tax compliance, higher levels of state ownership of banks, a more open financial system and stronger shareholder rights are associated with higher fixed-asset investment. Unexpectedly, common law, a developed economy, a larger banking system, an explicit bankruptcy code and weaker creditor rights are associated with less fixed-asset investment.

Lower corruption, lower start-up costs and higher creditor rights are associated with higher current-asset investment.

Conclusions and future research

Conclusions

- East Asian firms have a distinctive and striking financial structure. They rely to a considerable degree on external finance rather than on retained earnings, and much of that finance comes from stock markets.
- Only Japan, Korea and India conform to the stereotype of debt-financed corporate structure.
- In the aftermath of the Asian financial crisis, there was a dramatic change in the financial structure of firms and their sources of finance. The transition to the new structure took several years to achieve.
- For firms' financial-structure choices (i.e. debt levels, equity levels, maturity structure and retained earnings), firm-level, industry-level and country-level variables all matter.
- Thus, firm financing choices are not common across countries, even though firm characteristics do matter.
- This is consistent with other literature that finds that country variables matter for financial structure, but it is the first demonstration for the East Asian economies alone.
- The use of debt is greater when a country has common (rather than civil) law, has higher levels of corruption, a larger banking sector and higher levels of state ownership of banks and is a developed economy.
- There is no perceptible effect of shareholders' or debt holders' rights.

- Openness of the financial system has no effect on the overall choice of debt ratio but does increase the use of long-term debt (and reduces short-term debt).
- Firms' sources of finance (i.e. the structure of their fund-raising) have no influence on the change in investment in either long- or short-term assets.
- Only country-level variables have an effect (consistent with other research).
- The main variables supporting the creation of assets are lower corruption, lower start-up costs for new business, a higher level of state ownership of banks (perhaps the result of the large weight of China in the sample) and an open financial system.
- Stronger shareholders' rights also have a significant effect.

Future research

The current research has compiled a very large database of company accounting data that demonstrates what can be done even with the limitations of currently available data.

There is enormous scope for more research that can inform an understanding of how the financial system is structured, how it connects with the corporate sector's real activities, and what elements of policy and institutional structure make a difference. To develop specific policy recommendations, we suggest the following further research:

- a closer look at individual country results to see how countries have changed over time and what has determined those changes; this would be better achieved by using fixed-effects panel data estimation methods;
- separation of individual elements of the financial-openness measures and the inclusion of regional integration measures to consider the effects of financial liberalization and integration on the financial structure and behaviour of firms;
- the inclusion of better measures of financial-market development;
- other measures of different types of investment, such as R&D, which is a crucial element in growth and productivity;
- closer examination of structural breaks around times of crisis, to see whether finance sources and structure impact on investment more at certain times and under certain circumstances.

Appendix 1: results tables

Tables 5.a1.1–5.a1.6 give the results for the regressions, explaining the choice of each of the financial-structure variables. Tables 5.a1.7 and 5.a1.8 give the results for regressions explaining the change in investment in tangible assets (property, plant and equipment) and in current assets.

Table 5.a1.1 Total debt/total finance

Variable	*Coef.*	*t-statistics*	*P-value*
tangible	0.2147967	5.65	0.000
profit	–0.0019585	–0.99	0.320
size	0.0235452	7.18	0.000
m_b	5.89e–06	3.56	0.000
div_dum	–0.073453	–3.99	0.000
law	0.0510641	2.34	0.019
corrupt	0.0186969	4.31	0.000
enforce_du~t	0.0002817	2.07	0.039
taxevas	0.016249	1.32	0.186
start-up_co~t	–0.0263369	–0.41	0.681
bankdeposi~p	0.0218991	2.20	0.028
deposit_in~e	–0.0168976	–0.90	0.370
bankstate	0.061523	3.63	0.000
openness	–0.0018508	–0.21	0.830
income	0.0554457	3.59	0.000
reorg	–0.0369542	–1.61	0.108
miller	0.0621813	1.51	0.131
_Iindust_8	–0.0938547	–3.53	0.000
_Iindust_9	0.2482043	7.42	0.000
_Iindust_10	–0.0874373	–4.67	0.000
_Iindust_16	–0.156324	–4.12	0.000
_Iindust_21	–0.1854775	–4.20	0.000
_cons	–0.2053378	–2.78	0.006

Notes: Only industry dummies with a P of .001 or less have been included in the tables. Number of obs = 91,918; R-squared = 0.2292; Root MSE = 0.1713.

Table 5.a1.2 Total debt plus trade credit/total finance

Variable	*Coef.*	*t-statistics*	*P-value*
tangible	0.0409238	4.01	0.000
profit	–0.0020694	–1.08	0.282
size	0.0271438	7.25	0.000
m_b	6.65e–06	3.90	0.000
div_dum	–0.0765193	–3.42	0.001
law	0.0784962	2.57	0.010
corrupt	0.0125895	2.49	0.013
enforce_du~t	0.0001911	0.98	0.329
taxevas	–0.0166862	–1.19	0.235
startup_co~t	–0.1109728	–1.32	0.186
bankdeposi~p	0.0486097	4.48	0.000
deposit_in~e	–0.0185104	–1.08	0.279
bankstate	0.0704777	5.01	0.000
openness	0.0060221	0.58	0.560
income	0.0563452	3.17	0.002
reorg	–0.0500276	–1.98	0.048
miller	0.0837131	1.50	0.134

Continued

Table 5.a1.2 Continued

Variable	*Coef.*	*t-statistics*	*P-value*
_Iindust_8	–0.1004735	–3.28	0.001
_Iindust_9	0.2495399	10.73	0.000
_Iindust_16	–0.1658329	–4.33	0.000
_Iindust_21	–0.2082075	–5.09	0.000
_Iindust_23	0.1074116	7.56	0.000
_cons	0.0638888	0.57	0.572

Note: Number of obs = 91,916; R-squared = 0.2364; Root MSE = 0.1902.

Table 5.a1.3 Retained earnings/shareholders' equity

Variable	*Coef.*	*t-statistics*	*P-value*
tangible	–0.7023238	–0.13	0.896
profit	2.242583	2.69	0.007
size	1.061307	1.67	0.095
m_b	–0.0109832	–0.79	0.429
div_dum	3.72845	2.69	0.007
law	1.476316	0.37	0.711
corrupt	1.574422	3.15	0.002
enforce_du~t	–0.0008221	–0.05	0.958
taxevas	7.824188	4.61	0.000
startup_co~t	–3.398072	–0.26	0.792
bankdeposi~p	–2.544971	–1.22	0.224
deposit_in~e	1.719604	0.93	0.352
bankstate	10.60071	7.48	0.000
openness	0.9458251	0.79	0.427
income	0.0846882	0.06	0.955
reorg	–2.16044	–0.75	0.454
miller	13.28458	2.00	0.045
_cons	–55.24883	–5.66	0.000

Note: Number of obs = 91,944; R-squared = 0.0038; Root MSE = 129.7856.

Table 5.a1.4 Long-term debt/total finance

Variable	*Coef.*	*t-statistics*	*P-value*
tangible	0.1851676	6.67	0.000
profit	–0.0008804	–1.34	0.181
size	0.0209732	7.59	0.000
m_b	6.21e–06	5.34	0.000
div_dum	–0.0347795	–6.13	0.000
law	0.1460649	5.61	0.000
corrupt	–0.0042395	–2.55	0.011
enforce_du~t	–0.0002936	–1.44	0.149
taxevas	–0.0501534	–4.47	0.000

Continued

Table 5.a1.4 Continued

Variable	*Coef.*	*t-statistics*	*P-value*
startup_co~t	–0.0984596	–1.71	0.088
bankdeposi~p	0.0143888	1.19	0.232
deposit_in~e	–0.0089322	–0.64	0.522
bankstate	–0.0181173	–0.80	0.424
openness	0.0146491	2.96	0.003
income	0.0022558	0.15	0.879
reorg	–0.0365448	–1.87	0.061
miller	0.0461133	1.00	0.315
_Iindust_7	0.0614651	5.67	0.000
_Iindust_9	0.1998528	6.66	0.000
_cons	0.0508133	0.91	0.362

Note: Number of obs = 91,934; R-squared = 0.2973; Root MSE = 0.1101.

Table 5.a1.5 Short-term debt/total finance

Variable	*Coef.*	*t-statistics*	*P-value*
tangible	0.0298037	1.51	0.132
profit	–0.0010838	–0.81	0.416
size	0.0025538	2.28	0.023
m_b	–3.16e–07	–0.42	0.677
div_dum	–0.038722	–2.81	0.005
law	–0.0948951	–4.58	0.000
corrupt	0.0229242	4.58	0.000
enforce_du~t	0.0005754	6.45	0.000
taxevas	0.0663039	6.00	0.000
startup_co~t	0.0722868	1.93	0.054
bankdeposi~p	0.0076561	0.55	0.586
deposit_in~e	–0.0080042	–0.57	0.571
bankstate	0.0796828	5.01	0.000
openness	–0.0165479	–3.09	0.002
income	0.0533869	2.85	0.004
reorg	–0.0003924	–0.03	0.980
miller	0.0161676	0.26	0.794
_Iindust_4	–0.0880793	–4.52	0.000
_Iindust_7	–0.0794157	–5.41	0.000
_Iindust_8	–0.055409	–3.69	0.000
_Iindust_13	–0.0679676	–4.26	0.000
_Iindust_16	–0.0890191	–4.35	0.000
_Iindust_17	–0.0560176	–3.74	0.000
_Iindust_20	–0.0630637	–4.93	0.000
_Iindust_21	–0.0908602	–3.67	0.000
_cons	–0.2559502	–3.49	0.000

Note: Number of obs = 91,933; R-squared = 0.1409; Root MSE = 0.1236.

Table 5.a1.6 Trade credit/total finance

Variable	*Coef.*	*t-statistics*	*P-value*
tangible	–0.1736383	–4.65	0.000
profit	–0.0001351	–0.54	0.587
size	0.0035974	4.02	0.000
m_b	7.60e–07	2.52	0.012
div_dum	–0.0030248	–0.68	0.496
law	0.0274353	2.75	0.006
corrupt	–0.0061018	–4.10	0.000
enforce_du~t	–0.0000899	–1.23	0.220
taxevas	–0.0329664	–8.04	0.000
startup_co~t	–0.0843965	–2.73	0.006
bankdeposi~p	0.0267527	4.02	0.000
deposit_in~e	–0.0016499	–0.16	0.875
bankstate	0.0089752	0.94	0.347
openness	0.0078736	2.20	0.028
income	0.0009315	0.18	0.859
reorg	–0.0129973	–1.61	0.108
miller	0.0218234	1.13	0.260
_Iindust_5	0.0803013	7.74	0.000
_Iindust_14	0.0413365	3.71	0.000
_Iindust_19	0.0578412	5.07	0.000
_Iindust_23	0.1271955	4.99	0.000
_cons	0.268934	5.96	0.000

Note: Number of obs = 91,973, R-squared = 0.3203; Root MSE = 0.0900.

Table 5.a1.7 Investment in property, plant and equipment

Variable	*Coef.*	*t-statistics*	*P-value*
chg_ltd	–4.96e–08	–0.16	0.870
chg_std	9.69e–08	0.65	0.515
chg_tc	3.81e–07	0.84	0.398
chg_re	1.21e–07	1.65	0.099
law	–5.247312	–2.67	0.008
corrupt	–0.5419505	–5.21	0.000
enforce_du~t	–0.0251875	–4.10	0.000
taxevas	1.224491	3.49	0.000
startup_co~t	–15.70504	–5.39	0.000
bankdeposi~p	–2.476196	–2.92	0.004
deposit_in~e	–0.1899943	–0.30	0.766
bankstate	3.684801	3.45	0.001
openness	0.0106528	0.06	0.954
income	–5.82652	–5.38	0.000
reorg	–2.906417	–2.58	0.010
miller	–7.308702	–1.99	0.047
creditor_r~s	–2.03561	–7.06	0.000
share_rights	3.502545	5.00	0.000
_Iindust_6	0.6546698	3.35	0.001

Continued

Table 5.a1.7 Continued

Variable	*Coef.*	*t-statistics*	*P-value*
_Iindust_7	1.054598	3.21	0.001
_Iindust_14	0.6743884	3.83	0.000
_cons	3.709195	3.06	0.002

Note: Change in retained earnings, change in long-term debt; change in short-term debt and change in trade credit are defined as t–t–1. Number of obs = 64,515; R-squared = 0.0007; Root MSE = 53.4648.

Table 5.a1.8 Investment in current assets

Variable	*Coef.*	*t-statistics*	*P-value*
chg_ltd	5.18e–08	0.20	0.845
chg_std	–4.68e–07	–2.06	0.040
chg_tc	5.96e–07	0.94	0.349
chg_re	–7.01e–08	–0.53	0.595
law	–11.56963	–0.76	0.448
corrupt	–2.469467	–1.86	0.064
enforce_du~t	–0.0224026	–2.14	0.033
taxevas	–1.717838	–1.90	0.058
startup_co~t	–22.59532	–1.16	0.244
bankdeposi~p	1.530191	0.79	0.430
deposit_in~e	0.0892354	0.12	0.904
bankstate	11.44514	0.93	0.353
openness	0.1455602	0.27	0.786
income	–14.21094	–1.48	0.140
reorg	–4.026255	–0.74	0.462
miller	–9.066622	–0.62	0.538
creditor_r~s	1.089851	1.96	0.050
share_rights	6.678921	1.07	0.283
_cons	6.240801	0.76	0.447

Note: Number of obs = 66,246; R-squared = 0.0006; Root MSE = 89.8051.

Appendix 2: variable definitions

Independent variables

Leverage in period t (a) or leverage (a)

Definition: total debt/market value, where total debt is defined as the book value of current and long-term interest-bearing debt, and market value is defined as the market value of common equity plus book value of preferred stock plus total debt.

Calculating formula:

$$Leverage(a)_t = \frac{DLC_t + DLTT_t}{CSHO_{t,\,last\ trading\ day} \times PRCCD_{t,\,last\ trading\ day} + PSTK_t + DLC_t + DLTT_t}$$

Leverage in period t (b) or leverage (b)

Definition: total debt/market value, where total debt is defined as the book value of current and long-term interest-bearing debt plus trade credit, and market value is defined as the market value of common equity plus book value of preferred stock plus total debt.

Calculating formula:

$$Leverage(b)_t = \frac{DLC_t + DLTT_t + AP_t}{CSHO_{t,\,last\ trading\ day} \times PRCCD_{t,\,last\ trading\ day} + PSTK_t + DLC_t + DLTT_t + AP_t}$$

Debt maturity in period t (a) or DM (a)

Definition: long-term debt/total debt * total debt, defined as the book value of current and long-term interest-bearing debt.

Calculating formula:

$$DM(a)_t = \frac{DLTT_t}{DLC_t + DLTT_t}$$

Debt maturity in period t (b) or DM (b)

Definition: long-term debt/total debt * total debt, defined as the book value of current and long-term interest-bearing debt plus trade credit.

Calculating formula:

$$DM(b)_t = \frac{DLTT_t}{DLC_t + DLTT_t + AP_t}$$

Shareholder equity ratio in period t or SEMR

Definition: shareholders' equity/total assets.

Calculating formula:

$$EMR_t = \frac{SEQ_t}{AT_t}$$

Long-term debt maturity ratio in period t or LTMR

Definition: long-term debt/total assets.

Calculating formula:

$$LTMR_t = \frac{DLTT_t}{AT_t}$$

Short-term debt maturity ratio in period t or STMR

Definition: short-term debt/total assets.

Calculating formula:

$$STMR_t = \frac{DLC_t}{AT_t}$$

Trade credits maturity ratio in period t or TCMR

Definition: trade credits/total assets.

Calculating formula:

$$TCMR_t = \frac{AP_t}{AT_t}$$

Proportions of fixed investment in period t (a) or PFI (a)

Definition: change in fixed assets/total investable funds, where total investable funds are defined as change in current liabilities plus change in long-term liabilities plus change in issued equity plus cash flow from operations.

Calculating formula:

$$PFI(a)_t = \frac{(AT_t - ACT_t) - (AT_{t-1} - ACT_{t-1})}{OANCF_t + [(LT]_t - LT_{t-1}) + (CSTK_t - CSTK_{t-1})}$$

Proportions of fixed investment in period t (b) or PFI (b)

Definition: change in gross PP&E/total investable funds, where total investable funds are defined as change in current liabilities plus change in long-term liabilities plus change in issued equity plus cash flow from operations.

Calculating formula:

$$PFI(b)_t = \frac{PPEGT_t - PPEGT_{t-1}}{OANCF_t + [(LT]_t - LT_{t-1}) + (CSTK_t - CSTK_{t-1})}$$

Proportions of current investment in period t or PCI

Definition: change in current assets/total investable funds, where total investable funds are defined as change in current liabilities plus change in long-term liabilities plus change in issued equity plus cash flow from operations.

Calculating formula:

$$PCI_t = \frac{(ACT_t - ACT_{t-1})}{OANCF_t + [(LT]_t - LT_{t-1}) + (CSTK_t - CSTK_{t-1})}$$

FINCF/OANCF ratio in period t or FOR

Definition: net financing cash flow/net operating cash flow.

Calculating formula:

$$FOR_t = \frac{FINCF_t}{OANCF_t}$$

Retained earnings ratio in period t or RER

Definition: change in retained earnings/(change in long-term debt + change in common stock capital).

Calculating formula:

$$RER_t = \frac{RE_t - RE_{t-1}}{(DLTT_t - DLTT_{t-1}) + [(CSTK]_t - CSTK_{t-1})}$$

FINCF/OANCF ratio in period t or FOR

Definition: net financing cash flow/net operating cash flow.

Calculating formula:

$$FOR_t = \frac{FINCF_t}{OANCF_t}$$

RE/TF ratio in period t or RE/TF

Definition: retained earnings/total financing, where total financing is defined as shareholders' equity plus total debts plus trade credit.

Calculating formula:

$$\frac{RE}{TF_t} = \frac{RE_t}{SEQ_t + DLTT_t + DLC_t + AP_t}$$

LTD/TF ratio in period t or LTD/TF

Definition: long-term debts/total financing, where total financing is defined as shareholders' equity plus total debts plus trade credit.

Calculating formula:

$$\frac{LTD}{TF_t} = \frac{DLTT_t}{SEQ_t + DLTT_t + DLC_t + AP_t}$$

STD/TF ratio in period t or STD/TF

Definition: short-term debt/total financing, where total financing is defined as shareholders' equity plus total debts plus trade credit.

Calculating formula:

$$\frac{STD}{TF_t} = \frac{DLC_t}{SEQ_t + DLTT_t + DLC_t + AP_t}$$

TC/TF ratio in period t or TC/TF

Definition: trade credit/total financing, where total financing is defined as shareholders' equity plus total debts plus trade credit.

Calculating formula:

$$\frac{AP}{TF_t} = \frac{AP_t}{SEQ_t + DLTT_t + DLC_t + AP_t}$$

CS/TF ratio in period t or CS/TF

Definition: the residual value of total financing, representing the equity capital proportion in financing, where total financing is defined as shareholders' equity plus total debts plus trade credit.

Calculating formula:

$$\frac{CS}{TF_t} = 1 - \frac{RE}{TF_t} - \frac{LTD}{TF_t} - \frac{STD}{TF_t} - \frac{TC}{TF_t}$$

CRE/TF ratio in period t or CRE/TF

Definition: change in retained earning/total financing, where total financing is defined as shareholders' equity plus total debts plus trade credit.

Calculating formula:

$$\frac{CRE}{TF_t} = \frac{RE_t - RE_{t-1}}{SEQ_t + DLTT_t + DLC_t + AP_t}$$

CLTD/TF ratio in period t or CLTD/TF

Definition: change in long-term debt/total financing, where total financing is defined as shareholders' equity plus total debts plus trade credit.

Calculating formula:

$$\frac{CLTD}{TF_t} = \frac{DLTT_t - DLTT_{t-1}}{SEQ_t + DLTT_t + DLC_t + AP_t}$$

CSTD/TF ratio in period t or CSTD/TF

Definition: change in short-term debt/total financing, where total financing is defined as shareholders' equity plus total debts plus trade credit.

Calculating formula:

$$\frac{CSTD}{TF_t} = \frac{DLC_t - DLC_{t-1}}{SEQ_t + DLTT_t + DLC_t + AP_t}$$

CTC/TF ratio in period t or CTC/TF

Definition: change in trade credit/total financing, where total financing is defined as shareholders' equity plus total debts plus trade credit.

Calculating formula:

$$\frac{CTC}{TF_t} = \frac{AP_t - AP_{t-1}}{SEQ_t + DLTT_t + DLC_t + AP_t}$$

CCS/TF ratio in period t or CCS/TF

Definition: change in long-term debt/total financing, where total financing is defined as shareholders' equity plus total debts plus trade credit.

Calculating formula:

$$\frac{CCS}{TF_t} = \frac{CSTK_t - CSTK_{t-1}}{SEQ_t + DLTT_t + DLC_t + AP_t}$$

Data item list

ACT	current assets – total
AP	accounts payable – trade
AT	assets – total
CEQ	common/ordinary equity – total
CSHO	common shares outstanding
CSHR	common/ordinary shareholders
CSTK	common/ordinary stock (capital)
DLC	debt in current liabilities – total
DLTT	long-term debt – total
FINCF	financing activities – net cash flow
LCT	current liabilities – total
LT	liabilities – total
OANCF	operating activities – net cash flow
PPEGT	property, plant and equipment – total (gross)
PSTK	preferred/preference stock (capital) – total
RE	retained earnings
SEQ	stockholders' equity – total

Table 5.a2.1 Industry dummies definitions

	Industry	*SIC*
1	Agriculture, forestry and fishing	1 + 2 + 7 + 8 + 9
2	Automotive	55 + 75
3	Chemical	28 + 29
4	Communication	48
5	Construction	15 + 16 + 17
6	Electronics	36 + 38
7	Electricity, gas and sanitary services	46 + 49
8	Entertainment	78 + 79 + 84
9	Banks	60
10	Insurance	64
11	Brokers, real estate and other	62 + 65 + 67
12	Food and beverage	20
13	Hotels	70
14	Manufacturing	22 + 23 + 24 + 25 + 30 + 31 + 32 + 35 + 37 + 39
15	Metal fabrication	33 + 34
16	Mining	10 + 12 + 13 + 14
17	Newspapers	27
18	Paper and pulp	26
19	Retail	52 + 53 + 54 + 56 + 57 + 58 + 59
20	Services	43 + 72 + 73 + 76 + 80 + 81 + 82 + 83 + 86 + 87 + 88 + 89
21	Tobacco	21
22	Transport	40 + 41 + 42 + 44 + 45 + 47
23	Wholesale	50 + 51
24	Other	91 + 92 + 93 + 94 + 95 + 96 + 97 + 99

Table 5.a2.2 Definitions and data sources of country-level variables

Variable	*Description*	*Source*
Common law	A 0 or 1 dummy variable indicating whether a country adopts the common law system.	Treisman (2000)
Corruption index	An index ranging from 0 to 10, with larger value indicating more severe corruption.	Corruption perception index, Transparency International
Creditor rights	An index aggregating creditor rights – restrictions for a debtor to file for reorganization; secured creditors are able to seize their collateral after the reorganization petition is approved; secured creditors are paid first out of the	Djankov *et al.* (2007)

Continued

Table 5.a2.2 Continued

Variable	*Description*	*Source*
	proceeds of liquidating a bankrupt firm; management does not retain administration of its property pending the resolution of the reorganization. The index ranges from 0 (weak creditor rights) to 4 (strong creditor rights).	
Shareholder rights	Aggregate index of shareholder rights. The index is formed by summing: (1) vote by mail; (2) shares not deposited; (3) cumulative voting; (4) oppressed minority; (5) pre-emptive rights; and (6) capital to call a meeting.	Djankov *et al.* (2008)
Contact enforcement	Estimated duration, in calendar days, between the moment of issuance of judgment and the moment the creditor obtains payment.	Djankov *et al.* (2003)
Tax evasion	Executives' assessment of how important tax evasion is in their country (the lower the measure, the more rampant is tax evasion).	Djankov *et al.* (2009)
Business start-up cost	The cost of obtaining legal status to operate a firm as a share of per capita GDP.	Djankov *et al.* (2003)
Deposits	A proxy for the degree of financial intermediation of a country, measured as the country's deposits (liquid liability) over GDP.	International financial statistics, International Monetary Fund
Deposit insurance	Dummy variable equal to 1 if bank deposits are insured by government.	Demirguc-Kunt *et al.* (2005)
State control	An index measuring the proportion of a country's banks that are state controlled, where a bank is defined to be state controlled if the state's voting rights exceed 10 per cent.	Caprio *et al.* (2005)
Openness	An index that measures the extent of openness in capital account transactions. Higher values represent more open economies.	Chinn and Ito (2008)
Developed economy	A 0 or 1 dummy variable indicating whether the country is classified as developed according to the World Bank classification based on countries' gross national income levels.	World development indicators, World Bank
Bankruptcy code	A proxy for the existence of an explicit bankruptcy code, measured as a dummy variable equal to 1 if an insolvent firm is most likely to undergo a reorganization proceeding.	Djankov *et al.* (2008)
Tax	Estimate of the Miller tax ratio equal to (1 – [(after all tax value of $ dividends)/ (after all tax value of $ interest)]) calculated using statutory tax rates.	Doing business, Pricewaterhouse-Coopers

Appendix 3: financial structure: individual country results

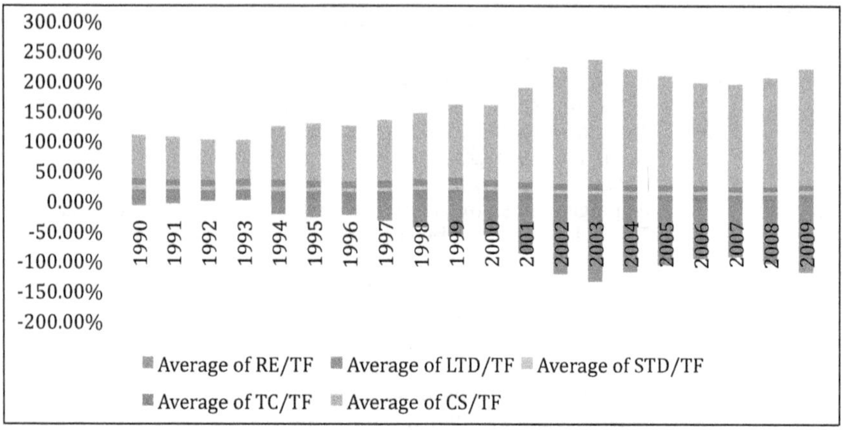

Figure 5.a3.1 Australia

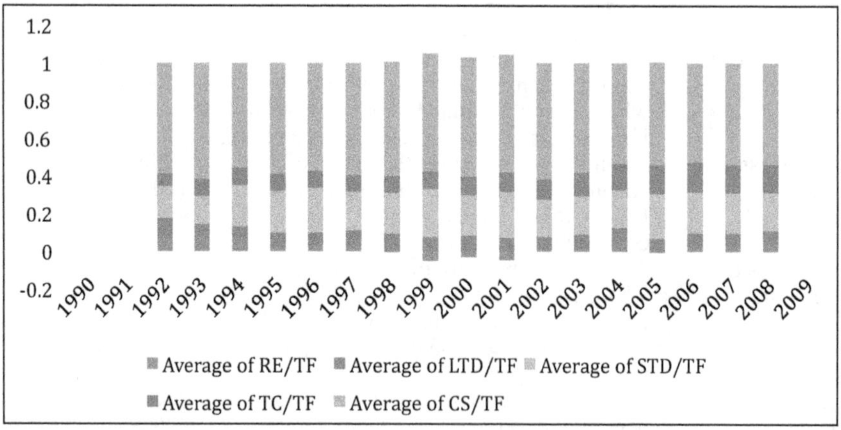

Figure 5.a3.2 China

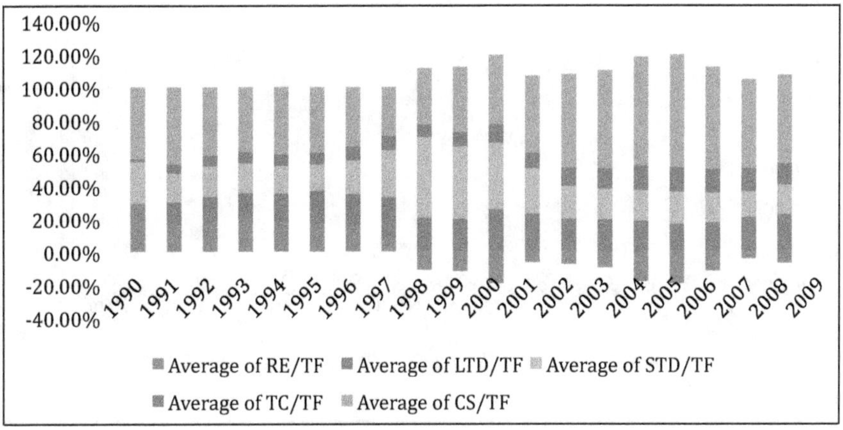

Figure 5.a3.3 Indonesia

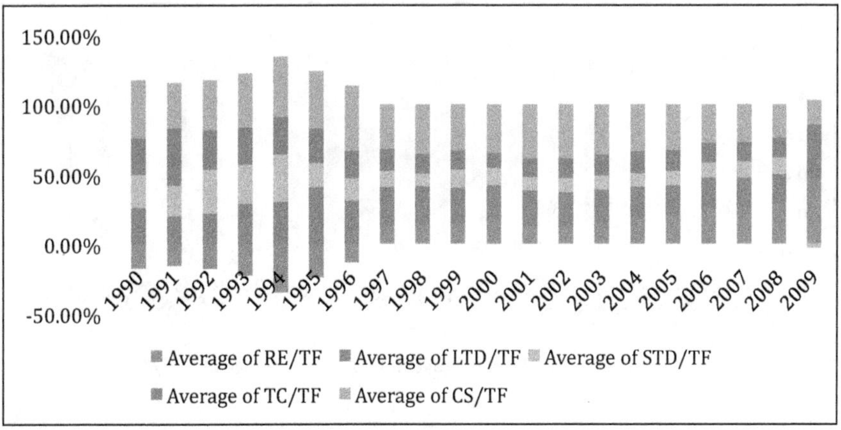

Figure 5.a3.4 India

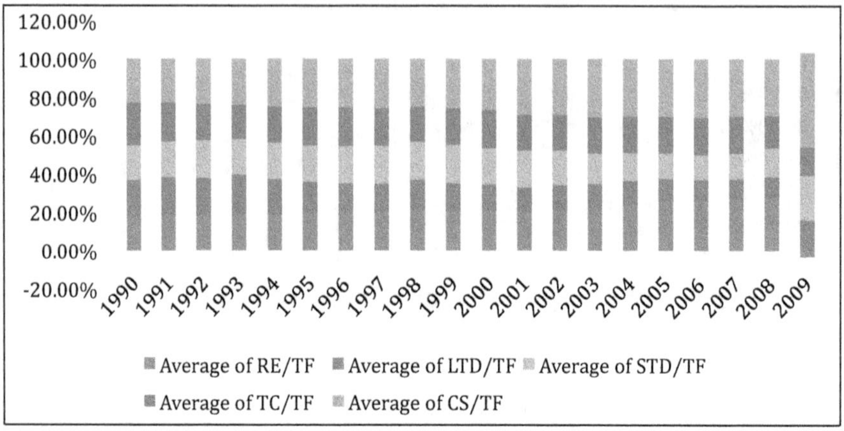

Figure 5.a3.5 Japan

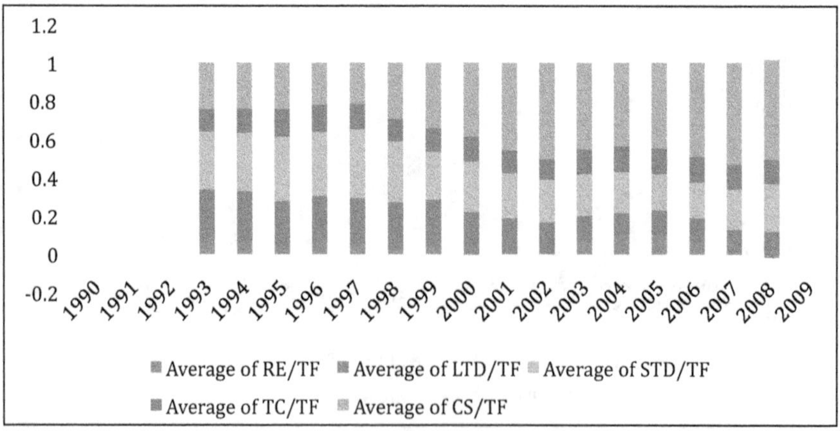

Figure 5.a3.6 Korea

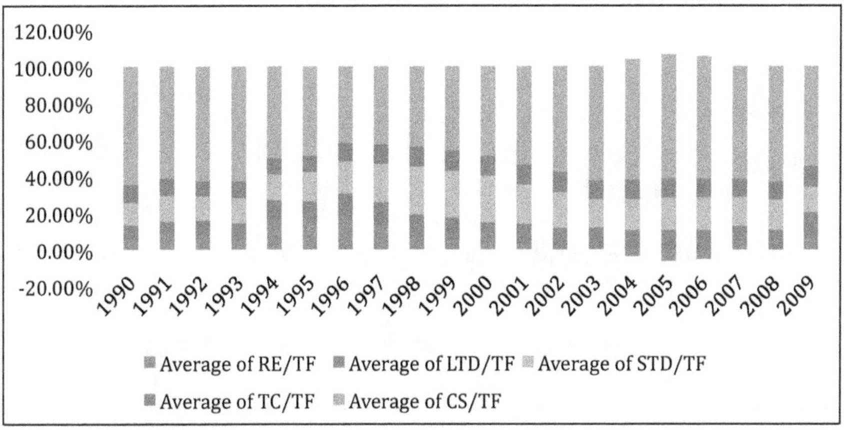

Figure 5.a3.7 Malaysia

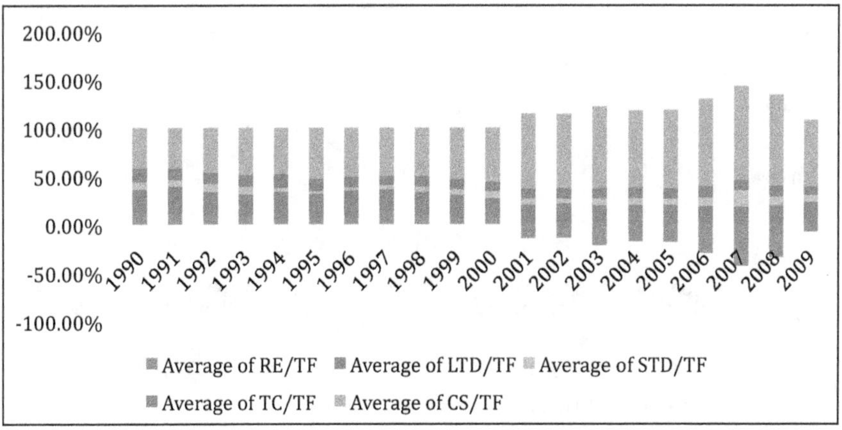

Figure 5.a3.8 New Zealand

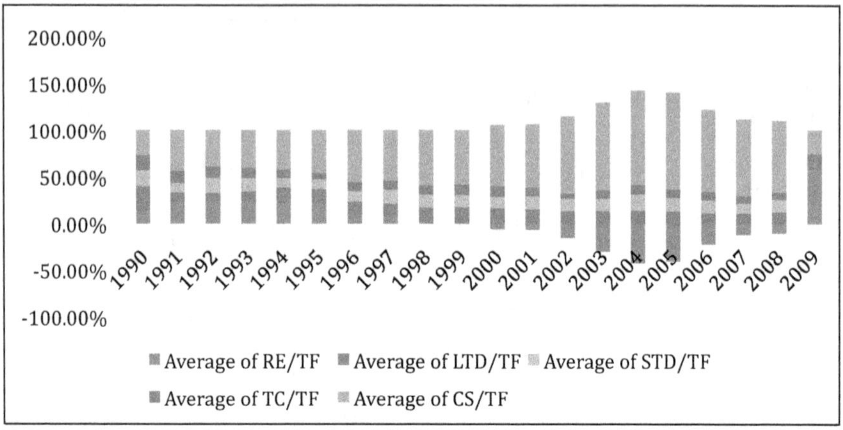

Figure 5.a3.9 Philippines

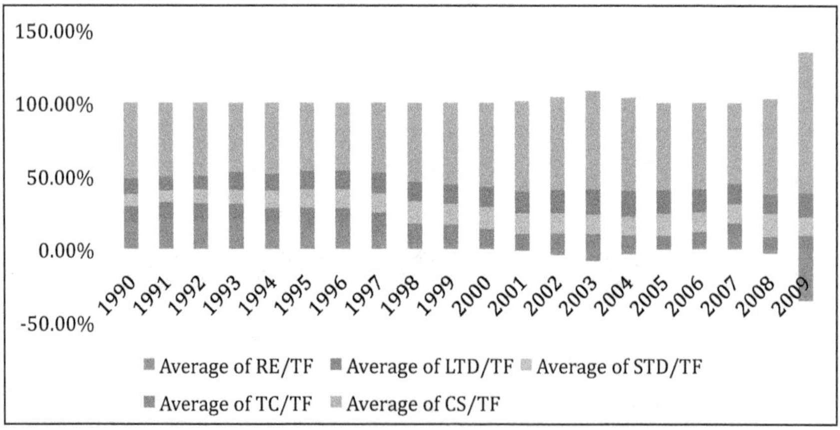

Figure 5.a3.10 Singapore

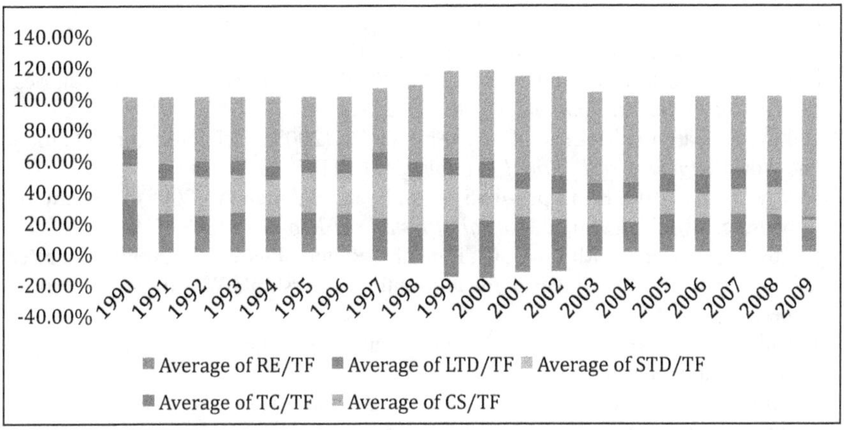

Figure 5.a3.11 Thailand

Appendix 4

Table 5.a4.1 R^2 for separate regressions

R-squared	*All variables*	*Firm only*	*Industry only*	*Country only*
Td_ta	0.2454	0.1689	0.1067	0.0657
Td_tc_ta	0.2517	0.1481	0.1520	0.1038
Re_shf	0.0043	0.0034	0.0006	0.0006
Ltd_ta	0.3119	0.2058	0.1039	0.0533
Std_ta	0.1597	0.0511	0.0854	0.0935
Tc_ta	0.3371	0.2197	0.2311	0.0890

Note

1 We are grateful to Yifei (Lance) Wang for his excellent research assistance.

References

Caprio, G., Laeven, L. and Levine, R. (2005) 'Governance and bank valuation', Working Paper, World Bank and University of Minnesota.

Carlin, W. and Mayer, C. (2003) 'Finance, investment and growth', *Journal of Financial Economics*, 69: 191–226.

Chinn, M.D. and Ito, H. (2008) 'A new measure of financial openness', *Journal of Comparative Policy Analysis: Research and Practice*, 10: 309–22.

Corbett, J. (2009) 'Corporate financial structure in East Asia: what do we know?', in C. Findlay, F. Parulian and J. Corbett (eds), *Linkages between Real and Financial Aspects of Economic Integration in East Asia*, Report 2009, No. 1, Jakarta: ERIA.

Demirguc-Kunt, A., Karacaovali, B. and Laeven, L. (2005) 'Deposit insurance around the world: a comprehensive database', World Bank Working Paper.
Djankov, S., La Porta, R., Lopez-de-Silanes, F. and Shleifer, A. (2003) 'Courts', *Quarterly Journal of Economics*, 118: 453–517.
Djankov, S., McLiesh, C. and Shleifer, A. (2007) 'Private credit in 129 countries', *Journal of Financial Economics*, 84: 299–329.
Djankov, S., Hart, O., McLiesh, C. and Shleifer, A. (2008) 'Debt enforcement around the world', *Journal of Political Economy*, 116: 1105–49.
Djankov, S., La Porta, R., Lopez-de-Silanes, F. and Shleifer, A. (2008) 'The law and economics of self-dealing', *Journal of Financial Economics*, 88: 430–65.
Djankov, S., Ganser, T., McLiesh, C., Ramalho, R. and Shleifer, A. (2009) 'The effect of corporate taxes on investment and entrepreneurship', World Bank Working Paper.
International Monetary Fund, International Financial Statistics, available at: www.imf.org/external/data.htm.
La Porta, R., Lopez-de-Silanes, F., Shleifer, A. and Vishny, R. (1998) 'Law and finance', *Journal of Political Economy*, 106: 1113–55.
PricewaterhouseCoopers, Doing Business, available at: www.pwc.com/gx/en/index.jhtml?ld=no.
Transparency International, Corruption Perception Index, available at: http://cpi.transparency.org/cpi2011/.
Treisman, D. (2000) 'The causes of corruption: a cross-national study', *Journal of Public Economics*, 76: 399–457.
Wharton Research Data Services, available at: http://wrds.wharton.upenn.edu/ (accessed 8 June 2012).
World Bank, World Development Indicators, available at: http://data.worldbank.org/data-catalog/world-development-indicators.

6 FDI, financial constraints and productivity

Firm-level study in Vietnam

Shandre M. Thangavelu
Department of Economics, National University of Singapore[1]

Christopher Findlay
School of Economics, University of Adelaide[2]

Aekapol Chongvilaivan
Institute of Southeast Asian Studies[3]

Introduction

Foreign direct investment (FDI) has been the key engine of growth for developing countries for the past decades. Developing countries have increasingly relied on FDI as a key engine of output, employment and productivity growth. The underlying rationale for attracting FDI in host countries rests with productivity spillovers associated with FDI, whereby positive externalities generated by multinational activities allow indigenous firms to pick up their productivity. Based on the transaction costs theory of FDI (Caves, 1996), multinational enterprises (MNEs) exploit superior knowledge (e.g. technological and informational advantage, managerial expertise and superior organizational structure) transferred from their foreign parents to compensate for the higher operating costs incurred in the host markets. MNEs are therefore expected to demonstrate higher performance in terms of profitability and productivity than domestically owned firms.

The productivity characteristics of MNEs and their foreign affiliates have been examined extensively in the literature. There is some evidence that foreign affiliates exhibit higher productivity performance than domestically owned firms. For instance, Aitken and Harrison (1999), using micro data on firms in Venezuela, showed that MNEs outperform domestically owned firms. The superior productivity performance of foreign affiliates in developing countries has been confirmed by Arnold and Javorcik (2009) for Indonesia; Sabirianova *et al.* (2005) for the Czech Republic; and Javorcik (2004) for Lithuania. A few studies found that the productivity advantage of MNEs' affiliates also prevails in developed countries, such as Girma and Görg (2007) and Griffith (1999) for the United Kingdom; Benfratello and Sembenelli (2006) for Italy; and Doms and Jensen (1998) for the United States. However, these existing studies compare productivity between MNEs and domestically owned firms, thereby neglecting the effects of difference in degree of foreign ownership within a firm on its productive performance. For instance, if a foreign stake matters to the productivity advantage of a firm, one should expect that greenfield FDI would outperform a partially foreign-owned firm.

In addition to heterogeneous degrees of foreign ownership, our empirical analyses add two other new elements of firm-specific characteristics into this strand of literature. First, we incorporate financial attributes into our empirical framework, which builds upon a body of the existing empirical findings that point to the negative effects of financial constraints on firm survival and development (Demirguc-Kunt and Maksimovic, 1998; Beck *et al.*, 2005; Levine, 2005). The mechanism through which financial health shapes the productivity prospects of a firm is that availability of funds stands it in good stead to leverage on ample business opportunities, to make superior investment decisions and ultimately to enjoy exceptional business capacity and the ability to survive in the market. Addressing this issue of financial constraints is vital, as this has affected multinational activities, especially in developing countries where the development of financial markets is usually limited. A recent study by Alfaro *et al.* (2006) shows that firms in countries with well-developed financial markets tend to experience positive gains in FDI. Thus, reducing the financial constraints of firms by developing financial markets could have positive impacts on their productivity.

Recent studies highlight the importance of financial markets in inducing innovation and entrepreneurship with the presence of FDI activities. Countries with better-developed financial markets increase innovative activities in the domestic economy and thus will have higher spillover and innovation in open economies with trade and FDI (Alfaro *et al.*, 2004). Financial markets can increase innovation and productivity with the presence of multinational firms in the following ways. First, domestic firms rely on external firms to finance their innovative and investment activities from multinational activities. Second, the presence of foreign firms will induce new technologies to be introduced into an economy, thereby increasing entrepreneurial activities. Well-developed financial markets will increase these entrepreneurial activities. This chapter also studies the impact of financial constraints on innovation of firms with the presence of foreign ownership. Finally, well-functioning financial markets enhance the potential for FDI to create backward linkages and transfer technologies in the domestic economy (Javorcik and Spatareanu, 2008).

The second firm-specific treatment is as follows. This study examines the productivity performance of firms by focusing on the effects of high-tech-capital accumulation (e.g. computers and automated machinery) on productivity, as in Oliner and Sichel (2000), Siegel (1997) and Siegel and Griliches (1992).[4] However, the roles of human-capital utilization have not been sufficiently emphasized, even if the developing Asian countries, including Vietnam, have flourished on swift development towards a knowledge-intensive economy, where richly skilled labour sources serve as a key catalyst of sustainable productivity growth. Therefore, it may be interesting to control for the effects of human-capital utilization in addition to high-tech-capital accumulation.

This chapter empirically examines linkages between TFP and firm characteristics using a panel of 5,302 firms in Vietnam, spanning the period 2002–8. The focus on Vietnam is motivated by two main considerations. First, foreign ownership has been increasingly important to output and employment growth in the Vietnamese economy (see Table 6.2). Second, the past decade witnessed rapid proliferation of multinational activities as a result of its market-driven momentum towards trade and investment liberalization, coupled with several policy initiatives such as tax exemption, legal reforms and improved institutional infrastructure (see Table 6.3).

Taking into account the unobserved productivity shocks, unobserved firm heterogeneity and endogeneity of variables, among other relevant econometric issues, our empirical results indicate that firms with higher foreign ownership tend to exhibit higher TFP. One implication may be that, if employed, FDI promotion policy is better redirected towards greenfield FDI instead of joint ventures, if the policymakers' objective is to maximize benefits from productivity spillovers. In other results, financial constraints appear to have a negative impact on a firm's productivity performance. We also find robust evidence of scale efficiency. The estimates further point to positive contributions of high-tech- and human-capital accumulations to TFP enhancement. We find only weak evidence that international trade exposure helps Vietnamese firms advance their productive performance.[5]

The organization of this chapter is as follows. The next section discusses the derivation of TFP using the Levinsohn–Petrin (LP) framework. The following section depicts data sources and measurement, followed by a section discussing the model and empirical methodology. Another section presents and analyses the empirical results, before the final section concludes and draws policy implications.

Derivation of the TFP measure – the LP framework

In this chapter, we adopt the semi-parametric framework of Levinsohn and Petrin (2003) to estimate the TFP in order to control for unobserved firm-specific productivity shocks. We adopt the LP framework owing to the availability of material inputs data and also owing to the lack of consistent investment data.

A crucial issue of production function estimations concerns the potential correlation between unobservable firm-specific productivity shocks and input levels, which, as is well known, makes the standard ordinary least squares (OLS) estimates biased and inconsistent (Griliches and Mairesse, 1998). There are at least two econometric approaches to TFP measurement that the existing literature conventionally utilizes to control for the unobservables. One is the

Olley–Pakes TFP measurement, in which investment serves as a proxy for these productivity shocks (Olley and Pakes, 1996); the other builds upon production theory and was first introduced by Levinsohn and Petrin (2003) using intermediate input proxies.

In this chapter, we employ the LP TFP measurement, as in Levinsohn and Petrin (2003), for two main reasons. First, a proxy of investment is not valid in our case, owing to the absence of investment information. In contrast, the LP TFP measurement is strictly data-driven now that our dataset provides complete information on the use of materials. More importantly, even if the investment data were available, the estimates would suffer from the truncation of all the establishments reporting 'zero' investment.

We assume that a firm's production technology takes the log-linearized Cobb–Douglas functional form:

$$y_t = \beta_0 + \beta_l l_t + \beta_k k_t + \beta_m m_t + \omega_t + \eta_t \tag{6.1}$$

where y_t is the logarithm of the firm's gross output in year t, l_t and m_t denote the log-levels of freely variable inputs labour and materials, respectively, and k_t refers to the logarithm of quasi-fixed input capital. A productivity shock to a firm's technology (6.1) is assumed to be additively separable and comprises two components: a transmitted component (η_t) and an independently and identically distributed component (ω_t). It should be highlighted that the former is correlated with input choices and is the source of simultaneity biases, whereas the latter is not.

Levinsohn and Petrin write the demand for m_t just as a function of the two state variables, ω_t and k_t. They show that this function is monotonically increasing in ω_t and k_t and allows inversion of the demand for m_t. Therefore, the unobservable ω_t can be rewritten as a function of k_t and m_t:$\omega_t = \omega_t(k_t, m_t)$. As in Olley and Pakes (1996), we assume that ω_t follows a first-order Markov process: $\omega_t = E\left[\omega_t \middle| \omega_{t-1}\right] + \xi_t$, where ξ_t is a shock to productivity that is uncorrelated with k_t, but not necessarily with l_t. With this identification, the production technology (6.1) can be expressed as:

$$y_t = \beta_l l_t + \phi_t(k_t, m_t) + \eta_t \tag{6.2}$$

where

$$\phi_t(k_t, m_t) = \beta_0 + \beta_k k_t + \beta_m m_t + \omega_t(k_t, m_t)$$

The estimation can be done in two steps. We first carry out a third-order polynomial approximation to estimate the conditional moments $E(y_t | k_t, m_t)$ and $E(l_t | k_t, m_t)$. The second step pertains to solving the generalized methods of moments (GMM) minimization problem to identify β_k and β_m.

The LP estimation of a firm's production technology (6.2) is reported in Table 6.1. The Wald's test of returns to scale implies increasing returns for

Table 6.1 Levinsohn–Petrin estimation of production technology

Dependent variable:	
l_t	0.3357*** (0.0435)
m_t	0.065 (0.2121)
k_t	0.6716*** (0.1714)
No. obs.	1,825
Wald's test of returns to scale	3.31*

Notes: (1) ***, * statistically significant at 1 and 10%, respectively; and (2) Wald's test is Chi-squared distributed against the null that the production technology is constant returns to scale.

the estimated production function, even though the null of constant returns to scale cannot be rejected at the 5 per cent level of significance. Having obtained the parameter estimates of the production technology, we then generate the predictions as a proxy of firm-specific TFP.

Data construction

We construct our dataset of firms from *Annual Statistical Censuses and Surveys: Enterprises* from 2002 to 2008, gathered by the General Statistics Office of Vietnam. It provides firm-level information on foreign ownership and production characteristics, such as the number of workers, gross revenue, working capital, materials, profits and export/import status, on top of financial attributes such as liquid assets, fixed assets, liabilities and equity, among many others.

Firms in our dataset operate in a wide range of economic sectors, most of which are concerned with manufacturing and service activities such as trade, hotels and restaurants, and real-estate business and consultancy. Table 6.2 indicates that the relative performance of MNEs in Vietnam compared with state and non-state enterprises is striking. The growth rate of outputs during the period 2000–8 reached 10.4 per cent. This figure is much higher than the average GDP growth rate of 7.5 per cent. Likewise, multinationals seemed to be increasingly important in terms of employment, with 20.41 per cent employment growth per annum. As portrayed in Table 6.3, although the proportion of MNEs was stable, the number of foreign affiliates increased exponentially throughout the period 2002–8. They accounted for approximately 3.19–3.89 per cent of surveyed firms during the period 2002–8. Interestingly, approximately 70–80 per cent of MNEs relate to greenfield FDI (100 per cent foreign capital). These figures point to a pivotal role of greenfield FDI in the Vietnamese economy.

For estimation efficiency, our dataset is cleaned in the following ways. First, we exclude firms from the dataset that do not report foreign ownership. Firms that do not have a complete record throughout the period of 2002–8 are also dropped to avoid data-entry errors. Therefore, our firm-level panel comprises a total of 5,302 annual observations, spanning the years 2002–8.[6]

Table 6.2 Output and employment growth by ownership, 2000–8

	Output growth (% p.a.)	*Employment growth (% p.a.)*
Total	7.5	2.3
State	6.8	1.85
Non-state	7.3	1.93
Foreign firms	10.4	20.41

Source: General Statistics Office, Vietnam

Table 6.3 Surveyed firms by foreign ownership characteristics

	2002	*2003*	*2004*	*2005*	*2006*	*2007*	*2008*
	Number of firms						
Total	51,680	62,908	72,012	91,756	112,950	131,318	155,771
Foreign firms	2,011	2,308	2,641	3,156	3,697	4,220	4,961
Foreign capital (100%)	1,294	1,561	1,869	2,335	2,852	3,342	4,018
Joint venture	717	747	772	821	845	878	943
	Percentage of firms						
Total	100.00	100.00	100.00	100.00	100.00	100.00	100.00
Foreign firms	3.89	3.67	3.67	3.44	3.27	3.21	3.19
Foreign capital (100%)	2.50	2.48	2.60	2.55	2.52	2.54	2.58
Joint venture	1.39	1.19	1.07	0.89	0.75	0.67	0.61

Source: General Statistics Office, Vietnam

Empirical framework and estimations

We now turn to a formal analysis of productivity effects associated with FDI and financial characteristics. Our empirical strategy is to incorporate FDI and financial constraint variables, in addition to the conventional determinants of productivity spillovers, into the econometric specification. We adopt the following reduced-form econometric model to estimate the productive performance of firms:

$$TFP_{it}^{L-P} = \alpha_0 + \alpha_1 \ln FDI_{it} + \alpha_2 \ln LIQUIDITY_{it} + \alpha_3 \ln LEVERAGE_{it}$$

$$+ \alpha_4 \ln SIZE_{it} + \alpha_5 \ln COM_{it} + \alpha_6 \ln HUMANK_{it} + \alpha_7 XM_{it} + \mu_i + u_{it} \quad (6.3)$$

where the subscript *i* indexes firms, and *t*, time. TFP_{it}^{L-P} refers to total factor productivity, measured by the LP approach, μi represents the firm-specific fixed effects, and u_{it} is the error term.

Central to our empirical analysis are the variables of foreign ownership and financial characteristics. The existing literature conventionally employs the dummies of foreign ownership as a proxy of FDI (Griffith, 1999; Girma at al., 2004; Benfratello and Sembenelli, 2006; Arnold and Javorcik, 2009). Nevertheless, this FDI measurement does not take into account changes in foreign ownership within firms and may lead to biased estimates of FDI contribution to firm performance. In addition, the use of the FDI dummies confines the scope of empirical evidence to a comparison between foreign-owned and domestic firms, while relative performance of firms with different degrees of foreign ownership, e.g. a performance comparison between greenfield FDI and joint venture, remains unexplored. To tackle these issues, our proxy of FDI abstracts from the traditional measure, utilizing the ratio of investment capital undertaken by foreign parties to total registered capital, denoted by FDI_{it}.

Two variables enter our econometric specification as proxies of financial health. The first is liquidity, denoted by $LIQUIDITY_{it}$, and is measured by the ratio of liquid (short-term) assets to total assets. A firm with higher liquidity is expected to be more resilient to unexpected financial shocks, to grow faster and therefore to be more productive (Beck *et al.*, 2005). In addition, the ratio of liabilities to equity, $LEVERAGE_{it}$, is meant to capture the degrees of credit constraints facing a firm. This financial variable has been adopted in studies of financial development as access to external finance and the existence of financial constraints can have crucial effects on the firm's ability to improve its productivity performance and stay in the market (Levine, 2005; Aghion *et al.*, 2007).

Apart from the explanatory variables representing foreign ownership and financial constraints, we also controlled for several firm-specific characteristics using the conventional determinants of productivity performance. First, our estimated production function, shown in Table 6.1, exhibits increasing returns to scale, suggesting the existence of scale effects on TFP. Firm size, $SIZE_{it}$, is measured by total sales to control for the effects of scale economies on productivity performance.[7] Second, high-tech-capital accumulation is an important engine of growth in developing economies. It has been a source of policy and academic debates that investment in high-tech-capital upgrades operating performance and profitability, thereby enhancing productivity growth (Morrison and Berndt, 1991; Siegel and Griliches, 1992).[8] Analogous to the measure employed by Oliner and Sichel (1994, 2000), COM_{it} aims to account for high-tech-capital investment and is proxied by the number of computers used per worker.

Another crucial source of productivity growth is human-capital utilization. It has been widely observed that developing economies have paved the way towards knowledge-intensive economies through higher rates of investment in education, training and R&D activities since the 1990s. It may be interesting to investigate empirically the roles of human-capital uses in explaining firm productivity performance in Vietnam. We employ the ratio of skilled to total workers as a proxy of human-capital intensity, denoted by $HUMANK_{it}$.

We also included a variable to capture the role of exports in the productivity of firms. Firms operating in export markets tend to enjoy higher productivity growth. In principle, such activities can generate positive externalities, e.g. technological and informational spillovers in terms of better access to new technology and technical assistance, through international contacts and competition (Evenson and Westphal, 1995; Clerides *et al.*, 1998). Nevertheless, our dataset does not provide information on volumes of international trade. Hence, we resort to the second-best measure of international trade exposure to control for the effects of export-market linkages on productivity performance using the dummy XM_{it}. It takes values of unity if the firms engage in export/import activities and nil otherwise.

The simplest way to obtain parameter estimates in our base-line econometric specification (6.3) is to carry out the standard OLS estimations. However, our concern is that OLS estimations tend to convey biased estimates owing to firm heterogeneity. The unobservable firm heterogeneity seems plausible, given the knowledge that firms operate in a wide range of economic activities, such as manufacturing, financial intermediation, trade, real estate and consultancy services. To control for unobservable firm heterogeneity, we make use of fixed-effects (FE) and random-effects (RE) estimations. The former is undertaken by using OLS with heteroscedasticity-robust estimators to take into account the heteroscedasticity problem that arises from variation in firm size, whereas the latter is obtained by GLS with the Swamy–Arora estimators.

FE and RE estimates may also be biased and inconsistent, however. The reason is that all of our structural variables, e.g. FDI, financial characteristics, high-tech-capital investment, human-capital utilization and export/import status, are very likely to be endogenously determined by other, unobserved variables. If the potential endogeneity bias problem exists, FE and RE estimates are not consistent and asymptotically efficient. There are at least two standard approaches to account for the potential endogeneity biases. The first is to employ the valid IVs – ones that are exogenous and strongly correlated with endogenous explanatory variables. However, this approach is data-intensive and thus may be inappropriate for our dataset. Alternatively, we go for the second approach, whereby lags of structural variables are chosen as IVs to correct any simultaneity bias in the estimations, using GMM to obtain two-step estimators (Arellano and Bover, 1995; Blundell and Bond, 1998). In so doing, our base-line econometric specification (6.3) is modified as follows:

$$\begin{aligned} TFP_{it}^{L-P} &= \alpha_0 + \alpha_1 TFP_{it-1}^{L-P} + \alpha_2 \ln FDI_{it} + \alpha_3 \ln LIQUIDITY_{it} \\ &+ \alpha_4 \ln LEVERAGE_{it} + \alpha_5 \ln SIZE_{it} + \alpha_6 \ln COM_{it} + \alpha_7 \ln HUMANK_{it} \\ &+ \alpha_8 XM_{it} + \mu_i + u_{it} \end{aligned} \tag{6.4}$$

where α_1 captures partial dynamic adjustments of TFP_{it}^{L-P}.

Tables 6.a.1 and 6.a.2 in the Appendix summarize statistics of the above-mentioned structural variables and present their correlation matrix, respectively. One concern was that the correlation among firm characteristics may exist now that a foreign stake, for instance, tends to affect decisions on financing, firm size, high-tech-capital investment, human-capital utilization and export/import status. However, the correlation matrix in Table 6.a.2 indicates that the correlation coefficients between different firm attributes are satisfactorily low. This implies that the multicollinearity may not pose a serious problem in our estimation.

Empirical results

Our empirical framework comprises two parts. The first deals with the estimation of LP TFP using the estimated production function reported in Table 6.1. Having obtained LP TFP, we then produce parameter estimates based on our econometric specification (6.3).

Table 6.4 reports preliminary estimates of the econometric specification. The first column portrays the OLS estimates with the heteroscedasticity-robust

Table 6.4 OLS, FE and RE estimations for LP TFP

Dependent variable: TFP_{it}^{L-P}			
Independent variable	*OLS*	*FE*	*RE*
$\ln FDI_{it}$	0.4603***	1.013***	0.5249***
	(0.1164)	(0.3255)	(0.1302)
$\ln LIQUIDITY_{it}$	1.650***	1.427***	1.613***
	(0.3034)	(0.5214)	(0.1328)
$\ln LEVERAGE_{it}$	0.2041***	0.1351*	0.1906***
	(0.0647)	(0.0724)	(0.0584)
$\ln SIZE_{it}$	0.7095***	1.170***	0.7811***
	(0.0997)	(0.2649)	(0.1107)
$\ln COM_{it}$	0.7441***	0.8439***	0.7816***
	(0.1352)	(0.1967)	(0.1328)
$\ln HUMANK_{it}$	0.4166**	0.5521*	0.4205**
	(0.1869)	(0.3136)	(0.1853)
$\ln XM_{it}$	0.2037	–0.5079	–0.0113
	(0.3210)	(0.3458)	(0.2828)
Constant	1.204	–0.9246	1.020
	(0.8292)	(2.155)	(0.8620)
No. of obs.	726	726	726
R-squared	0.1734	0.1495	—
Wald's Chi-squared	—	—	124.50***
Breusch–Pagan test	—	—	5.13**

Notes: (1) Heteroscedasticity-robust standard errors in parentheses for OLS and RE; (2) RE estimates are based on GLS with the Swamy–Arora estimators; (3) the Breusch–Pagan test statistic is Chi-squared distributed under the null hypothesis that there are no random effects; and (4) ***, ** and * statistically significant at 1, 5 and 10%, respectively.

estimators. As emphasized earlier, the OLS estimates tend to be biased owing to the unobservable firm heterogeneity. We address this econometric issue by utilizing FE and RE estimations, reported in the second and third columns, respectively. Even though the parameter estimates are consistent in terms of signs and statistical significance across all estimations, the Breusch–Pagan test in the last row of Table 6.4 rejects the null hypothesis of no random effects at the 5 per cent level of significance and is thus in favour of RE estimates.

Table 6.5 accounts for the possibility that our dependent variable may be endogenously determined by other unobserved variables, in which case even FE and RE estimates are biased and inconsistent. We tackle this issue by employing the two-step Bond–Blundell estimations with GMM, where our structural variables are instrumented by their lags.[9] As shown in Table 6.5, the first column reports the full model GMM estimation (Model 1). We then perturb the baseline model by dropping $HUMANK_{it}$ and XM_{it} from the specification (Model 2). The last column excludes only XM_{it} (Model 3). We

Table 6.5 GMM estimations for LP TFP

Dependent variable: TFP^{L-P}_{it}			
Independent variable	*Model 1*	*Model 2*	*Model 3*
TFP^{L-P}_{it-1}	–0.0184	0.0847	0.0688
	(0.1316)	(0.1406)	(0.1313)
$\ln FDI_{it}$	0.6629**	0.7090**	0.6306**
	(0.2728)	(0.2984)	(0.2658)
$\ln LIQUIDITY_{it}$	1.648***	1.244**	1.738***
	(0.6277)	(0.5909)	(0.6533)
$\ln LEVERAGE_{it}$	0.1437*	0.1581**	0.1672**
	(0.0814)	(0.0790)	(0.0738)
$\ln SIZE_{it}$	0.9460***	0.9776***	0.9136***
	(0.2793)	(0.2614)	(0.2388)
$\ln COM_{it}$	0.9080***	0.8399***	0.9027***
	(0.2819)	(0.2493)	(0.2485)
$\ln HUMANK_{it}$	0.6598	—	0.8540**
	(0.4166)		(0.4319)
$\ln XM_{it}$	–0.3789	—	—
	(0.5459)		
Constant	0.2390	–1.778	0.0654
	(2.954)	(2.348)	(2.505)
No. of obs.	309	381	380
Wald's Chi-squared	34.17***	33.72***	33.72***
No. of IVs	15	17	17
Sargan test	7.88	11.90	10.78

Notes: (1) The Blundell–Bond estimates are based on GMM with the two-step estimators; (2) the maximum lag for AR tests is two; (3) standard errors in parentheses; (4) ***, ** and * statistically significant at 1, 5 and 10%, respectively; and (5) the Sargan test is chi-squared distributed under the null hypothesis that over-identifying restrictions are valid.

examine the over-identifying restrictions using the Sargan test reported in the last row of Table 6.5. The null of valid over-identifying restrictions cannot be rejected across all specifications. The Sargan test is therefore in favour of our treatment of lagged endogenous variables as if they were exogenous, and substantiates our well-specified econometric model. Interestingly, the coefficients of TFP_{it-1}^{L-P} are statistically insignificant across all specifications, suggesting that firms in Vietnam respond promptly to productivity shocks.[10]

Our parameter estimates are strikingly robust across all estimation strategies and specifications, as the different estimation techniques and model specifications in Tables 6.4 and 6.5 produce qualitatively identical results. The robust estimates imply that firm heterogeneity and endogeneity biases may not pose a serious problem in our case. The main findings can be summarized as follows.

First, the degrees of foreign ownership contribute positively to the TFP of firms in Vietnam. The coefficients of FDI_{it} are positive and statistically significant at 1 per cent for OLS, FE and RE estimations and 5 per cent for the GMM estimations. The productivity premium offered by an acquisition of a domestic firm by foreign investors can be explained by superior know-how, technology and organizational management, which may be transferred easily across borders from the parent to subsidiaries abroad (Markusen, 2002). However, the observed productivity-enhancement effects in principle could also be market-driven, in the sense that the foreign parents tend to acquire the best-performing indigenous firms.

Empirical evidence that points to a positive correlation between foreign ownership and productivity advantage is not new. Our results are consistent with a substantial body of existing empirical studies that have asserted productivity effects of FDI across a number of industries and countries, such as Arnold and Javorcik (2009), Girma and Görg (2007), Girma *et al.* (2001) and Doms and Jensen (1998), among many others. These studies usually regard the productivity advancement associated with FDI as MNEs' technological advantage vis-à-vis domestic firms and leave out changes in foreign ownership within firms. Our empirical finding pushes forward the existing literature on this subject by showing that firms with higher foreign ownership (e.g. greenfield FDI) tend to be more productive than others with low foreign ownership (e.g. joint ventures).

Second, the financial health of firms matters to TFP. Our estimates associated with financial variables, $LIQUIDITY_{it}$ and $LEVERAGE_{it}$, are positive and statistically significant, at at least 10 per cent across all estimations and specifications. Firms with stretched financial constraints, either in terms of low liquidity ($LIQUIDITY_{it}$) or limited access to external sources of funds ($LEVERAGE_{it}$), tend to be characterized by inferior productivity performance. Financial characteristics have effects on market-selection mechanisms and investment decisions, thereby shaping growth prospects (Levine, 2005). Our empirical results also confirm the findings of past studies that liquidity helps ease obstacles facing firms and, hence, augments productivity performance (Demirguc-Kunt and Maksimovic, 1998; Beck *et al.*, 2005), and that limited access to external credit imposes constraints on development, innovation and overall investment decisions (Becchetti and Trovato, 2002).

Third, scale efficiency appears to play a major role in improving the productivity performance of firms in Vietnam. The coefficients of $SIZE_{it}$ exhibit a positive sign and are strongly significant at 1 per cent across all estimations and specifications. Therefore, our empirical exercise is consistent with the productivity-analysis literature, which underscores the role of changes in scale for productivity growth, such as Balk (2001).

Fourth, firms with large high-tech-capital accumulation and intensive human-capital utilization tend to outperform others. The coefficients of COM_{it} appear to be positive and statistically significant at 1 per cent across all estimations and specifications, even though the GMM estimates of $HUMANK_{it}$ seem to be vulnerable to econometric specifications. As portrayed in Table 6.4, the GMM results show the positive, statistically significant coefficient only when XM_{it} is dropped. Our empirical results point to investment in high-tech equipment and human resources as a key driver of productivity performance among firms in Vietnam. In addition, our empirical framework sheds light on the literature on the linkage between capital formation and productivity growth, such as Siegel and Griliches (1992) and Siegel (1997), which emphasizes the role of high-tech capital such as computers and automated machinery in enhancing industrial productivity. We further show that human capital is equally important.

Finally, we find only weak evidence that international trade exposure is correlated with the productivity of firms in Vietnam. The coefficients of the export/import dummy, XM_{it}, turn out to be statistically insignificant, with mixed signs across all estimations and specifications. Although measurement biases may account for the weak evidence of linkages between participation in international trade and productivity performance, our empirical findings are consistent with a number of cross-country studies that show that productivity improvements associated with international trade are small. These include Greenaway and Kneller (2007) for the United Kingdom; Aw *et al.* (2000) for South Korea; Bernard and Jensen (1995) for the United States; and Clerides *et al.* (1998) for Colombia, Mexico and Morocco.

Conclusions

This chapter empirically examines the determinants of productivity performance using micro-level panel data of firms in Vietnam from 2002 to 2008. Our empirical framework builds upon a well-established body of the literature on the effects of foreign ownership and firm performance, incorporating financial variables and other conventional determinants of firm productivity measured by the LP TFP. We attempt to control for several econometric issues and find the following interesting results.

First, and perhaps most importantly, the degree of foreign ownership is positively correlated with productivity performance. This implies that, not just the presence of, but also higher degrees of, foreign ownership are associated with higher productivity performance in affiliate firms in the host country. Our result also supports the recent industrial development policy in Vietnam that focuses on raising the cap on foreign ownership.[11] Our empirical exercises reveal that such a policy potentially helps local firms pick up their productivity performance and maintain their competitiveness in the international market. At least, these results indicate the value of a more careful assessment of its costs and benefits.

Our empirical framework identifies several characteristics of multinational activities that produce high productivity performance. A positive correlation between size and productivity performance points to the existence of scale efficiency, whereby production factors employed in-house can advance their sophistication through an expansion of production scale. Investment in high-tech capital (e.g. computers and automated machinery) and utilization of human capital (e.g. education and training) serve as key engines of productivity enhancement among firms in Vietnam.

Furthermore, financial constraints also have an influence on firms' productivity performance. We show that firms operating in an environment with more liquidity and more access to external credit demonstrate better productivity performance. The result of our study is consistent with the recent evidence that firms in well-developed financial markets tend to experience greater positive gains from multinational activities (Alfaro *et al.*, 2006). Well-developed financial markets will support firms' investment activities to reorganize their production structure, to adopt new technologies and to support the development of new industries that could create linkages (suppliers) with multinational companies.

Appendix

Table 6.a.1 Summary of statistics

Variable	*Obs.*	*Mean*	*S.D.*	*Min.*	*Max.*
ln*FDI*	5,158	–0.2833	0.4515	–4.382	1.099
ln*LIQUIDITY*	5,138	–0.5264	0.7160	–6.598	0.0533
ln*LEVERAGE*	1,845	–0.6158	2.411	–10.55	6.743
ln*SIZE*	4,905	9.136	2.475	0.6932	17.99
ln*COM*	4,642	–2.028	1.126	–5.622	2.481
ln*HUMANK*	5,078	–1.121	0.7046	–4.727	0
ln*XM*	3,401	0.8944	0.3073	0	1

Table 6.a.2 Correlation matrix of structural variables

	FDI	*LIQUIDITY*	*LEVERAGE*	*SIZE*	*COM*	*HUMANK*	*XM*
FDI	1.000						
LIQUIDITY	–0.0117	1.000					
LEVERAGE	–0.0185	0.0816	1.000				
SIZE	–0.0318	0.0965	0.2064	1.000			
COM	0.0586	0.1319	–0.0634	–0.2767	1.000		
HUMANK	0.0248	–0.0895	–0.0579	–0.1830	0.1102	1.000	
XM	0.0415	–0.0351	–0.1375	–0.1255	0.0130	–0.0655	1.000

Note: All variables are represented in logarithmic forms, except for *XM*.

Notes

1 Corresponding author: Department of Economics, National University of Singapore, AS2 Arts Link 1, Singapore 117570. Tel: +65–6516–6835; email address: ecssmt@nus.edu.sg.
2 School of Economics, The University of Adelaide, Napier Building, The University of Adelaide SA, Australia 5005. Tel: +61–8-8303–4768; email address: christopher.findlay@adelaide.edu.au.
3 Institute of Southeast Asian Studies (ISEAS), 30 Heng Mui Keng Terrace, Singapore 119614. Tel: +65–6870–4509; email address: aekapol@iseas.edu.sg.
We would like to thank ERIA for the financial support for this project. The chapter was presented at ERIA Workshop Programme, 'Linkages between Real and Financial Aspects of Economic Integration in East Asia', Singapore, 28 February 2010. We would like to thank Shujiro Urata, Jenny Corbett, Tony Cavoli, Victor Pontines, Friska Parulian, Kazuki Onji and Reza Siregar for their helpful comments on the earlier draft.
4 Their empirical evidence points to a significant contribution of high-tech-capital investment such as computers, data-processing equipment, automated machinery and information technology (IT) capital, to total factor productivity.
5 The weak evidence may be attributable to measurement biases. Our proxy of international trade exposure pertains to dummies of export and import activity, instead of the intensity of exports and imports, owing to the lack of export- and import-volume data.
6 We are not able to include the 2006 survey in the dataset now that the firm codes are absent.
7 An alternative measurement of firm size is the amount of labour. However, this seems inappropriate in our case owing to the potential multicollinearity with COM_{it}.
8 However, empirical evidence regarding the linkages between high-tech-capital accumulation and productivity growth is rather mixed. Whereas Morrison and Berndt (1991), using the US firm-level data, find that the contribution of high-tech-capital investment to productivity growth is small, Siegel and Griliches (1992) draw rather contrasting conclusions, that high-tech-capital formation is a crucial source of economic growth.
9 We also carry out the Arellano–Bond estimations using GMM and the two-step estimators. The results are qualitatively identical to those of the Blundell–Bond estimations in Table 6.5. The results are available upon request.
10 The insignificant coefficients of TFP^{L-P}_{it-1} are consistent with the fact that our results are strikingly robust when the dynamic specifications with the GMM estimations are undertaken in lieu of the baseline specification.

11 In June 2009, the Vietnamese government announced an increase in the ceiling foreign ownership ratio from 30 to 49 per cent.

References

Aghion, P., Fally, T. and Scarpetta, S. (2007) 'Credit constraints as a barrier to the entry and post-entry growth of firms', *Economic Policy*, 22: 731–79.

Aitken, B. and Harrison, A. (1999) 'Do domestic firms benefit from direct investment? Evidence from Venezuela', *American Economic Review*, 89: 605–18.

Alfaro, L., Chanda, A., Kalemli-Ozcan, S. and Sayek, S. (2004), 'FDI and economic growth: the role of local financial markets', *Journal of International Economics*, 64: 89–112.

Alfaro, L., Chanda, A., Kalemli-Ozcan, S. and Sayek, S. (2006) 'How does foreign direct investment promote economic growth? Exploring the effects of financial markets on linkages', Department of Economics Working Paper, 07–013, Harvard University, United States.

Arellano, M. and Bover, O. (1995) 'Another look at the instrumental-variable estimation of error-components models', *Journal of Econometrics*, 68: 29–52.

Arnold, J.M. and Javorcik, B.S. (2009) 'Gifted kids or pushy parents? Foreign direct investment and plant productivity in Indonesia', *Journal of International Economics*, 79: 42–53.

Aw, B.-Y., Chung, S. and Roberts, M.J. (2000) 'Productivity and turnover in the export market: micro-level evidence from the Republic of Korea and Taiwan (China)', *World Bank Economic Review*, 14: 65–90.

Balk, B.M. (2001) 'Scale efficiency and productivity change', *Journal of Productivity Analysis*, 15: 159–83.

Becchetti, L. and Trovato, G. (2002) 'The determinants of growth of small and medium sized firms: the role of the availability of external finance', *Small Business Economics*, 19: 291–306.

Beck, T., Demirguc-Kunt, A. and Maksimovic, V. (2005) 'Financial and legal constraints to firm growth: does firm size matter?', *The Journal of Finance*, 60: 137–77.

Benfratello, L. and Sembenelli, A. (2006) 'Foreign ownership and productivity: is the direction of causality so obvious?', *International Journal of Industrial Organization*, 24: 733–51.

Bernard, A.B. and Jensen, J.B. (1995) 'Exporters, jobs, and wages in U.S. manufacturing, 1976–87', *Brooking Papers on Economic Activity, Microeconomics*, 67–119.

Blundell, R. and Bond, S. (1998) 'Initial conditions and moment restrictions in dynamic panel data models', *Journal of Econometrics*, 87: 115–43.

Blundell, R. and Bond, S. (2000) 'GMM estimation with persistent panel data: an application to production functions', *Econometric Review*, 19: 321–40.

Caves, R. (1996) *Multinational Enterprise and Economic Analysis* (2nd Edition), Cambridge: Cambridge University Press.

Clerides, S.K., Lach, S. and Tybout, J.R. (1998) 'Is learning by exporting important? Micro-dynamic evidence from Colombia, Mexico, and Morocco', *Quarterly Journal of Economics*, 113: 903–48.

Demirguc-Kunt, A. and Maksimovic, V. (1998) 'Law, finance, and firm growth', *The Journal of Finance*, 53: 2107–37.

Doms, M.E. and Jensen, J.B. (1998) 'Comparing wages, skills, and productivity between domestically and foreign-owned manufacturing establishments in the United States', in *Geography and Ownership as Bases for Economic Accounting*, eds R. Baldwin, R. Lipsey and J.D. Richardson, Chicago: Chicago University Press, pp. 235–55.

Evenson, R. and Westphal, L. (1995) 'Technological change and technology strategy', in *Handbook of Development Economics, Volume 3*, eds T.N. Srinivasan and J. Behrman, Amsterdam: North-Holland.

Girma, S. and Görg, H. (2007) 'Multinationals' productivity advantage: scale or technology?', *Economic Inquiry*, 45: 350–62.

Girma, S., Greenaway, D. and Wakelin, K. (2001) 'Who benefits from foreign direct investment in the UK?', *Scottish Journal of Political Economy*, 48: 119–33.

Girma, S., Görg, H. and Strobl, E. (2004) 'Exports, international investment, and plant performance: evidence from a non-parametric test', *Economics Letters*, 83: 317–24.

Greenaway, D. and Kneller, R. (2007) 'Industry differences in the effect of export market entry: learning by exporting?', *Review of World Economics*, 143: 416–32.

Griffith, R. (1999) 'Using the ARD establishment level data to look at foreign ownership and productivity in the United Kingdom', *The Economic Journal*, 109: F416–42.

Griliches, Z. and Mairesse, J. (1998) 'Production functions: the search for identification', in *Econometrics and Economic Theory in the Twentieth Century: The Ragna Frisch Centennial Symposium*, ed. S. Strøm, New York: Cambridge University Press, pp. 169–203.

Javorcik, B. (2004) 'Does foreign direct investment increase the productivity of domestic firms? In search of spillovers through backward linkages', *American Economic Review*, 93: 605–27.

Javorcik, B.S. and Spatareanu, M. (2008) 'Liquidity constraints and linkages with multinationals', Working Papers 2008-005, Department of Economics, Rutgers University, Newark.

Levine, R. (2005) 'Finance and growth: theory and evidence', in *Handbook of Economic Growth Volume 1*, eds P. Aghion and S. Durlauf, Amsterdam: North-Holland, pp. 865–934.

Levinsohn, J. and Petrin, A. (2003) 'Estimating production functions using inputs to control for unobservables', *The Review of Economic Studies*, 70: 317–41.

Markusen, J.R. (2002) *Multinational Firms and the Theory of International Trade*, Cambridge, MA: MIT Press.

Morrison, C. and Berndt, E.R. (1991) 'Assessing the productivity of information technology equipment in U.S. manufacturing industries', NBER Working Paper, no. 3582.

Oliner, S. and Sichel, D. (1994) 'Computers and output growth revisited: how big is the puzzle?', *Brooking Papers on Economic Activity*, 273–334.

Oliner, S. and Sichel, D. (2000) 'The resurgence of growth in the late 1990s: is information technology the story?', *Journal of Economic Perspectives*, 14: 3–22.

Olley, S. and Pakes, A. (1996) 'The dynamics of productivity in the telecommunications equipment industry', *Econometrica*, 64: 1263–89.

Petrin, A., Poi, B.P. and Levinsohn, J. (2004) 'Production function estimation in Stata using inputs to control for unobservables', *Stata Journal*, 4: 113–23.

Sabirianova, K., Svejnar, J. and Terrell, K. (2005) 'Distance to the efficiency frontier and FDI spillovers', *Journal of the European Economic Association: Papers and Proceedings*, 3: 576–86.

Siegel, D. (1997) 'The impact of computers on manufacturing productivity growth: a multiple-indicators, multiple-causes approach', *Review of Economics and Statistics*, 79: 68–78.

Siegel, D. and Griliches, Z. (1992) 'Purchased services, outsourcing, computers, and productivity in manufacturing', NBER Working Paper, no. 3678, and in *Output Measurement in the Service Sector*, ed. Z. Griliches, Chicago: University of Chicago Press.

7 Did domestic banks amplify the global financial crisis in East Asia?

Jenny Corbett
Australia–Japan Research Centre, Crawford School, Australian National University

Prasanna Gai
Faculty of Business and Economics, University of Auckland

Kazuki Onji
Australia–Japan Research Centre, Crawford School, Australian National University

Introduction

Did the financial sector in East Asia amplify the shock from the GFC? Evidently, the global fall in the demand for industrial produce manufactured in East Asia was behind the declines in exports from Asia. Conventional wisdom also suggests that the financial sector in East Asia withstood the GFC relatively well (Pomerleano, 2009). The shock to the real sector is probably the main factor behind the decline, but, given the well-established body of literature linking financial shocks and loan supplies (e.g. Peek and Rosengren, 1997), one would suspect that the output decline in Asia after the Lehman Brothers shock of September 2008 might have been amplified by the transmission of financial shocks into the real sector, even with a relatively healthy financial sector.

In a complementary analysis, Siregar (2010) examined the role played by credits extended through international trades – another channel of the financial crisis transmission mechanism considered by Amiti and Weinstein (2009) in the context of the Japanese financial crisis in the 1990s. We focus instead on the role of loans extended by domestic financial institutions, or the lending channel of financial-sector transmission. Our aim in this chapter is to consider whether the lending channel of the GFC transmission amplified the GFC shock in East Asia, paying particular attention to the variations in the transmission mechanism across economies in the region.

We explore two possible channels: (1) direct holding of Lehman stock and (2) reliance on the money market as a source of funding. With regards to the latter, Raddatz (2009) observed that financial institutions worldwide have increasingly relied on wholesale funding to supplement demand deposits as a source of funds (Adrian and Shin, 2009), and that the short-term wholesale funds collapsed during the GFC. Indeed, the stock price of banks with larger dependence on wholesale funding fell faster at the time of the Lehman shock in September 2008 (Raddatz, 2009). Understanding the regional diversity in the transmission channel of financial crisis is important in identifying the potential policy needs of the banking sector in East Asia.

This chapter is organized as follows. The next section considers a visual examination of the relationship between exports and industrial production. There is then a section discussing evidence from micro- and macro-level analyses, before the concluding section.

Exports and industrial productions

Our basic proposition is that the industrial production decline might have been driven by the global financial linkage – not just the response to rapid decline in external demands. We first look at the data to see whether this is a reasonable proposition. The following set of figures show industrial production and exports from East Asian economies. Figure 7.1 shows that, for Japan, Singapore, South Korea, Taiwan and Thailand, the fall in production appears to lead to, or coincide with, the fall in exports. In the Philippines, the export decline clearly leads to the decline in industrial production. Sharp declines in both export and industrial production clearly indicate the response to external demand. For Japan and Taiwan, however, declines in industrial production precede the sharp decline in exports. This suggests that other mechanisms might have been at work. Figure 7.2 shows that, for China, Indonesia and Malaysia, the impact of industrial production is proportionally low. Overall, the evidence warrants further examination of the global financial linkage.

Analysis

Macro-level evidence: did firms substitute towards commercial papers?

It is informative to examine the ratio of commercial papers to bank loans in uncovering a credit crunch. Kashyap *et al.* (1993) pioneered this approach in the context of the monetary transmission mechanism. The intuition behind Kashyap *et al.* (1993) is the substitutability of sources of external finance: if the quantity demanded for loans remains constant at a given interest rate, but the quantity of bank loans supplied at the respective interest rate falls, firms fill the shortfall by issuing commercial papers. An increased ratio of commercial papers to bank loans is interpreted as evidence consistent with the lending channel. Kashyap *et al.* (1993) find statistically significant increases in commercial-paper issues relative to bank loans after tightening of the monetary policy. In the current application, an increase in this variable is taken as evidence consistent with the contraction of loan supplies relative to loan demands. Importantly, an increase in the mix variable is consistent with the lending channel, but admits an alternative explanation. As elaborated by Oliner and Rudebusch (1993) and Kashyap and Stein (1995), commercial papers are typically issued by large firms, and so the mix can increase when small firms demand fewer credits while large firms maintain credit demand. We think that the analysis of mix provides a good starting point, but caution is needed in interpretation.

We have implemented the analysis of mix focusing on Korea, Japan and Taiwan, owing to the availability of data for these countries. The analytical

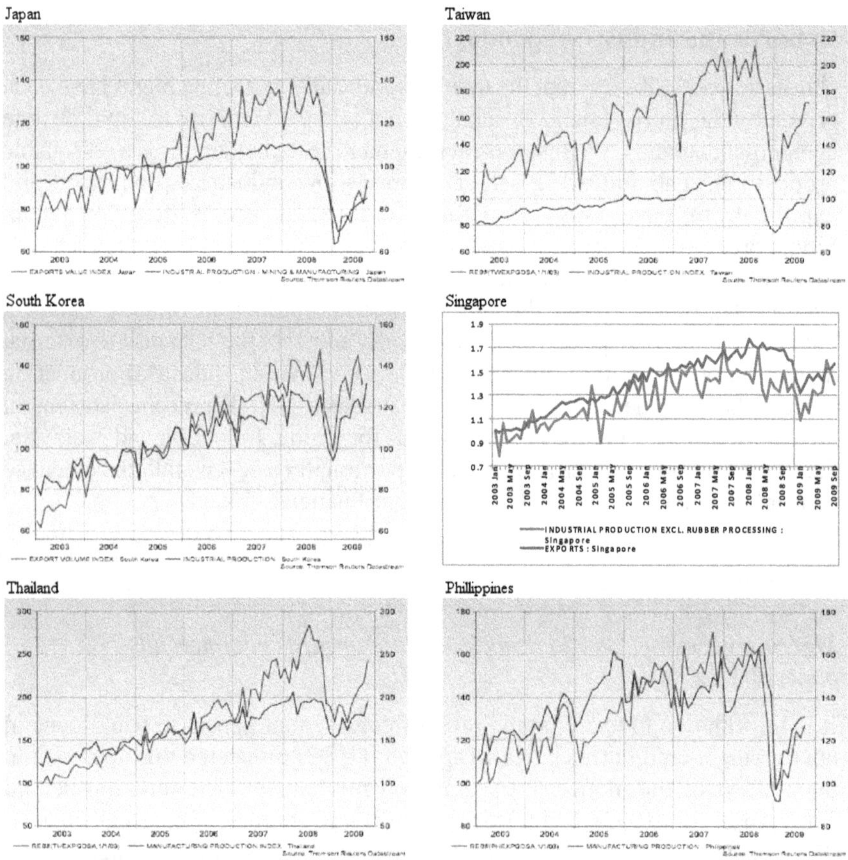

Figure 7.1 Export fall leading to or coinciding with the decline in industrial production

Notes: The left axis is for an export value index (light-coloured line). The right axis is for an industrial production index (dark-coloured line).
Source: Author. Data source is Datastream

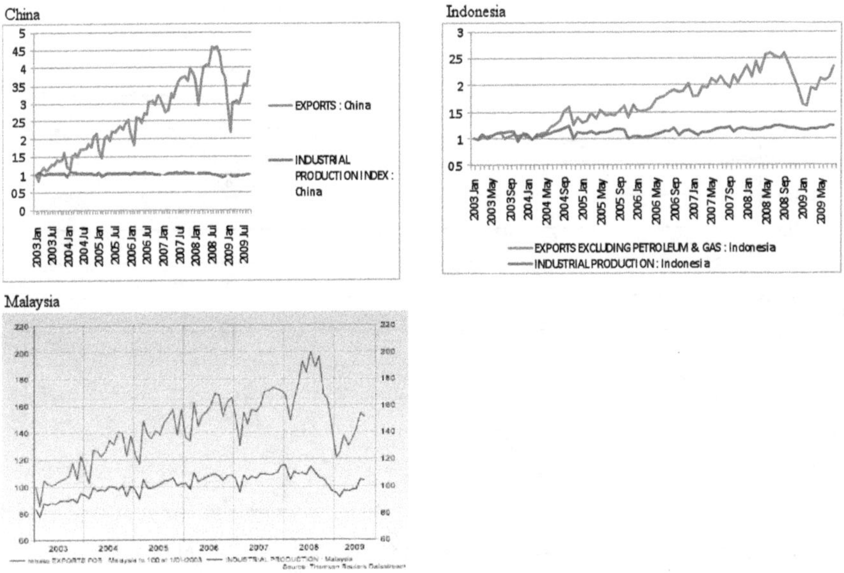

Figure 7.2 No apparent relationship between exports and industrial production

Notes: The left axis is for an export value index (light-coloured line). The right axis is for an industrial production index (dark-coloured line).
Source: Author

details are reported in Corbett *et al.* (2010). Figure 7.3 reproduces their analysis, showing the log of bank loans, the log of commercial papers and the mix for the three economies, from 2007Q2 to 2009Q2. For convenience of visual comparison, the values in those figures are rescaled by subtraction of the 2008Q3 value. For instance, 0.1 point in the top two panels indicates a value of 10 percentage points higher than the base period. Korean and Taiwanese firms rely more on the commercial papers than Japanese firms; in 2008Q3, the values of commercial papers are 9.5 per cent and 8.7 per cent of total bank loans, respectively. The share of commercial papers for Japanese firms is 4.0 per cent.

Figure 7.3a presents the amount of bank loans in logarithmic form. Bank loans in Korea are increasing over the period. The apparent kink at the 2008Q3 shows that the growth rate slows down after the Lehman shock.[1] Surprisingly, Japanese bank loans increased sharply in 2008Q4 by approximately 10 percentage points, and reverted to the base level in 2009Q2. Taiwanese bank loans increased until 2008Q3 and declined thereafter. Figure 7.3b presents the amount of commercial papers in logs. The volume of commercial papers increases for Korea, remains roughly the same for Taiwan, but declines sharply for Japan (with approximately a 40 per cent reduction in outstanding commercial papers from 2008Q3 until 2009Q2).

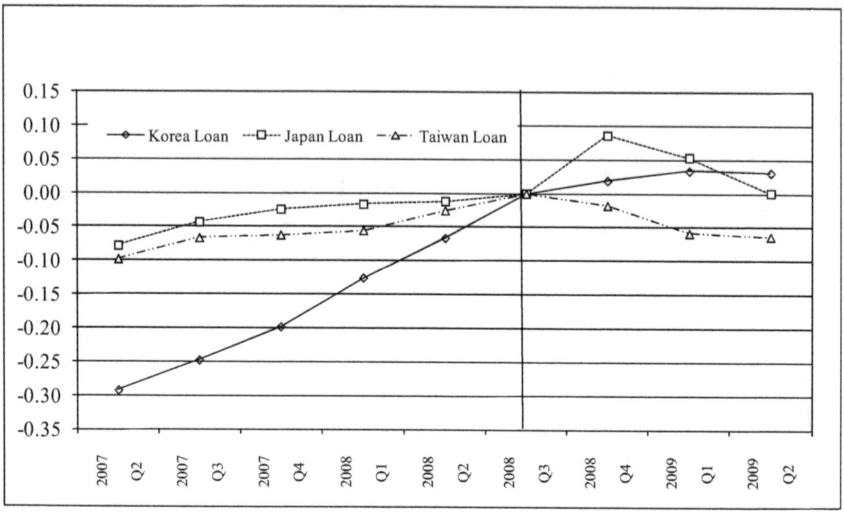

Figure 7.3a Changes in short-term external finance around the Lehman Brothers shock: commercial bank loans, shown as log of native currencies

Source: Author

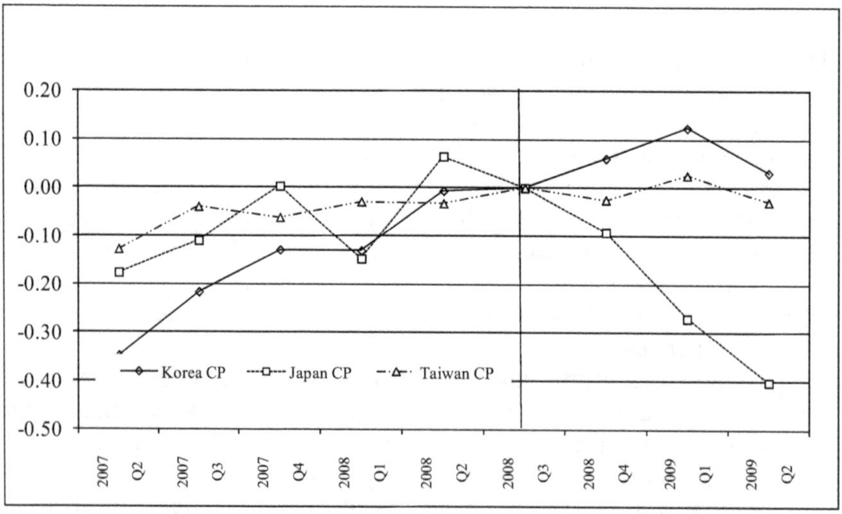

Figure 7.3b Changes in short-term external finance around the Lehman Brothers shock: commercial paper, shown as log of native currencies

Source: Author

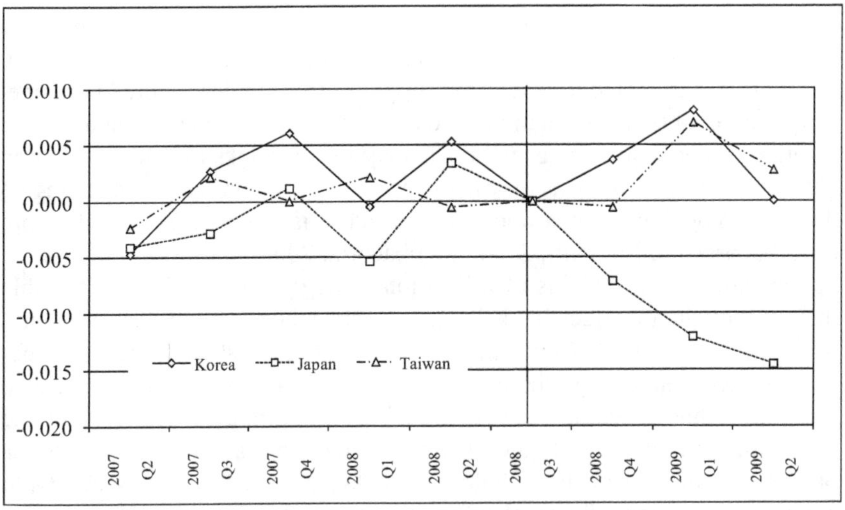

Figure 7.3c Changes in short-term external finance around the Lehman Brothers shock: commercial paper as a fraction of short-term external finance

Source: Author

Figure 7.3c shows the ratio of commercial papers to bank loans. The mix variable for Korea increased initially and reverted to the 2008Q3 level in 2009Q2. Likewise for Taiwan, the mix variable increased in 2009Q1 but reverted. These patterns for Korea and Taiwan suggest that firms temporarily resorted to commercial papers, possibly owing to an increased difficulty in obtaining bank loans. Notably, the mix variable in Japan fell by 1.5 percentage points from 2008Q3 to 2009Q2. According to the conventional wisdom of Japanese economists, a main bank – the largest lender to a company – extended loans to its main clients in response to the GFC; consequently, those firms that did not have close ties with a main bank were more severely hit. This is despite the supposed decline in the role of the main bank, which played the key monitoring role under the 'traditional' Japanese economic system, as documented in Hoshi *et al.* (2009). If anything, this result for Japan indicates the persistent role of main banks in the country.

In summary, our analysis suggests a diverse experience among Korea, Japan and Taiwan. The bank-lending channel might have been at work in Korea and Taiwan.

Micro-level analysis

Empirical approach

Our next approach is an adaptation of a one-step procedure considered by Kashyap and Stein (2000) in their study of the credit channel in the monetary transmission mechanism. A study of the monetary transmission mechanism is relevant to the transmission of the financial crisis, because of the similarity in the identification problem (Borensztein and Lee, 2002): a monetary-policy contraction is expected to reduce the supply of loans under the credit-channel story, but an observed reduction in loans may in fact be due to a contraction in aggregate demand; a financial crisis may induce banks to lend less, but an observed reduction in loans may likewise be due to a contraction in aggregate demand. A variant of this one-step procedure is common in the literature (Gambacorta and Mistrulli, 2004; Gambacorta, 2005).

The essential idea of this identification strategy is to see if a key variable that is thought to affect bank loans matters when it should be relevant. Kashyap and Stein (2000) posit that a bank's liquidity should affect whether the bank reduces loans in the face of a monetary contraction. Their one-step procedure thus examines the relationship between loan growth and the interaction term between liquidity and monetary contraction. We posit that a bank's dependence on the wholesale market affects the bank's ability to extend loans during a financial crisis. In our model, we examine the relationship between loan growth and the interaction term between wholesale dependence and the period of financial crisis.

Data

The main dataset is based on the balance sheets and income statements of banks based in ten Asian regions from BankScope. The data used in our analysis account for missing observations and organizational changes (i.e. mergers and acquisitions). Corbett *et al.* (2010) elaborate the sample selection protocol. This sample selection process left us with 747 banks, or about 80 per cent of the original sample size.

The measure of exposure to Lehman Brothers and its subsidiaries is based on the list of individual Asian financial institutions summarized and reported by Reuters on 25 September 2008.[2] This report lists individual banks and the amount of exposure in millions of US dollars, assembling information from reports by major financial firms and the Lehman's Chapter 11 bankruptcy filing. The Reuters report does not include individual information for Korean banks. We drop Korea from our analysis when examining the Lehman exposure, because we lack information on Korea.

Table 7.1 reproduces the summary by countries reported in Corbett *et al.* (2010). In seven Asian economies included in this report, the total exposure is estimated to be US$6.1 billion. Not all information on individual banks is reported; the sum of individual-level information is $3.6 billion, or 58.5 per cent of the total. In particular, the Bank of Korea estimates the exposure to be $1.34 billion – the second largest amount in the region, following Japan. Unfortunately, the Reuters' report does not include individual information for Korean banks.

Table 7.1 The exposure to the Lehman Brothers' bankruptcy: Asian financial institutions

	Reuters sample	*Estimated total*
Japan	1,721	2,200
Korea	n.a.	1,340
Taiwan	641	1,200
Hong Kong	398	—
China	385	—
Philippines	242	386
Thailand	101	124
Singapore	93	—
Total	3,581 (58.5%)	6,126
Japan, Taiwan, Philippines, Thailand	2,705 (69.1%)	3,910

Notes: Units are in US$ millions. The estimated totals are based on respective agencies for countries: S&P for Japan; the Bank of Korea for Korea (includes the exposure to Merrill Lynch); the regulatory agency for Taiwan; the Philippines *Daily Inquirer*, on the basis of its hearing on the central bank, for the Philippines.
Source: Author's summary from Reuters

Table 7.2 shows the summary statistics by bank type. Figures are in current US dollars. The cooperative banks, nearly all of which are from Japan, have the highest representation. The second largest group comprises the commercial banks. Other banks total just twenty-four, or 3.2 per cent of the total number of banks. The last three columns of the table report, respectively, the change in total loans over 2007–8, the measure of money-market dependence, and the fraction of banks that were exposed directly to the Lehman Brothers bankruptcy. Notably, investment banks reduced lending on average by 5.4 percentage points, and had high money-market dependence, as well as a high exposure to the Lehman shock.

Table 7.3 presents the summary by economies, excluding cooperative banks. Japan has the highest representation in this sample, with 111 banks. As noted elsewhere in studies that draw data from BankScope, this reflects the oversampling of banks from advanced economies. For other economies, banks in the sample are limited to larger banks.

Table 7.4 lists banks with a positive Lehman exposure from the sample of banks used in the analysis. The list is ordered by the amount of exposure relative to total assets in 2008. The exposure, on average, was 0.49 per cent of assets, indicating that the banks in general were diversified. Aozora Bank of Japan had the most exposure in terms of the absolute amount. However, the Reuters report notes that Aozora's net exposure could have been less than $25 million, owing to hedging and collateral. Inevitably, the true extent of exposure is difficult to assess, but these are the best available data we were able to obtain.

Table 7.2 Summary statistics by bank type

	All years (in US$ million)				*2008*		
	Number of banks	*Total loan*	*Total deposit*	*Total liabilities*	*Loan growth*	*Money market dependence*	*Lehman Brothers exposure (fraction)*
Types							
Commercial banks	301	15,684	20,086	24,093	0.204	0.062	0.060
		(37,962)	(52,809)	(66,464)	(0.318)	(0.115)	
		3,376	3,376	3,376	300	301	301
Cooperative banks	422	2,510	4,271	5,312	0.291	0.007	0.002
		(11,540)	(23,482)	(32,636)	(0.147)	(0.030)	
		4,322	4,322	4,322	422	422	422
Investment banks	11	8,923	5,045	14,704	-0.054	0.153	0.182
		(21,839)	(9,034)	(34,370)	(0.546)	(0.302)	
		95	95	95	11	11	11
Islamic banks	5	1,428	2,671	2,767	0.345	0.001	0.000
		(782)	(1,552)	(1,612)	(0.769)	(0.001)	
		33	33	33	5	5	5
Savings banks	8	2,271	13,286	24,028	0.102	0.001	0.125
		(3,521)	(32,564)	(44,966)	(0.102)	(0.002)	
		55	55	55	8	8	8
Total	747	8,225	11,111	13,590	0.249	0.031	0.029
		(27,171)	(39,573)	(50,893)	(0.252)	(0.090)	
		7881	7881	7881	746	747	747

Source: Author

Estimation model

The most parsimonious specification we have considered is as follows:

$$\Delta \ln L_{it} = \pi \Delta \ln L_{it-1} + \alpha M_{it} + \sum_{t=2007}^{2008} \beta_t D_t + \sum_{t=2007}^{2008} \left[\psi M_{it} D_t \right] + \sum_{j=2}^{10} \theta_j R_j \quad (7.1)$$

$$+ \sum_{t=1995}^{2006} \rho_t D_t + \sum_{k=1}^{5} \omega_k S_k + u_{it}$$

L_{it} = total loans of bank *i* at time *t*. Following Kashyap and Stein (2000), a change in loans is regressed on its lag. M_{it} is the measure of money-market dependence. Here, the measure is defined as a dummy for the ratio of total deposits to the money-market funding when it is in the top twenty-fifth percentile of the distribution of the ratio at a given point in time, *t*. The set of highly dependent banks varies across years, depending on ranking. The advantage of this specification is that, as most banks in the bottom seventy-fifth percentile are close to zero, we can capture the average loan growth for banks at the higher end of the distribution.

D_{2008} is a dummy variable for the year 2008. Banks around the region adopt different timings for the financial year: many end on 31 December, while all Japanese banks and some Malaysian and Filipino banks end on 31 March. For the latest financial-year data, most banks have one quarter after September 2008, while those in Japan, Malaysia and the Philippines have two quarters.

Table 7.3 Summary statistics by economies

	All years (in US$ million)				*2008*		
	Number of banks	*Total loan*	*Total deposit*	*Total liabilities*	*Loan growth*	*Money market dependence*	*Lehman Brothers exposure (fraction)*
Regions							
China	43	22,981	36,802	40,889	0.314	0.107	0.070
		(62,012)	(105,830)	(115,446)	(0.342)	(0.177)	
		364	364	364	43	43	43
Hong Kong	14	6,062	11,469	13,018	0.027	0.023	0.143
		(8,737)	(17,119)	(20,054)	(0.200)	(0.031)	
		56	56	56	14	14	14
Indonesia	41	1,104	1,868	2,176	0.157	0.035	0.000
		(2,231)	(4,309)	(4,971)	(0.239)	(0.063)	
		416	416	416	41	41	41
Japan	111	21,255	26,122	31,991	0.295	0.047	0.045
		(43,006)	(53,870)	(75,006)	(0.066)	(0.079)	
		1611	1611	1611	111	111	111
Korea	13	23,473	17,973	32,284	–0.169	0.271	NA
		(36,845)	(27,946)	(45,535)	(0.040)	(0.168)	
		152	152	152	13	13	13
Malaysia	30	2,816	4,159	4,596	0.022	0.035	0.000
		(6,040)	(8,026)	(8,957)	(0.481)	(0.097)	
		302	302	302	29	30	30
Philippines	18	1,051	1,829	2,075	0.247	0.008	0.167
		(1,347)	(2,407)	(2,713)	(0.828)	(0.012)	
		72	72	72	18	18	18
Singapore	9	9,484	13,878	16,485	0.101	0.139	0.111
		(16,261)	(25,617)	(29,603)	(0.264)	(0.312)	
		38	38	38	9	9	9
Taiwan	27	11,745	16,418	20,136	0.105	0.057	0.222
		(12,528)	(19,986)	(25,294)	(0.229)	(0.110)	
		337	337	337	27	27	27
Thailand	19	8,304	9,642	10,588	0.186	0.061	0.053
		(8,719)	(9,863)	(10,619)	(0.425)	(0.128)	
		211	211	211	19	19	19
Total	325	15,164	19,418	23,643	0.195	0.062	0.065
		(37,221)	(51,699)	(65,258)	(0.337)	(0.125)	
		3559	3559	3559	324	325	325

Source: Author

Table 7.4 The list of banks exposed to the Lehman Brothers' bankruptcy

ID	*Bank name*	*Country*	*Exposure (US$mn)*	*Ratio to asset*
853	RCBC Savings Bank Inc	Philippines	40	0.0407
77	Citibank (Hong Kong) Limited	Hong Kong	275	0.0211
858	Bank of Nova Scotia Asia Ltd (The)	Sinagpore	93	0.0143
837	Bank of Commerce	Philippines	15	0.0074
168	Aozora Bank	Japan	463	0.0069
483	Mizuho Trust & Banking Co., Ltd	Japan	382	0.0055
848	Metropolitan Bank & Trust Company	Philippines	71	0.0054
875	Bank of Kaohsiung	Taiwan	18	0.0031
889	EnTie Commercial Bank	Taiwan	24	0.0027
924	Bangkok Bank Public Company Limited	Thailand	101	0.0021
633	Shinsei Bank Limited	Japan	231	0.0020
893	Hua Nan Commercial Bank	Taiwan	93	0.0017
70	Bank of East Asia Ltd	Hong Kong	54	0.0014
218	Chuo Mitsui Trust & Banking Co. Ltd (The)	Japan	144	0.0009
879	Cathay United Bank Co. Ltd	Taiwan	33	0.0008
24	China Merchants Bank Co. Ltd	China	70	0.0003
628	Shinkin Central Bank	Japan	93	0.0003
45	Industrial Bank Co. Ltd	China	34	0.0002
913	Taiwan Business Bank	Taiwan	7	0.0002
656	Sumitomo Mitsui Banking Corporation	Japan	177	0.0002
4	Bank of China Limited	China	129	0.0001
898	Mega International Commercial Bank Co. Ltd	Taiwan	n.a.	n.a.
			121	0.0056

Source: Author

The differences in fiscal year pose some inconvenience in interpretation. We define 'year' to be the calendar year in which a financial year began.

The coefficient on the interaction term, ψ, is of main interest. If the GFC affected money-market-dependent banks more, we would expect to observe a slower loan growth, or a contraction, for banks with higher money-market dependence. The Lehman shock occurred in September 2008, so those impacts are captured on the coefficient on $M_{it} \times D_{2008}$. We have included the interaction term with year 2007, as the subprime mortgage crisis in the United States began in 2007.

Our empirical model allows for heterogeneity in average growth rates by country and by bank type. R_j is the economic region dummy for the ten economies: (1) China; (2) Hong Kong; (3) Indonesia; (4) Japan; (5) Korea; (6) Malaysia; (7) the Philippines; (8) Singapore; (9) Thailand; and (10) Taiwan. China is the omitted category. D_t is the year dummy. S_k is a dummy for bank type: (1) commercial banks; (2) corporative banks; (3) investment banks; (4) Islamic banks; and (5) savings banks. Commercial banks are the omitted category. u_{it} is a heteroscedastic and idiosyncratic error term assumed to be serially uncorrelated.

We have tried various specification checks reported in Corbett *et al.* (2010). First, we have considered various forms of money-market-dependence measure, including linear, quadratic and step functions. Second, ordinary least squares (OLS) estimates produce unbiased estimates under the assumption that u_{it} is white noise. To be consistent with Kashyap and Stein (2000), who report OLS estimates, we take OLS estimates as our baseline. To check the robustness of the baseline OLS estimates, we have implemented the difference general method of moment (GMM) (Arellano and Bond, 1991) and system GMM (Blundell and Bond, 1998).

Results from the full sample

Table 7.5 presents the estimation results from OLS, difference GMM and system GMM. The lag of the dependent variable is highly significant across all specifications. The first column indicates a strong negative association between high money-market dependence and low loan growth in 2008 but not in 2007. The coefficient is negative and is significant at the 1 per cent level.

Table 7.5 OLS estimates: whole sample

	(1)	*(2)*	*(3)*	*(4)*
		Difference	*System*	
	OLS	*GMM*	*GMM*	*OLS*
L. First Difference of LN (Loan)	0.186**	0.188**	0.214**	0.186**
	(0.039)	(0.044)	(0.012)	(0.040)
HIGHDEP	0.017**	0.014	0.025*	0.014*
	(0.006)	(0.014)	(0.011)	(0.006)
HIGHDEP x YEAR 2007	0.001	–0.039+	–0.035+	0.010
	(0.016)	(0.022)	(0.018)	(0.018)
HIGHDEP x YEAR 2008	–0.108**	–0.174**	–0.175**	–0.082**
	(0.025)	(0.032)	(0.020)	(0.026)
POSITIVE EXPOSURE				–0.023
				(0.017)
POS EXPO X YEAR 2007				–0.005
				(0.037)
POS EXPO X YEAR 2008				–0.017
				(0.037)
Constant	0.238**	0.142**	0.146	0.250**
	(0.025)	(0.036)	(0.127)	(0.028)
Observations	6341	5587	6341	6218
m2		0.170	0.212	0.36

Note: Robust standard errors in parentheses; + significant at 10%; * significant at 5%; ** significant at 1%. Year dummies and a full set of control variables are included but are not shown.
Source: Author

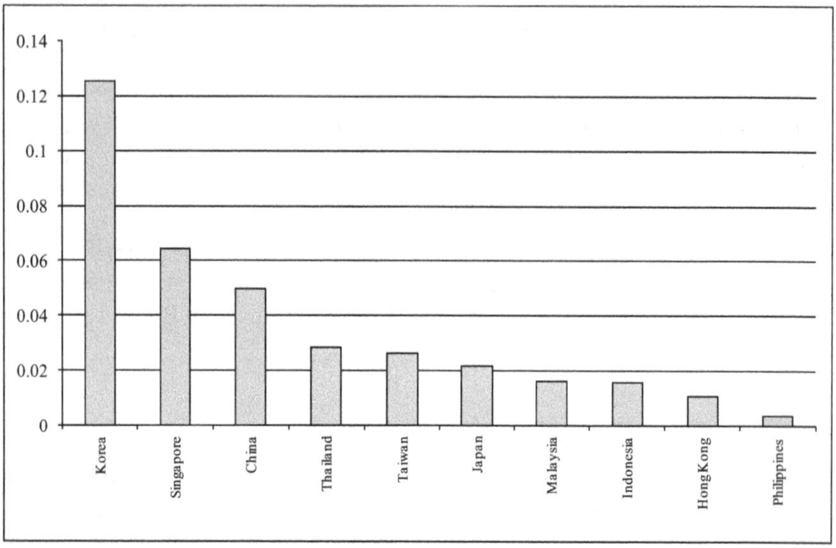

Figure 7.4 Heterogeneity in the impacts through the lending channel
Source: Author

The magnitude of the coefficient on the interaction term with year 2008 indicates that the loans from the banks in the top twenty-fifth percentile of money-market dependence grew on average by 10.8 percentage points less than the other category. Difference GMM and system GMM produce qualitatively similar results. The interaction terms with the 2008 dummy are negative and significant, indicating that the result is not sensitive to the assumption of no individual specific trend implicit in the OLS specification. Interestingly, the interaction terms with the 2007 dummy are significant, but this result is not robust to alternative functional-form assumptions.

To gauge the differences in the GFC impacts through the lending channel across the East Asian economies, Figure 7.4 presents the estimated impact of the GFC through money-market funding. Higher values indicate greater impacts of the GFC through the lending channel. The estimate implies that Korea was affected the most, followed by Singapore and China. The Philippines, Hong Kong and Indonesia were not affected much. Pomerleano (2009) observes that Korea was unique in having guaranteed loans for small- and medium-sized enterprises by the middle of 2009, and this relatively aggressive policy stance in Korea seems to back the result. Taking the estimates at face value, the importance of the lending channel appears to be heterogeneous across economies.

Results from the country subsample

Thus far, we have pooled ten economies in our sample. Heterogeneous business environments across economies provide variations in the money-

Table 7.6 OLS estimates: country by country

	China	*Hong Kong*	*Indonesia*	*Japanese cooperatives*	*Japanese banks*	*Korea*
HIGHDEP x YEAR 2008	0.003 (0.088)	0.370* (0.136)	–0.026 (0.099)	–0.006 (0.009)	0.020* (0.010)	–0.064 (0.048)
R-squared	0.05	0.31	0.15	0.34	0.39	0.21
Observations	280	28	316	3456	1366	123
	Malaysia	*Philippines*	*Singapore*	*Thailand*	*Taiwan*	
HIGHDEP x YEAR 2008	–0.347 (0.301)	–0.284+ (0.149)	0.278+ (0.152)	0.096 (0.105)	0.036 (0.055)	
R-squared	0.11	0.42	0.66	0.15	0.20	
Observations	243	36	20	169	281	

Notes: Robust standard errors in parentheses; + significant at 10%; * significant at 5%; ** significant at 1%.
Source: Author

market dependence necessary in identification. To see if the transmission channel differed, we repeated the analysis for the subsample of banks from each economy. However, subsamples are quite small for some economies, and so the results need to be viewed with caution.

We made two main adjustments. First, the cut-off for high dependence is the top thirty-fourth percentile of the distribution of the ratio of money-market funding to total liabilities. Second, we split the Japanese sample into cooperative banks and all other banks, as the sample size is relatively large.

Table 7.6 presents the summary of the main coefficients. Estimates are generally imprecise, as expected from smaller sample sizes and from a lower within-country variation in the money-market dependence. Notable exceptions are Hong Kong, Singaporean and Japanese banks that have positive and significant coefficients. For those countries, on average, banks with higher money-market dependence increased loans faster than other, less-dependent banks in the other countries. A possible explanation is the 'flight to quality'. These three economies are relatively advanced. To the extent that banks operating in these economies are considered more secure in the eye of lenders, perhaps owing to their better regulatory environments, those banks may see an inflow of funding. The result for Hong Kong and Singapore, however, should be viewed with caution, given the small sample size.

Malaysia and the Philippines have negative coefficients. Although the Philippines subsample is too small to draw reliable inferences, the results show that Malaysian banks with higher money-market dependence grew slower than their peers within the Malaysian economy. Although the overall importance of the lending channel was low in Malaysia according to the prior analysis, this result suggests that the GFC constrained credit to some extent in Malaysia. Interestingly, many Malaysian and Filipino banks have their financial year ending in

Table 7.7 Loan growth (2007–8) by Lehman exposure

	Positive exposure	*No exposure*	*Difference*
Loan growth	0.190 (0.156)	0.259 (0.250)	0.069 [0.058]
Number of observations	22	711	—

Notes: Standard deviations in parentheses. P-value for a two-tailed t-test with unequal variance in brackets. The sample is from 2008 and excludes Korea.
Source: Author

March, as noted above. It is possible that the longer coverage post-September 2008 in the sample might have made it easier to find the effects for those economies. The estimate for Korea, which has the highest average dependency ratio within our sample, is not significant, but this is probably owing to the low within-economy variation and to the small sample size (thirteen banks).

Did Lehman-exposed banks reduce lending more?

As a preliminary examination of the effects of the direct exposure to the Lehman shock on lending, Table 7.7 compares the means of loan growth from 2007–8 for those with any exposure to the Lehman shock with those without. The sample excludes Korea, as we do not have bank-level information on exposure for Korean banks. On average, the total amount of loans, in US dollars, increased by 25.8 and 19.3 per cent, respectively, for those with and without exposure. This difference in the mean is significant at the 10 per cent level. Thus, a simple comparison suggests the negative impact of direct exposure to the Lehman shock.

We have tried incorporating a dummy variable for positive exposure in the baseline model. The coefficient on the interaction term between the exposure dummy and the 2008 dummy is not significant. Thus, the direct exposure of the Lehman shock alone does not appear to be important in explaining the lending behaviour of banks. One possible explanation is that there was a measurement error in the Lehman exposure that attenuated the estimated effects. At face value, however, the results suggest that banks were sufficiently hedged against the Lehman shock.

Conclusion

In summary, we implemented two complementary techniques to study the impacts of the GFC on the supply of bank loans in East Asia. Following Kashyap *et al.* (1993), we first examined the aggregate data on the ratio of commercial papers to bank loans for Korea, Japan and Taiwan. We then applied the two-step regression procedure considered by Kashyap and Stein (2000) on ten East Asian economies. The results suggest that Korea experienced a temporary credit crunch as a result of the GFC. In contrast, Japanese banks appeared to have countered the GFC shock by increasing lending, suggesting that the main bank system is still alive. Data limitation restricts us from offering strong conclusions for other economies, but the impacts on most ASEAN countries in our sample would have been negative but small. Malaysia exhibited some indication of a credit crunch, but the extent of this credit crunch is estimated to be much smaller than for Korea. Taiwan also exhibited symptoms of a credit crunch in our analysis of macro variables, but this result was not corroborated in the analysis of bank-level data. Banks from mainland China were predicted to be affected, but their actual performance, in terms of the number of loans extended, was robust, suggesting some other factor was in operation in China.

A rough estimate is that a maximum of 3 per cent of lending was reduced through the lending channel of the GFC transmission, but the substitution of sources of funding would have reduced the impact. Overall, our exercise indicates that the GFC was transmitted through the lending channel to East Asian economies, but the effects were heterogeneous within the region.

These results have implications for the financial integration in the region. Our findings suggest that a financial shock that originated in the United States had heterogeneous impacts on East Asian economies. An integration of the financial sector within a region would mean that a shock to one country is likely to transmit across national borders through the presence of foreign banks; see, for instance, Peek and Rosengren (1997). As a closer financial integration of East Asia is likely to increase the risk of exposure to external shocks, owing to easier transmission of shocks within the region, it seems worthwhile to develop a framework for containing a contagion via a weak link in the system. Such a framework might mandate cross-border support by injecting liquidity into economies that are hardest hit by an external shock. Although regulators must watch for moral hazards, a risk-sharing framework seems a necessary precondition for the financial sector to be integrated.

Finally, this chapter is an early attempt to understand the transmission of the current financial crisis to East Asia, and further work is necessary to form stronger conclusions. First, to better understand longer-term impacts, the sample needs to be extended to cover more post-crisis periods. Second, more detailed data are required for more precise inferences. For instance, quarterly data would enable researchers to pinpoint the timing of changes; narrower categories of loans would enable more precise analyses of the impacts on businesses; and greater coverage of smaller lending institutions, beyond that covered by BankScope, is necessary to limit any issues arising from a small sample. Third, having comprehensive regulatory data on banks around the region would be a significant contribution to research. Fourth, we were not able to conduct an analysis of mix variables for ASEAN owing to data limitation, although it would be of interest to see the behaviour of the variables. Last, our sample is restricted to banks that were operating in 2008 and does not include banks that were closed or absorbed. This restriction prevented us from comparing the impacts of the current GFC with the Asian financial crisis of 1998, which would be of great interest.

Notes

1 One might argue, on the basis of the continuous increase in loans, that Korea did not experience a 'credit crunch'. The question asked in this chapter is whether or

not the GFC led to a supply-driven contraction in credits. The slowdown in loan growth is consistent with banks reducing the supply of loans. Of course, the slowdown can be explained by the slowdown in loan demand. The point of looking at the mix is to gauge the demand condition by taking the commercial-paper issues as a benchmark for the demand condition.

2 Reuters website (http://uk.reuters.com/article/idUKMAN20091320080925, accessed 5 January 2010).

References

Adrian, T. and Shin, H.S. (2009) 'Money, liquidity, and monetary policy', *American Economic Review*, 99(2): 600–5.

Amiti, M. and Weinstein, D.E. (2009) 'Exports and financial shocks', NBER Working Paper, no. 15556, Cambridge, MA: NBER.

Arellano, M. and Bond, S. (1991) 'Some tests of specification for panel data: Monte Carlo evidence and application to employment equations', *Review of Economic Studies*, 58: 277–97.

Blundell, R. and Bond, S. (1998) 'Initial conditions and moment restrictions in dynamic panel data models', *Journal of Econometrics*, 87: 115–43.

Borensztein, E. and Lee, J.-W. (2002) 'Financial crisis and credit crunch in Korea: evidence from firm-level data', *Journal of Monetary Economics*, 49(4): 853–75.

Corbett, J., Gai, P. and Onji, K. (2010) 'The banking system in East Asia and the transmission of the global financial crisis', unpublished manuscript.

Gambacorta, L. (2005) 'Inside the bank lending channel', *European Economic Review*, 49(7): 1737–59.

Gambacorta, L. and Mistrulli, P.E. (2004) 'Does bank capital affect lending behavior?', *Journal of Financial Intermediation*, 13(4): 436–57.

Hoshi, T., Koibuchi, S. and Schaede, U. (2009) 'Changes in main bank rescues during the lost decade: an analysis of corporate restructuring in Japan, 1981–2007', paper presented at the NBER Japan Project Meeting, 30 June–1 July 2009.

Kashyap, A.K. and Stein, J.C. (1995) 'The impact of monetary policy on bank balance sheets', *Carnegie-Rochester Conference Series on Public Policy*, 42: 151–95.

Kashyap, A.K. and Stein, J.C. (2000) 'What do a million observations on banks say about the transmission of monetary policy?', *American Economic Review*, 90(3): 407–28.

Kashyap, A.K., Stein, J.C. and Wilcox, D.W. (1993) 'Monetary policy and credit conditions: evidence from the composition of external finance', *American Economic Review*, 83(1): 78.

Oliner, S.D. and Rudebusch, G.D. (1993) 'Is there a bank credit channel for monetary policy?', *Finance and Economics Discussion Series*, Federal Reserve Board, pp. 93–8.

Peek, J. and Rosengren, E.S. (1997) 'The international transmission of financial shocks: the case of Japan', *American Economic Review*, 87(4): 495–505.

Pomerleano, M. (2009) 'What is the impact of the global financial crisis on the banking system in East Asia?', ADBI Working Paper Series, no. 146.

Raddatz, C. (2009) 'When the rivers run dry: liquidity and the use of wholesale funds in the transmission of the US subprime crisis', World Bank Policy Research Working Paper, no. 5203.

Siregar, R. (2010) 'Trade financing and export performance in Asia', in C. Findlay, F. Parulian and J. Corbett (eds), *Linkages between Real and Financial Aspects of Economic Integration in East Asia*, ERIA Research Project 2009, no. 1, pp. 196–225.

8 Bank efficiency, regulation and response to crisis of financial institutions in selected Asian countries[1]

Shandre M. Thangavelu
Department of Economics, National University of Singapore

Christopher Findlay
School of Economics, University of Adelaide

Introduction

With the pace of financial-market liberalization, financial institutions are facing increasing competition and greater volatility from external shocks. In such an environment, efficient banks and financial institutions will have greater competitive advantage. Banking efficiency is also important to maintain the stability of the financial markets (Berger *et al.*, 1993; Schaeck *et al.*, 2009). Efficient banks are, in addition, better able to diversify their activities and channel funds effectively to economically viable activities in the economy, thereby providing greater stability for the economy.

A competitive environment is a spur to efficiency, but it may also increase risk-taking activities, as banks are forced to adopt non-traditional banking activities to maintain their share in the financial markets (Edwards and Mishkin, 1993). The regulatory concern is that competition in the financial market could lead to excessive risk-taking behaviour, leading to instability in the financial markets. The 2007 global crisis provides examples of banks' excessive off-balance-sheet activities. The traditional banking model was replaced by the 'originate and distribute' banking model, where loans are pooled, tranched and then resold via securitization (Brunnermeier, 2009). Financial innovation that had supposedly made the banking system more stable by transferring risk to those most able to bear it had an unprecedented credit expansion. To offload the risk, banks repackaged the loans and passed them on to other financial investors, through structured products often referred to as collateralized debt obligations (CDOs). Financial-market regulation plays an important role in maintaining a balance between competition and risk-taking activities in the financial sector, but in the process it may affect the efficiency of the financial institutions.

The determinants of efficiency of banks in the South-East Asian countries of Indonesia, Malaysia, the Philippines, Singapore, Thailand and Vietnam are discussed in this chapter, which covers nearly 600 banks, from 1994 to 2008. The study is expected to help improve the institutional, regulatory and supervisory framework of financial institutions in the region by identifying factors that could contribute to their efficiency.

There are four key aspects of the chapter. First, it studies the impact of financial-market regulation on bank efficiency. One of the objectives of bank regulation is to manage competition and risk-taking activities in the financial sector. In this case, bank regulation tends to retard competition and the innovative activities of financial institutions, thereby affecting the efficiency of financial institutions. Recent studies highlight the positive impact of regulation on banking activities, in terms of increased market monitoring and a better-quality contracting environment, which has a positive impact on bank efficiency (Gonzalez, 2009). In this chapter, we study the impact of bank regulation and supervision on bank efficiency in terms of the regulation of the activities that generate non-interest income, the intensity of monitoring of banks by private-sector organizations, and the extent of official supervision by the central bank. To our knowledge, this is the first study to address the impact of bank regulation and supervision on bank efficiency for South-East Asian banks.

The chapter also studies the impact of financial-market liberalization, in terms of opening up the financial sector to foreign participation and foreign ownership, on the efficiency of financial institutions. Foreign banks are generally restricted in entry and operations in Asia, and the penetration of foreign banks in Asia is much lower than in Central Europe and Latin America (Montgomery, 2003). Foreign banks in Asia are restricted in commercial-lending activities and limited to a few branches in comparison with the local banks. For example, in Indonesia, foreign banks are restricted geographically in lending activities in the Jakarta region and in taking time deposits. In most Asian countries, foreign banks are restricted in access to the central-bank discount window and to subsidized trade-credit facilities. In Korea, foreign banks are allowed to operate only restricted branches within the city area, thereby restricting their access to local-currency deposits; and the total amount of deposits they can accept is also restricted (Montgomery, 2003).

The impact of financial-market liberalization is an important talking point following the experience of the Asian crisis in 1997. Following the crisis, Singapore liberalized its financial sector by increasing the foreign ownership and participation of foreign banks in the domestic economy. In contrast, Malaysia adopted capital controls that limited the flow of capital and the role of foreign participation in the financial and domestic markets. Malaysian policies are argued by some to have led, in the short run, to a faster economic recovery, a smaller decline in unemployment and wages, and a more rapid turnaround of the stock market (Kaplan and Rodrik, 2001). However, there is no clear evidence of the impact of capital controls in the long run on bank efficiency. An understanding of the impact of foreign participation on the productive performance of banks in the long term is valuable. A recent study by Kose *et al.* (2009) also shows that financial openness has a robust, positive impact on TFP growth in the domestic economy. A study by Xu (2010) provides strong empirical evidence that foreign entry led to a more competitive and efficient banking industry in China. However, Obstfeld (2009) says that there is little evidence of a direct positive impact of financial openness on the economic welfare of developing countries. This chapter studies the impact of foreign ownership and participation in the financial markets on individual bank efficiency.

Our study further examines the impact of the off-balance-sheet activities of banks on their efficiency. Increasingly, banks are using off-balance-sheet activities in pursuit of higher profits and trying to satisfy the rising consumer demand for non-banking products. These off-balance-sheet activities could be associated with excessive risk-taking, which subsequently affects efficiency. There is little research that examines financial innovation in terms of the off-balance-sheet activities of South-East Asian banks, and this study fills this gap. Finally, this work contributes to the understanding of the risk of the misallocation of funds by banks arising from the moral-hazard issues associated with state influence and guarantees (Radelet and Sachs, 1998). We used a bank's equity-to-asset ratios and its corporate linkages, via its own ownership structure or its links to subsidiaries, to capture the impact of the related moral-hazard issues on productive performance.

The chapter is organized as follows. The next section discusses the methodology, and the construction of the data is presented in the third section. The results are presented in the fourth section, followed by the conclusion in the final section.

Empirical methodology

The chapter adopts a panel-data framework to study the determinants of bank efficiency. The regression equation is given as:

$$Bank\text{-}Efficient_{it} = \alpha_0+\alpha_1 Fin_{it}+\alpha_2 Reg_{it}+\alpha_3 Types_{it}+\mu_i+\theta_t+\varepsilon_{it} \quad (8.1)$$

where $Bank\text{-}Efficient_{it}$ is the bank efficiency measure of bank i in year t; Fin_{it} is the set of specific characteristics of bank i in year t; Reg_{it} is the set of bank regulatory and supervision variables; $Types_{it}$ captures the bank types; θ_t are dummies to capture any unobserved bank-invariant time effects not included in the regression; μ_i are unobservable bank-specific effects that vary across the banks but are constant over time; and ε_{it} are white-noise error terms.

We adopt fixed effects and random effects to estimate Equation (8.1). It is very likely that there are endogeneity problems in Equation (8.1) in terms of reverse causation, whereby bank regulation and supervision might be responding to the efficiencies of the bank. Thus, failure to account for the simultaneity problems might lead to biased estimation and coefficients.[2] To address this problem, we adopt the two-stage least square fixed-effects (FE2SLS) and two-stage least square random-effects (RE2SLS) estimators, as provided by Baltagi (2001). Both FE2SLS and RE2SLS are expected to control for the presence of unobservable bank-specific effects and potential endogeneity of bank efficiency.

Data and construction of variables

Data

The main bank-level data for the study are obtained from the BankScope Database. Bank-level information to estimate bank efficiency is taken from the BankScope Database. All data used are expressed in 1996 US dollar terms, and consolidated bank balance sheet and income statement data will be used whenever available. The construction of regulatory and supervisory variables is based on Barth *et al.* (2004, 2006) and the World Bank's Bank Regulation and Supervision Database. The full description of the data is given in Table 8.a.1 in the Appendix.

Variables

Bank efficiency measure

To measure bank efficiency, we adopted data envelopment analysis (DEA). This framework has been extensively used to study the efficiency of financial institutions, as in Casu *et al.* (2004), Gonzalez (2009), Isik and Hassan (2003), Leightner and Lovell (1998), Sturm and Williams (2004) and Wheelock and Wilson (1999).[3] A recent paper by Gonzalez (2009) used DEA to measure the bank efficiency of commercial banks in sixty-nine countries to study the impact of political economy variables on bank efficiency. Isik and Hassan (2003) utilized DEA to examine productivity growth and technical progress in Turkish commercial banks during the deregulation of financial markets in Turkey. Sturm and Williams (2004) adopted the DEA framework to study the efficiency of banking in Australia during the post-deregulation period of 1988 to 2001. Casu *et al.* (2004) examined the efficiency of European banks for the period 1994–2000 using the DEA framework and found Italian and Spanish banks had higher productivity increases compared with German, French and English banks.

DEA is a non-parametric method to estimate production functions, particularly the productive efficiency of decision-making units. DEA employs mathematical programming to estimate the trade-offs inherent in the empirical efficient frontier. The efficient frontier identified by DEA is the benchmark against which other decision-making units will be compared (see Gonzalez, 2009). Two alternative approaches can be employed in the determination of the efficient frontier: input-oriented and output-oriented approaches. In the input-oriented approach, the outputs of each decision-making unit are held at the current levels, and the minimal amount of inputs required by an efficient producer to produce those specific levels of outputs will be estimated. A comparison between this optimal level of inputs required and the actual level of inputs each producer uses will yield an efficiency measure for each decision-making unit. The output-oriented approach is similar, except that the inputs are kept fixed at the current levels, and the maximum amount of outputs that can be produced at those levels of inputs will be estimated and compared against the actual levels of outputs of each producer. In the estimation of the efficient frontier, either constant returns to scale (CRS) or variable returns to scale (VRS) can be assumed. DEA efficiency scores ranges between zero and one, with one being fully efficient.

DEA has several advantages in terms of its application to the financial sector. It does not require knowledge of the explicit functional form or assumptions with regard to its stochastic error terms, which is particularly important, as it is difficult to define the functional forms of bank production. Nor does it require a large sample size to implement. In this study, we adopt the input orientation to measure the efficiency of each bank with the assumptions of constant (Input CRS). As in Berger and Mester (1997), DeYoung and Nolle (1998) and Gonzalez (2009), we used three inputs – personnel expenses, book value of fixed assets and loanable funds (sum of deposits and non-deposit funds) – and two outputs – total loans and non-interest income. In this approach, a frontier is calculated for each individual country, and a bank's efficiency is measured relative to its country's own frontier (banks are equally weighted).

The average bank efficiency measure using DEA for the selected South-East Asian countries is given in Table 8.a.2 in the Appendix. Indonesia, Malaysia and Vietnam have experienced low levels of bank efficiency among the countries in the sample. In fact, the bank efficiency for Vietnam is lowest among the six South-East Asian countries, whereas Singapore and the Philippines have the highest. It is interesting to note that the banking efficiency of Malaysia is lower than that of Indonesia and Thailand, with a declining trend over time, except for 1999–2003. It will be interesting to examine whether this result is due to the capital controls and restrictions on foreign participation imposed by Malaysia since 1998, after the Asian crisis. We also notice that banking efficiency is declining for all South-East Asian banks, except for Vietnam's. Although the bank efficiency measures for the Philippines, Singapore and Thailand are relatively high, they also declined in recent years.

In this chapter, we adopt the two-stage framework to study the determinants of bank efficiency. The efficiency measure derived from DEA in the first stage is used as an independent variable in the second stage. Recent studies by Banker and Natarajan (2008), Simar and Wilson (2007) and Souza and Staub (2007) highlight that the two-stage analysis using DEA is viable and, under certain conditions, can even capture the non-parametric stochastic efficiency results.

Our measure of efficiency is based on activity, particularly loans and other banking activities that earn a fee, and might better be described as a productivity or technical efficiency measure. A more complete measure of efficiency would be based on profits or margins, and that extension is a topic for further work, which may also involve the application of other estimation methods, such as a stochastic frontier.

Bank regulation and supervision

The study uses three key regulatory and supervisory variables. The variable RESTRICT measures the extent of bank regulations that restrict activities that generate non-interest income. This variable indicates whether bank activities in the securities, insurance and real-estate markets, and bank ownership and control of non-financial firms, are unrestricted, permitted, restricted or prohibited. Higher values indicate a higher level of restriction.

The bank supervision variables are represented by the intensity of private monitoring (MONITOR) and official supervision of banks (OFFICIAL). Both variables were derived as given in Barth *et al.* (2004, 2006). The MONITOR index contains information regarding the external auditing of banks, ratings by international agencies, the availability of an explicit deposit insurance scheme, and the disclosure of risk-management procedures to the public. The OFFICIAL index provides information regarding the extent to which regulators have the authority to take regulatory actions. Higher values for MONITOR and OFFICIAL indicate greater private oversight and more official supervisory power, respectively.

Specific characteristics of financial institutions

We used several variables to capture specific banking activities that could directly affect the productive performance of banks. Several studies have highlighted the importance of capital requirements. Higher capital requirements will have a direct impact on the risk-taking activities of the owners of the bank. To capture this effect, we introduced the total-equity-to-total-assets ratio (TE_TA). To capture the liquidity effects of the banks, we used the loan-loss-reserve-to-total-loans ratio (LOANLR_GL), liquid-assets-to-total-assets ratio (LA_TA) and non-earning-assets-to-total-assets ratio (NEA_A). To account for the off-balance-sheet activities of banks, we used the off-balance-sheet-to-total-assets ratio (OFFBAL_A).

The impact of foreign ownership and partnership on bank performance is given by a dummy variable, FOREIGN, which represents majority foreign ownership of more than 50 per cent of the bank's equity. We also show whether the bank is a public bank (PUBLIC), wherein the government has more than 25 per cent ownership. To capture the moral-hazard issues related to banks taking ownership of banks and private companies taking ownership of banks, we introduce the dummy variable SUBSIDIARY, which indicates if the bank is a subsidiary or if it has a subsidiary. We also introduce dummy variables to capture the types of banking activity of the bank.

Results: determinants of bank efficiency

The key trends of TE_TA, LOANLR_GL, LA_TA, NEA_A and OFFBAL_A are given in Table 8.a.3 in the Appendix. We also present the plots of TE_TA, LOANLR_GL, LA_TA, NEA_A and OFFBAL_A in Figures 8.1–8.5. In Figure 8.1, TE_TA fell during the Asian crisis period of 1997–9 and then increased during the post-crisis period of 2000–8. Singapore and Thailand increased this ratio by nearly 20 per cent in 2000–8. The other selected ASEAN countries of Malaysia, Indonesia, the Philippines and Vietnam increased their TE_TA ratio by nearly 15 per cent. Indonesia experienced a TE_TA ratio of less than 5 per cent in 1997–9, which increased to nearly 15 per cent in 2000–8.

The LOANLR_GL ratio tends to increase during an economic crisis, which is shown clearly among the ASEAN countries in Figure 8.2. Most ASEAN countries increased their LOANLR_GL ratio in 2000–8 by between 5 and 10 per cent, except Vietnam. The higher LOANLR_GL indicates that the financial institutions were holding higher liquidity reserves to ride volatility

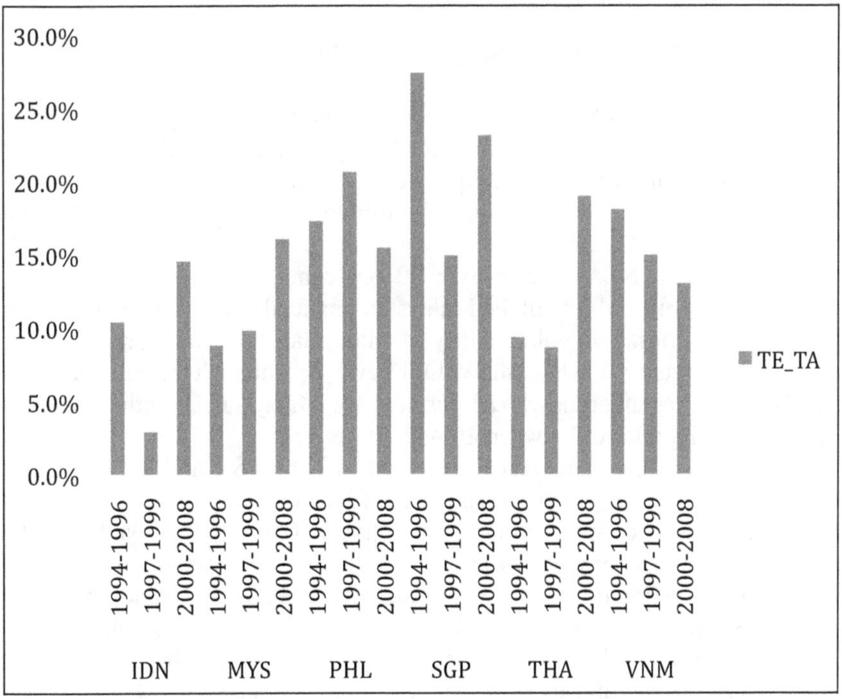

Figure 8.1 Total equity to total assets (TE_TA) for selected Asian countries

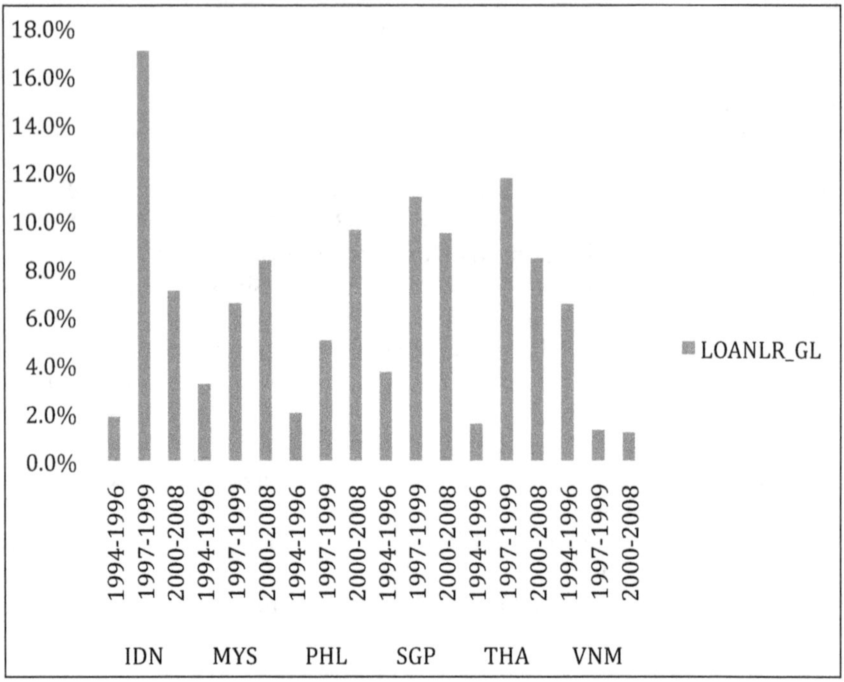

Figure 8.2 Loan loss reserve to total assets (LOANLR_GL)

in output in the post-Asian-crisis period. The higher liquidity-assets holding is also reflected by the LA_TA ratio for Malaysia in Figure 8.3, which shows that it was holding more than 25 per cent of liquid assets to total assets. In comparison, the other countries were holding more than 15 per cent of liquid assets to total assets.

In Figure 8.4, NEA_A was over 20 per cent for Malaysia in 2000–8, indicating the vulnerability of the Malaysian financial markets relative to other ASEAN countries. The vulnerability of Malaysian financial markets is also indicated in Figure 8.5, which shows OFFBAL_A. Although this ratio declined in 2000–8, it remained nearly 25 per cent for Malaysia. The other ASEAN countries had a ratio of between 10 and 20 per cent.

The results of the panel study are given in Tables 8.1 and 8.2. Table 8.1 reports the estimations based on the bank efficiency measurement using CRS and using FE and RE specifications, respectively. To account for bank-specific effects and endogeneity issues in our estimation, we adopted the two-stage least square estimation for fixed-effects (FE2SLS) and random-effects (RE2SLS) specifications proposed by Baltagi (2001). We used the liquid-assets-to-total-bank-deposits-and-borrowing ratio, the sample size for DEA estimation and types of bank as IVs in the estimation. The results of the FE2SLS and RE2SLS estimations are reported in Table 8.2. The results of our study are consistent across both the FE and RE specifications.

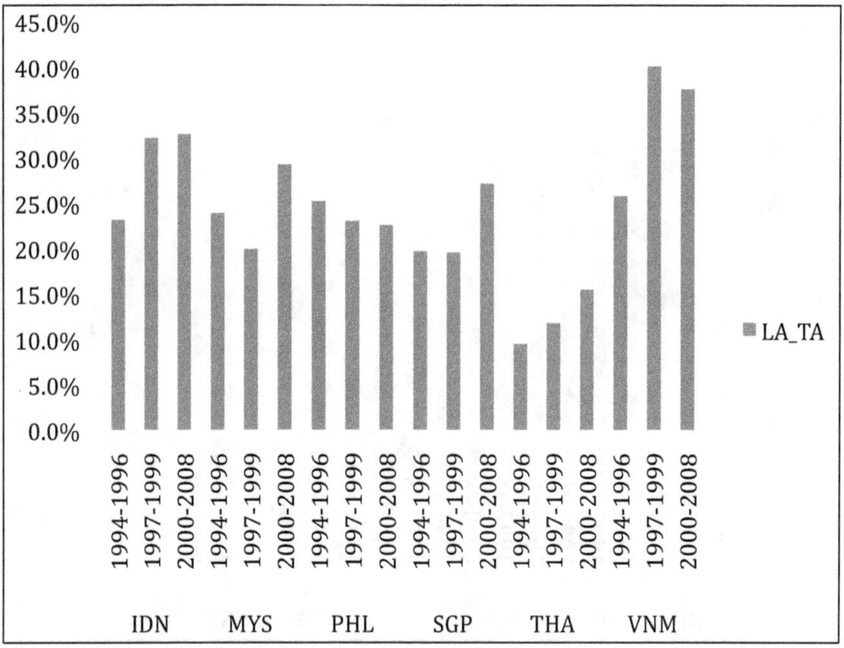

Figure 8.3 Liquid assets to total assets (LA_TA)

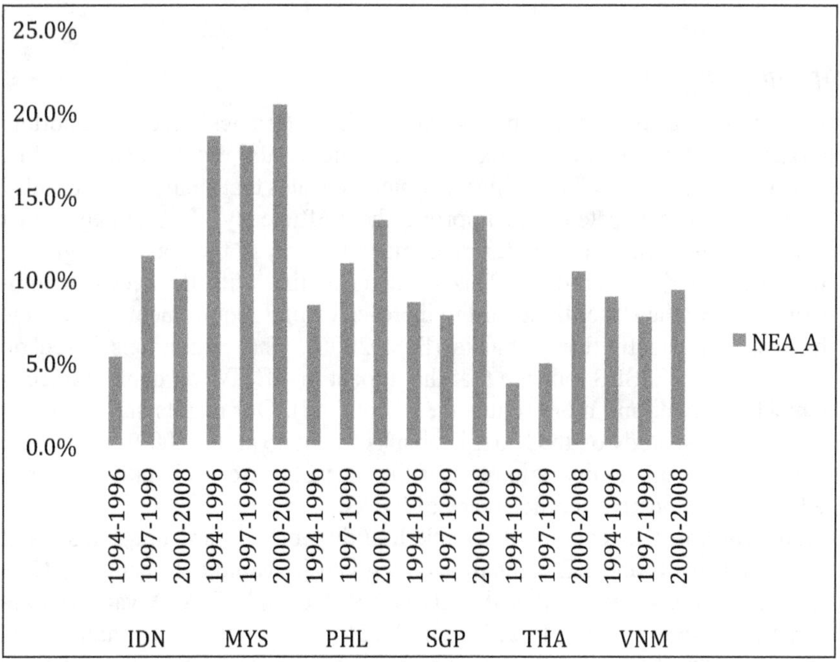

Figure 8.4 Total non-earning assets to total assets (NEA_A) for selected Asian countries

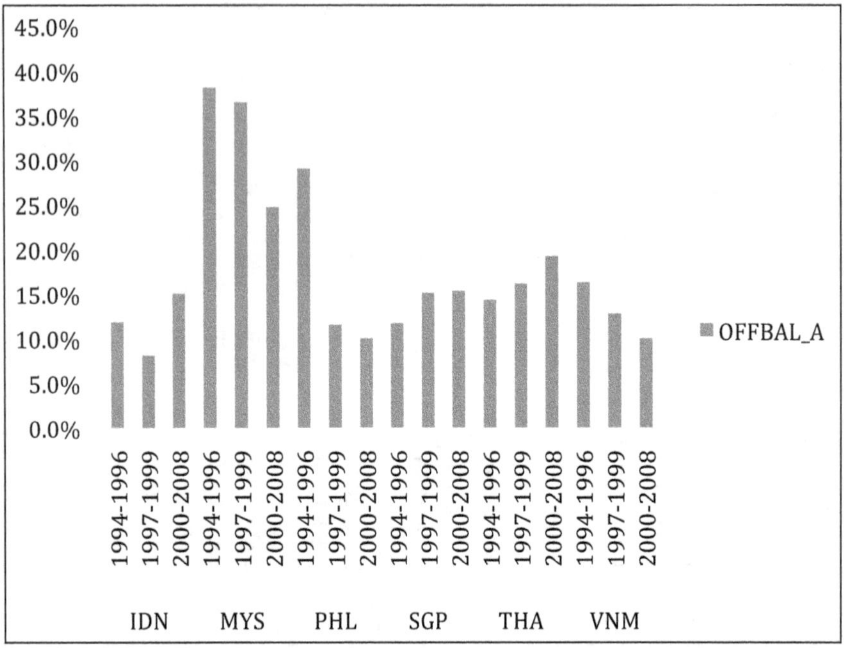

Figure 8.5 Off-balance-sheet activities to total assets (OFFBAL_A) of selected Asian countries

Specific bank characteristics

It is interesting to note that bank-specific characteristics have an important impact on the efficiency of banks. TE_TA, the capital requirement variable, is positive and statistically significant, which indicates that an increase in banks' capital requirements tends to improve their efficiency. This suggests that banks might experience better risk management if they assume greater ownership of their activities. This result is in line with the recent recommendation by the Basel II Accord to increase capital requirements to manage the risk-taking activities of banks (BIS, 2006). The estimations based on FE2SLS and RE2SLS indicate that the impact of TE_TA on bank efficiency is much stronger and more robust (see Table 8.2). Our results are consistent with the recent study on the Brazilian banks by Staub *et al.* (2009), who found that a higher bank equity ratio reduces the moral hazards of bankers and thus reduces the allocative inefficiencies of banks.

The variables to capture the bank liquidity effects are not statistically significant in FE and RE estimations, as given in Table 8.2, using the CRS measure. We also notice that the LOANLR_GL and NEA_A variables are statistically significant in FE2SLS and RE2SLS estimations, as indicated in Table 8.2. The provisions for more reserves to protect loan losses and more liquid assets tend to improve banks' overall productive performance.

Table 8.1 Determinants of bank efficiency based on constant returns to scale measure (CRS DEA–Input CRS) in selected South-East Asian banks

	FE(1)	*FE(2)*	*RE(1)*	*RE(2)*
TE_TA	0.257**	0.283**	0.243**	0.242**
	(2.280)	(2.490)	(2.540)	(2.150)
LOANLR_GL	0.074	0.078	0.099	0.035
	(0.820)	(0.843)	(0.790)	(0.401)
LA_TA	0.009	0.051	–0.066	0.019
	(0.140)	(0.701)	(–1.140)	(0.390)
NEA_A	0.135*	—	0.116	—
	(1.710)		(1.500)	
OFFBAL_A	–0.011***	–0.013***	–0.010***	–0.014***
	(–7.220)	(–7.424)	(–5.300)	(–7.820)
FOREIGN	0.029***	0.032***	0.053***	0.023***
	(3.531)	(3.805)	(5.660)	(2.730)
PUBLIC	0.015	0.014	0.023	0.004
	(0.962)	(0.930)	(1.550)	(0.320)
SUBSIDARY	–0.089***	–0.090***	–0.117***	–0.103***
	(–4.063)	(–4.071)	(–6.600)	(4.800)
RESTRICT	0.107***	0.099***	0.097***	0.096***
	(5.040)	(5.210)	(4.630)	(4.530)
MONITOR	–0.495***	–0.478***	–0.464***	–0.464***
	(–15.500)	(–15.750)	(–15.350)	(–15.350)
OFFICIAL	0.088**	0.078**	0.077**	0.073**
	(2.875)	(2.780)	(2.580)	(2.460)
Commercial banks	0.097***	0.106***	0.077	0.023
	(3.975)	(4.302)	(0.160)	(0.520)
Investment banks	0.192***	0.199***	0.114**	0.125**
	(6.330)	(6.550)	(2.260)	(2.600)
Finance and securities companies	0.202***	0.208***	0.101*	0.205**
	(5.280)	(5.260)	(1.610)	(2.355)
Savings banks	0.072	0.073	–0.069	–0.044
	(1.306)	(1.290)	(–0.710)	(–0.650)
Holding finance companies	0.069**	0.074**	–0.023	–0.011
	(2.510)	(2.680)	(–0.480)	(–0.220)
Government savings banks	0.228***	0.232***	0.129**	0.147**
	(5.510)	(5.710)	(2.170)	(2.631)
Islamic banks	0.222***	0.231***	0.100*	0.122**
	(5.090)	(5.320)	(1.650)	(1.920)
Others	0.089**	0.094***	–0.015	–0.086*
	(2.020)	(5.080)	(–0.260)	(–1.690)
Constant	1.710***	1.791***	1.851***	1.874***
	(4.450)	(5.080)	(4.420)	(4.650)
Country dummies	Yes	Yes	Yes	Yes
Time dummies	Yes	Yes	Yes	Yes
R-squared	0.550	0.549	0.556	0.551
Obs	1359	1359	1359	1359

Notes: * 10% level of significance; ** 5% level of significance; *** 1% level of significance; t-statistics in parentheses; FE – fixed effects; RE – random effects.

Table 8.2 Determinants of bank efficiency based on constant returns to scale measure (Input CRS) using IV estimation in selected South-East Asian banks

	FE2SLS		*RE2SLS*	
	(1)	*(2)*	*(3)*	*(4)*
TE_TA	0.606***	0.591***	0.567***	0.564***
	(6.240)	(8.260)	(5.460)	(5.560)
LOANLR_GL	0.117	0.113	0.060	0.060
	(0.820)	(0.640)	(0.340)	(0.430)
LA_TA	0.052	0.038	0.022	0.020
	(0.76)	(0.480)	(0.360)	(0.330)
NEA_A	—	0.049	—	0.008
		(0.330)		(0.070)
OFFBAL_A	–0.013***	–0.013***	–0.015***	–0.015***
	(–3.840)	(–3.230)	(–4.750)	(–4.130)
FOREIGN	0.028**	0.026**	0.019**	0.018*
	(2.630)	(2.550)	(1.940)	(1.670)
PUBLIC	0.011	0.012	0.001	0.002
	(0.710)	(0.790)	(0.120)	(0.110)
SUBSIDIARY	–0.091***	–0.081***	–0.094***	–0.095***
	(–3.580)	(–3.360)	(4.760)	(–4.020)
RESTRICT	0.112***	0.115***	0.179***	0.180***
	(5.360)	(4.260)	(17.660)	(15.750)
MONITOR	–0.502***	–0.508	–0.488***	–0.490***
	(–16.080)	(–11.700)	(–13.310)	(–12.530)
OFFICIAL	0.094***	0.098**	0.159***	0.160***
	(3.110)	(2.540)	(7.900)	(7.760)
Commercial banks	0.089**	0.086***	0.103**	0.103**
	(3.700)	(3.160)	(2.960)	(2.990)
Investment banks	0.164**	0.160***	0.184***	0.183***
	(6.730)	(5.780)	(4.860)	(5.180)
Finance and securities companies	0.201***	0.207***	0.220***	0.220***
	(5.280)	(5.071)	(4.310)	(4.810)
Savings banks	0.263***	0.262***	0.250***	0.250***
	(4.320)	(3.870)	(4.040)	(4.250)
Holding finance companies	0.051**	0.048*	0.059	0.058*
	(1.980)	(1.750)	(1.600)	(1.710)
Government savings banks	0.207***	0.205***	0.215***	0.218***
	(4.450)	(4.940)	(4.970)	(3.890)
Islamic banks	0.225***	0.220**	0.215**	0.214**
	(3.050)	(2.550)	(2.430)	(2.660)
Others	0.126**	0.123**	0.129*	0.128*
	(2.310)	(2.14)	(1.830)	(1.650)
Constant	1.621***	1.589***	1.680**	1.675**
	(4.610)	(3.530)	(2.840)	(2.010)
Country dummies	Yes	Yes	Yes	Yes
Time dummies	Yes	Yes	Yes	Yes
R-squared	0.590	0.589	0.591	0.590
Obs	1220	1220	1220	1220

Notes: * 10% level of significance; ** 5% level of significance; *** 1% level of significance; t-statistics in parentheses; FE2SLS – two-stage least square fixed effects; RE2SLS – two-stage least square random effects (Baltagi, 2001).

The off-balance-sheet effect of banks (OFFBAL_A) is negative and statistically significant at the 1 per cent level to both the FE and RE estimation specifications. It is also robust to the FE2SLS and RE2SLS estimations. The negative coefficient of off-balance-sheet activities indicates that constraining the non-traditional activities of banks will have a positive outcome on their efficiency.

Foreign participation and ownership in the financial sector have positive effects on banking efficiency (see the positive and statistically significant coefficient for the FOREIGN variable).

There is a negative coefficient on the SUBSIDIARY variable. This result is statistically significant at the 1 per cent level and robust to FE2SLS and RE2SLS estimations. This indicates that there are moral-hazard issues if banks take ownership of companies and if they are bought by corporations.

The results indicate that the types of banking activity have different impacts on the efficiency of banks in South-East Asia, and thus diversification of banking activities is important to maintain banking performance and efficiency.

Bank regulation and supervision

The results for the banking regulation and supervision variables of RESTRICT, MONITOR and OFFICIAL (described under 'Bank regulation and supervision' in the section on Variables) are statistically significant and robust to the FE2SLS and RE2SLS estimations.

The MONITOR variable in our study is negative and statistically significant at the 1 per cent level. This result is robust in our FE2SLS and RE2SLS specifications. It is supported by the recent study by Gonzalez (2009) that indicated a negative coefficient for intensity of private monitoring of financial markets. The negative coefficient in our study indicates that private monitoring does not yield a positive outcome for the financial markets in South-East Asia. It is likely that more-developed and well-diversified financial markets will rely heavily on the private sector to provide information on the activities of the banks for depositors and potential investors. However, given the stage of growth of the financial markets in South-East Asia and developing countries, private monitoring might not produce a positive impact in these countries, compared with those hosting well-developed financial markets. This result supports the views expressed during both the recent global financial crisis and the Asian crisis concerning the moral-hazard issues related to weak private-sector monitoring of the financial markets by rating agencies and private investors.

In contrast, the supervisory and regulatory role of the central bank seems to produce a positive outcome in terms of improvements in the bank efficiency of the financial institutions in South-East Asia. The RESTRICT variable that captures the restrictions on activities that generate non-interest income is positive and statistically significant. This suggests that the regulatory role of central banks in the region is crucial to bank efficiency. Monitoring and regulating the balance-sheet activities of banks tends to improve the productive performance of the banks in our sample. The coefficient on the bank supervisory variable (OFFICIAL) is also positive and statistically significant in our estimations. The transparency of the supervisory function and the official authority of the supervisory activities of the central bank improve banking efficiency. In comparison, the variable on the restriction of activities of non-interest income (RESTRICT) tends to have a higher coefficient in our estimation, indicating that restrictions on bank activities are associated with higher increments to bank efficiency, compared with the OFFICIAL variable.

Conclusion

This chapter looks at the determinants of the technical efficiency of banks in South-East Asia using individual bank data from 1994 to 2008. The study controlled for bank heterogeneity and endogeneity issues by adopting the two-stage least square estimation of fixed and random effects, as provided by Baltagi (2001).

The results highlight certain key activities that could be valuable to policymakers to improve banking efficiency and thereby stability in financial markets. More extensive non-traditional banking activities, in terms of off-balance-sheet activities, are associated with lower levels of efficiency. More extensive corporate linkages to a bank also tend to reduce efficiency. There are further implications of these linkages that may also have a direct impact on system stability. Based on the experience from the Asian crisis, linkages with corporations that may induce moral hazards have to be monitored, and the transparency of such relationships will be very important for the stability of the financial system.

Given the different stages of financial and economic development, a greater concentration on traditional banking activities, such as government savings banks and Islamic banking, has a positive impact on efficiency.

Compared with private-sector monitoring of financial activities, the role of banking regulation and supervision is important for the efficiency of banks in South-East Asia. Our results highlight the importance of bank regulation and supervision for improving bank efficiency in the region, compared with private-sector monitoring of banking activities. In particular, restrictions on banks' risky activities tend to produce more efficient banks. Thus, central banks in the region gain from a better system of monitoring and supervising the risk-sensitive activities of the banks.

The results of the chapter have important implications for liberalizing the financial sector in terms of increasing foreign ownership and participation, as they show that there are positive impacts on bank efficiency from foreign ownership and participation. The financial openness of the financial markets will be important for their development and regional integration.

Bank regulation and supervision are important for the efficiency of banks and for stability in the financial markets in South-East Asia. However, different types of bank regulation and supervision produce different results, and recognition of the impact of different policies will be important to achieve the desired outcomes. The right balance between creating a competitive market, including foreign participation, alongside prudent banking regulation and supervision will be important for banking efficiency and for stability in financial markets.

Appendix

Table 8.a.1 Description of variables

Period	*1994–2008*
Country	*Coverage of number of banks*
Indonesia	129
Malaysia	131
Singapore	110
Thailand	73
Philippines	83
Vietnam	43
Description	*Variables*
Total equity/total assets	TE_TA
Loan loss reserve/gross loans	LOANLR_GL
Liquid assets/total assets	LA_TA
Non-earning assets/assets	NEA_A
Off-balance-sheets/assets	OFFBAL_A
Majority foreign owned	FOREIGN
Public bank (> 25% government ownership)	PUBLIC
Subsidiary or has subsidiary	SUBSIDIARY
Bank regulation and supervision	
Bank regulation: restrictions on activities that generate non-interest income	RESTRICT
Bank supervision: intensity of private monitoring	MONITOR
Bank supervision: official supervision	OFFICIAL
Bank efficiency	
DEA efficiency, input CRS method	Input CRS
Sample size for DEA estimation for country year	DEAsize

Table 8.a.2 Average bank efficiency, 1994–2008

	Input CRS
	Indonesia
1994–2008	0.269
1994–8	0.210
1999–2003	0.430
2004–8	0.170
2007–8	0.184

Continued

Table 8.a.2 Continued

	Input CRS
	Malaysia
1994–2008	0.185
1994–8	0.150
1999–2003	0.231
2004–8	0.175
2007–8	0.187
	Singapore
1994–2008	0.761
1994–8	0.908
1999–2003	0.778
2004–8	0.616
2007–8	0.650
	Thailand
1994–2008	0.698
1994–8	0.752
1999–2003	0.621
2004–8	0.721
2007–8	0.714
	Philippines
1994–2008	0.860
1994–8	0.920
1999–2003	0.921
2004–8	0.740
2007–8	0.830
	Vietnam
1994–2008	0.060
1994–8	0.025
1999–2003	0.048
2004–8	0.105
2007–8	0.120

Table 8.a.3 The trends of key bank variables, 1994–2008 (%)

	Year	*TE_TA*	*LOANLR_GL*	*LA_TA*	*NEA_A*	*OFFBAL_A*
Indonesia	1994–6	10.4	1.8	23.1	5.3	11.8
	1997–9	2.9	17.0	32.2	11.3	8.1
	2000–8	14.5	7.1	32.6	9.9	15.0
Malaysia	1994–6	8.8	3.2	23.9	18.5	38.1
	1997–9	9.8	6.5	19.9	17.9	36.5
	2000–8	16.0	8.3	29.2	20.4	24.7

Continued

Table 8.a.3 Continued

	Year	*TE_TA*	*LOANLR_GL*	*LA_TA*	*NEA_A*	*OFFBAL_A*
Philippines	1994–6	17.2	2.0	25.2	8.4	29.0
	1997–9	20.6	5.0	23.0	10.9	11.5
	2000–8	15.4	9.6	22.5	13.5	10.0
Singapore	1994–6	27.3	3.7	19.7	8.5	11.7
	1997–9	14.9	10.9	19.5	7.8	15.1
	2000–8	23.1	9.4	27.1	13.7	15.3
Thailand	1994–6	9.3	1.5	9.5	3.7	14.3
	1997–9	8.6	11.7	11.8	4.9	16.1
	2000–8	19.0	8.4	15.4	10.4	19.2
Vietnam	1994–6	18.0	6.5	25.7	8.9	16.3
	1997–9	14.9	1.3	40.0	7.7	12.8
	2000–8	13.0	1.2	37.5	9.3	10.0

Notes

1 We would like to thank, first, Guo Jaijing and Xu Kaixian for their excellent research assistance and, second, ERIA for the financial support for the project that generated these chapters. This chapter was presented at the ERIA project, 'Linkages between Real and Financial Aspects of Economic Integration in East Asia', Singapore, 28 February 2010. We would like to thank Shujiro Urata, Jenny Corbett, Tony Cavoli, Victor Pontines, Friska Parulian, Kazuki Onji and Reza Siregar for their helpful comments on an earlier draft.

2 The FE2SLS and RE2LS estimations are expected to correct for the key endogeneity problems in the estimation, such as those related to bank regulation and supervision, and also any endogeniety effects from the TE–TA ratio.

3 See Berger and Humphrey (1997) for an application of DEA in the financial sector.

References

Baltagi, B.H. (2001) *Econometric Analysis of Panel Data*, New York: John Wiley and Sons.

Banker, R.D. and Natarajan, R. (2008) 'Evaluating contextual variables affecting productivity using data envelopment analysis', *Journal of Operations Research*, 56(1): 48–58.

Barth, J.R., Caprio Jr., G. and Levine, R. (2004) 'The regulation and supervision: what works best?', *Journal of Financial Intermediation*, 13: 205–48.

Barth, J.R., Caprio Jr., G. and Levine, R. (2006) *Rethinking Bank Supervision and Regulation: Until Angels Govern*, Cambridge, UK: Cambridge University Press.

Berger, A.N. and Humphrey, D.B. (1997) 'Efficiency of financial institutions: international survey and directions for future research', *European Journal of Operational Research*, 98: 175–212.

Berger, A.N. and Mester, L.J. (1997) 'Inside the black box: what explains differences in the efficiencies of financial institutions', *Journal of Banking and Finance*, 21: 895–947.

Berger, A.N., Hancock, D. and Humphrey, D.B. (1993) 'Bank efficiency derived from the profit function', *Journal of Banking and Finance*, 17: 317–47.

BIS (2006) 'International convergence of capital measurement and capital standards', Basel Committee on Banking Supervision, CH-4200 Basel, Switzerland.

Brunnermeier, M. (2009) 'Deciphering the liquidity and credit crunch 2007–2008', *Journal of Economic Perspective*, 23(1): 77–100.

Casu, B., Girardone, C. and Molyneux, P. (2004) 'Productivity change in European banking: a comparison of parametric and non-parametric approaches', *Journal of Banking and Finance*, 28(10): 2521–40.

DeYoung, R. and Nolle, D.E. (1998) 'Foreign-owned banks in the US: earning market share or buying it?', *Journal of Money, Credit and Banking*, 28: 622–36.

Edwards, F. and Mishkin, F.S. (1993) 'The decline in the traditional role of banks: implications for financial stability and regulatory policy', NBER Working Paper, no. 4993.

Gonzalez, F. (2009) 'Determinants of bank–market structure: efficiency and political economy variables', *Journal of Money, Credit and Banking*, 41(4): 736–54.

Isik, I. and Hassan, K. (2003) 'Financial deregulation and total factor productivity change: an empirical study of Turkish commercial banks', *Journal of Banking and Finance*, 27(8): 1455–85.

Kaplan, E. and Rodrik, D. (2001) 'Did the Malaysian capital controls work?', NBER Working Paper, no. 8142.

Kose, A., Prasad, E.S. and Terrones, M.E. (2009) 'Does openness to international financial flows raise productivity growth?', *Journal of International Money and Finance*, 28(4): 554–80.

Leightner, J.E. and Lovell, K. (1998) 'The impact of financial liberalization on the performance of Thai banks', *Journal of Economics and Business*, 50: 115–31.

Montgomery, H. (2003) 'The role of foreign banks in post-crisis Asia: the importance of method of entry', ADB Institute Research Paper, no. 51, ADB Institute, Tokyo.

Obstfeld, M. (2009) 'International finance and growth in developing countries: what have we learned?', NBER Working Paper, no. 14691.

Radelet, S. and Sachs, J. (1998) 'The onset of the East Asian financial crisis', NBER Working Paper, no. 6680.

Schaeck, K., Cihak, M. and Wolfe, S. (2009) 'Are competitive banking systems more stable?', *Journal of Money, Credit and Banking*, 41(4): 711–34.

Simar, L. and Wilson, P. (2007) 'Estimation and inference in two-stage, semi-parametric models of production process', *Journal of Econometrics*, 136: 31–64.

Souza, G. and Staub, R. (2007) 'Two-stage inference using data envelopment analysis efficiency measurements in univariate production models', *Transactions in Operations Research*, 14: 245–58.

Staub, R., da Silva e Souza, G. and Tabak, B.M. (2009) 'Evolution of bank efficiency in Brazil: a DEA approach', *Pesquisa Operacional na Gestão do Conhecimento*, XLI SBPO: 1616–28.

Sturm, J.-E. and Williams, B. (2004) 'Foreign banks entry, deregulation and bank efficiency: lessons from Australian experience', *Journal of Banking and Finance*, 28(7): 1775–97.

Wheelock, D.C. and Wilson, P.W. (1999) 'Technical progress, inefficiency, and productivity change in US banking, 1984–1993', *Journal of Money, Credit and Banking*, 31: 212–34.

Xu, Y. (2010) 'Towards a more accurate measure of foreign bank entry and its impact on domestic banking performance: a case of China', Crawford School of Economics.

9 Trade financing and export performance

Experiences of Indonesia, Korea and Thailand[1]

Reza Y. Siregar
The South-East Asian Central Banks (SEACEN) Research and Training Centre

Introduction

The rate of decline in global trade during the recent global financial crisis (GFC), also known as the subprime crisis, has been more severe and more widespread than during the era of the Great Depression of the 1930s. According to the WTO, world trade declined by about 12 per cent in 2009 and greatly exceeded the estimated loss of 5.4 per cent of the world GDP for the same year (Freund, 2009; Chor and Manova, 2010; Levchenko *et al.*, 2010). Accompanying this sharp fall in global trade, the joint IMF–Bankers' Association for Finance and Trade (BAFT) survey further found that the decrease in the value of trade finance accelerated between October 2008 and January 2009 in almost every region of the world (BAFT, 2009). Furthermore, the World Bank estimates that 85–90 per cent of the fall in world trade since the second half of 2008 is due to falling international demand, and 10–15 per cent is attributable to a fall in the supply of trade finance (Auboin, 2009).

Two contrasting trends emerged at the outset of the recent GFC in a number of key East and South-East Asian economies. On one hand, the resilient financial sectors, particularly the banking sector, in these Asian economies generally withstood the crisis and emerged relatively unscathed. In contrast to the period of the 1997–8 Asian financial crisis (AFC), as shown in Table 9.1, over the period 2007–9 the capital adequacy and liquidity positions of the banking sectors of these countries remain above the Basel requirements, and the level of non-performing loans has been kept at a relatively low level during recent years. However, the exports of key Asian economies have been impaired by the recent global financial meltdown, as illustrated in Table 9.2, and in Figures 9.1–9.3. For those economies most acutely affected by the AFC, namely Indonesia, Thailand and Korea, export contractions were significantly more severe during the GFC than during the AFC.

During the AFC, two key factors have frequently been underlined by early studies as the root causes of poor export/trade performance in the East and South-East Asian economies (Lane, 1999). The first is the exchange rate factor.

Table 9.1 Soundness indicators of selected East and South-East Asian countries

	Non-performing loans (% of bank loans)			*Risk-weighted capital adequacy ratio*			*Bank return on assets*	
	1999	*2007*	*2009*	*1999*	*2007*	*2009*	*1999*	*2009*
Indonesia	32.9	4.02	$3.9^{\text{Oct/}}$	–6.7	19.18	$17.5^{\text{Oct/}}$	–8.7	$2.7^{\text{Apr/}}$
Korea	8.3	0.64	$1.2^{\text{Sep/}}$	10.8	11.95	$14.3^{\text{Jun/}}$	–1.3	$0.5^{\text{Dec 08/}}$
Malaysia	16.6	6.4	$4.6^{\text{Apr/}}$	12.5	13.2	$14.1^{\text{Nov/}}$	0.7	$1.5^{\text{Dec 08/}}$
Philippines	14.6	4.45	$3.25^{\text{Sep/}}$	17.5	15.93	$15.48^{\text{Mar/}}$	0.4	$0.8^{\text{Mar/}}$
Singapore	5.3	1.5	$2.3^{\text{Sep/}}$	20.6	13.5	$16.5^{\text{Sep/}}$	1.2	$1.1^{\text{Dec 08/}}$
Taiwan	$4.9^{\text{Dec/}}$	1.83	$1.38^{\text{Sep/}}$	$11.2^{\text{Dec/}}$	10.8	$11.6^{\text{Sep/}}$	0.49	$0.3^{\text{Jun/}}$
Thailand	38.6	7.28	$5.31^{\text{Sep/}}$	12.4	15.38	$16.4^{\text{Sep/}}$	–5.7	$1.0^{\text{Dec 08/}}$

Source: James *et al.* (2008) and Siregar and Lim (2010)

The large swings, and especially the severe depreciation, of the local currencies have exacerbated the fundamental weaknesses of the affected economies. Depreciated currencies severely affected the financial institutions and their customers, and was a key factor leading to insolvency. The second factor is the scarcity of short-term trade financing facilities. The sudden drop in trade financing contributed directly to the sharp drops in Indonesia's exports and imports. Establishing possible links between trade financing and trade-sector performance is indeed crucial for a better understanding of the impacts of financial-sector crises on real sectors.

Supporting those early works on the 1997–8 AFC, more recent studies, such as Auboin (2009), BAFT (2009) and Claudio (2008), further underline the importance of trade financing in explaining slowdowns in trade activities. Claudio (2008) has further claimed that the role of trade financing has been strengthened by the structure of production lines through regional supply chains and the move to greater importance of cross-border dispersion of component production and assemblies within vertically integrated production processes in Asia.

The objective of our study is to explore empirically the role of trade financing in inducing the recent slowdown in trade activities in key economies of East and South-East Asia, namely Indonesia, Korea and Thailand. These three countries were selected because of their acute collapse in trade financing during the AFC. Yet, despite the severity of this crisis, virtually no empirical work has assessed the dependency of these countries' export sectors on the availability of trade financing at a country-specific level. The availability of official data on trade financing or credit remains a major obstacle to carrying out comprehensive empirical studies, which partly explains why early works on trade financing for emerging markets are relatively scarce and are mostly based on panel testing.[2]

This study extends the early works by focusing on individual countries and conducting empirical testing on each of those three countries' cases individually. This allows us to highlight and contrast different cross-country experiences. In particular, we hope to address the following set of policy concerns: First, did these economies experience equally severe export drops during the GFC and the AFC? Second, has trade financing contracted more sharply in the GFC compared with the AFC? Has trade financing played a role in explaining the drastic fall in exports of major South-East and East Asian economies during the past two decades, including the recent subprime financial crisis (the GFC)? Further, has the export sector's degree of dependence on trade financing heightened during times of economic crisis? More interestingly, is there any evidence to suggest that the impact of trade credit on export performance is highly dependent on the depth of financial development of the country?

The rest of the chapter is structured as follows. The next section presents the literature review and analyses key facts. The third section discusses the data, model specification and econometric testing. Key empirical findings are analysed and highlighted in the following section. Discussions on the appropriateness of the stimulus-policy measures implemented in these three economies are presented in the fifth section, and brief conclusions end the chapter.

Literature review and stylized facts

Literature review

A number of studies have, either directly or indirectly, addressed the question of whether trade financing matters for export activities. To begin with, Chor and Manova (2010) nicely sum up various cost factors that underscore the importance of trade financing for an exporting firm:

> Exporting is associated with additional outlays that further increase firms' reliance on external finance. Sunk and fixed costs specific to international trade include costs incurred in learning about the profitability of export opportunities; in making market-specific investments in capacity, product customization, and regulatory compliance; and in setting up and maintaining foreign distribution networks. Some variable trade costs, such as shipping and duties, may also have to be incurred before export revenues are realized. Exporters' need for working capital is further magnified by the fact that cross-border transactions on average take between 30–90 days longer to process than domestic sales.
>
> (Chor and Manova, 2010, p. 3)

It is important to acknowledge that trade financing, especially trade credit, has been commonly extended by both financial and non-financial institutions. The role of non-financial firms in providing trade credits is even more important in a country where the quality of financial intermediation is low (Fisman and Love, 2003). In short, trade credit may provide access to capital for firms that are unable to raise it through more traditional channels, such as the banking sector. Why do industrial firms extend trade credit, when financial institutions, such as banks, could provide that facility? A number of possible motives have been theoretically supported (Petersen and Rajan, 1997). More importantly, the motives clearly accentuate the benefits of trade credits for export performance.

According to the financing motive, imperfect capital markets enable suppliers to finance borrowing firms at a lower cost than financial institutions (Smith, 1987). In their work, Petersen and Rajan (1995) demonstrate that suppliers of trade credit have a long-term interest in the survival of the borrower. Credit suppliers are willing to subsidize borrowers with lower interest rates as they expect to reap a higher return from future activities.

In addition, according to the transaction theory of trade credit, firms can economize on the joint costs of exchange by using trade credits. Many have demonstrated theoretically that trade-credit providers have information advantages to sort 'buyers' of their trade financing (Smith, 1987; Biais *et al.*, 1993; Brennan *et al.*, 1998). Banks can get such necessary information, but, through their normal course of business activities, firms may be able to get it faster and more accurately. In addition, suppliers of trade credit have the advantage with regard to collateral – better collateral is provided, because more durable goods tend to be exchanged in the business transactions, and thus greater credit can be offered by the supplier (Mian and Smith, 1992). Ferris (1981) has also demonstrated that trade credit may reduce transaction costs for the borrower. Rather than paying bills every time goods are delivered, the firm might want to schedule the payment on a monthly basis, for instance. Transaction costs could also be lowered, as trade finance could allow the firm to retain inventory and manage it better.

Some empirical works have closely examined the bond between the availability of finance and firm/sector performance and found that the growth of firms depends heavily on the availability of trade finance. Fisman and Love (2003) further claim that, where the quality of financial intermediation is low, firms relying more on trade finance tend to grow faster. Studies have also arrived at a general agreement that the role of trade finance/credit in export performance is even more formidable during crises or recessionary periods. Dell'Ariccia *et al.* (2008) show that, during periods of financial distress, industries that depend more on external finance are hurt disproportionately more. In a related study, Borensztein and Panizza (2006) find that industries with a higher propensity to export are more adversely affected during periods of sovereign defaults. Similarly, Braun and Larrain (2005) demonstrate that, during a recession, industries that depend relatively more on external finance are adversely affected to a greater extent.

Despite anecdotal evidence that the contraction of trade financing may have affected the trade performance of the emerging economies, including those in Asia, only a few empirical studies have been conducted. In addition, past empirical works have largely applied panel testing, thereby failing to capture country-specific experiences. Ronci (2005), for instance, carried out panel testing on ten countries, including a number of the South-East and East Asian economies. The study examines the impacts of world-trade volume, price factors (export and import prices), trade finance and banking crises on export and import volumes.[3] Given data availability, this study revisits the set of issues discussed above and further enhances the analyses by comparing and contrasting the experiences of the three major Asian economies.

Brief facts

Although Asia has not been at the epicentre of the recent global financial meltdown, the real sectors, particularly the trade sectors, of major economies in the region have been widely affected, and the real GDP of Thailand and Korea contracted during the first two quarters of 2009. In fact, the adverse

Table 9.2 The tales of two crises*

Country	*The 1997 financial crisis*		*The subprime crisis*	
	Export	*Trade financing*	*Export*	*Trade financing*
Indonesia	–27% (Quarter 3, 1997–Quarter 1, 1999)	–38% (Quarter 3, 1997–Quarter 3, 1998)	–38% (Quarter 3, 2008–Quarter 1, 2009)	–22% (Quarter 3, 2008–Quarter 1, 2009)
Korea	–17% (Quarter 4, 1997–Quarter 3, 1998)	–17% (Quarter 2, 1997–Quarter 1, 1998)	–35% (Quarter 3, 2008–Quarter 1, 2009)	–7% (Quarter 3, 2008–Quarter 3, 2009)
Thailand	–11% (Quarter 4, 1997–Quarter 2, 1998)	–35% (Quarter 1, 1997–Quarter 3, 1998)	–31% (Quarter 3, 2008–Quarter 1, 2009)	–38% (Quarter 3, 2008–Quarter 1, 2009)

*Note: I limit the observation period to an eight-quarter span following the peak amount prior to the outbreak of the crisis.
Source: CEIC database, the websites of Bank Indonesia, Bank of Korea and Bank of Thailand, and the author's own calculation

impacts of the GFC on the export performance of these three economies have been much more severe than during the AFC. In particular, Thailand and Korea have seen their exports in recent years contract by more than twice the reported rates in the 1997–8 period, as shown in Table 9.2.

As the GFC unfolded, the availability of trade finance declined, and its cost increased. Liquidity pressure in mature markets led to general scarcity of capital in the global market in recent years. The fall in trade finance was also fuelled by the collapse and closure of critical market participants, such as Lehman Brothers. Subsequently, banks in developed countries are now required to hold more capital at home and provide less liquidity to the banks and non-bank financial institutions in the emerging economies (ICC, 2009).

However, the size of the collapse (in percentage terms) in trade financing during the recent GFC has been significantly smaller for Indonesia and Korea and only marginally greater for Thailand compared with the corresponding rates recorded during the AFC, as illustrated in Table 9.2 and in Figures 9.1–9.3. By eyeballing the reported trends on export and trade credit, one could be tempted to argue that the cut in trade finance had a rather limited contribution, or was not the main determining factor of the sharp falls in exports of these three major Asian economies during the recent economic turmoil.

Moreover, the relative amount of trade credit over total exports has been the highest for Korea when compared with Indonesia and Thailand (Figure 9.4). In fact, it is clear from Figures 9.1–9.3 that the actual amount of trade financing to Korea dwarfed the amounts enjoyed by the other two countries. This seems to suggest that the Korean trade sector has the greatest access to trade credit, and that Korean traders have been more heavily

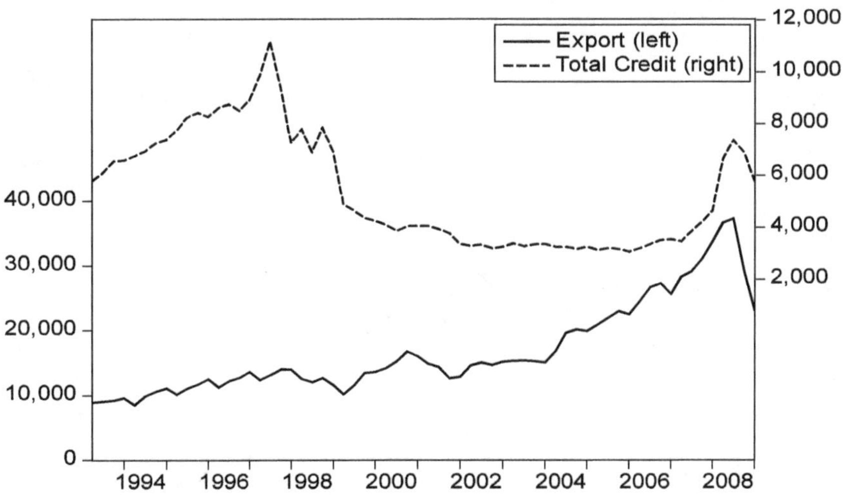

Figure 9.1 Quarterly exports and export credit of Indonesia (US$ million)

Source: Bank Indonesia database and CEIC database

dependent on trade credit. This fact is indeed consistent with the findings of Iacovone and Zavacka (2009) and Kroszner *et al.* (2007), that exporters from developed economies with a more developed financial sector are likely to have better access to trade financing.

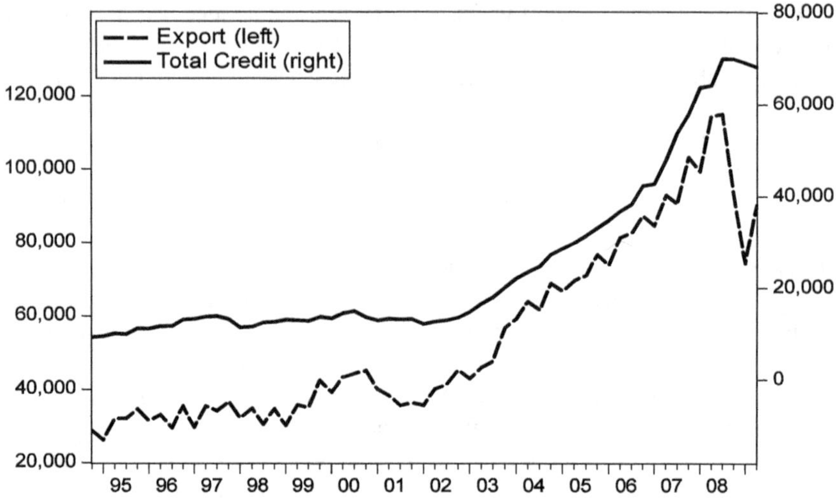

Figure 9.2 Quarterly exports and trade credit of Korea (US$ million)

Source: Bank of Korea website

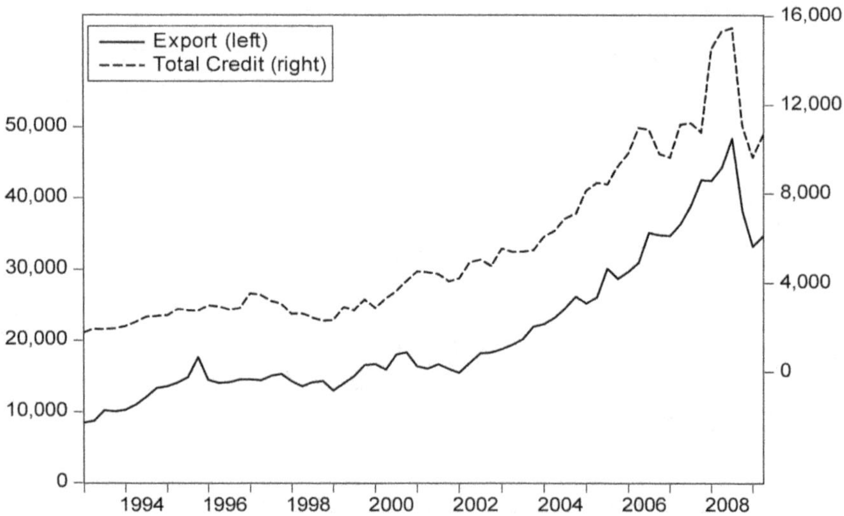

Figure 9.3 Quarterly exports and trade credit of Thailand (US$ million)

Source: Bank of Thailand website and CEIC database

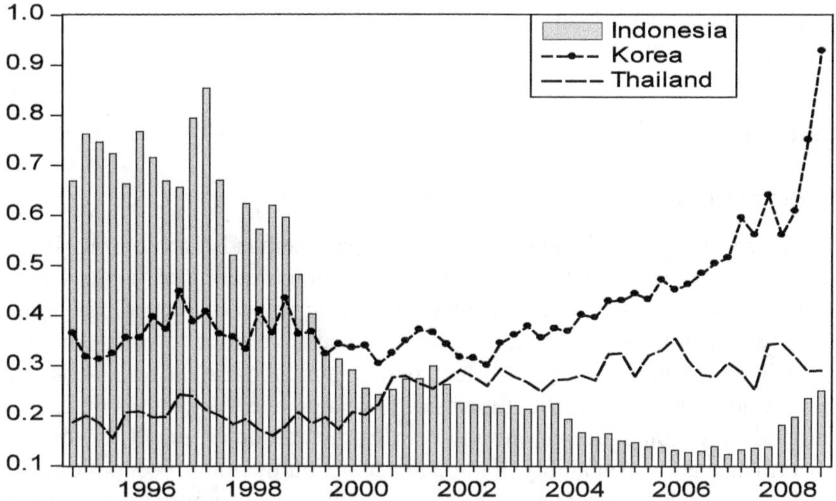

Figure 9.4 Quarterly ratio of trade financing to total exports

Source: Bank of Indonesia, Bank of Korea, Bank of Thailand and author's own calculations

It is interesting to compare the trends of trade financing of these three countries over the past two decades. Indonesia and Korea, in particular, reported distinctive experiences. On one hand, Indonesia attracted steady, strong flows of export credits, ranging from 65 per cent to 85 per cent of total exports on a quarterly basis during the pre-1997 financial crisis. However, following the outbreak of financial and political turmoil in 1998, export credit declined from the third quarter of 1998 to the first quarter of 2006. By the second quarter of 2007, the ratio of export credit to total exports was only about 12 per cent. In a mirror image, the trend for Korea was the opposite: between early 1993 and late 2003, the ratio of trade credit to total exports was in the range of 35–40 per cent. From late 2005 and early 2006, the ratio surged as high as 90 per cent. Interestingly, Thailand seems to have managed a very steady ratio of around 20–30 per cent for the last 15 years.

The overall impact of trade credit on export performance should arguably be influenced, not only by the severity of the fall, but also by the persistence of weak trade credit. During the AFC, export credit in Indonesia contracted for twelve consecutive quarters, from the first quarter of 1997. In Korea, the reported total credit, particularly short-term credit, contracted between the third quarter of 1997 and the first quarter of 1999. The persistence of the contraction in trade credit was also reported for Thailand for about nine quarters, from the first quarter of 1997. Unfortunately, data availability only allows us to analyse up to the second quarter of 2009, but the data seem to suggest that the degree and persistence of the trade credit contraction during the GFC were less than reported in the AFC. It is interesting to note that the amount of quarterly export credit to Indonesia (measured in US dollars) has never returned to its peak of the third quarter of 1997. In contrast, the average values of trade credits to Korea and Thailand in 2008 were more than five times the levels in 1997.

Empirics

Model specification

There are two primary determinants of export demand (Dornbusch, 1988; Hooper and Marquez, 1993). The first is the foreign-income variable, which measures the economic activity and the purchasing power of the trading-partner country ('income effect'). The second is the relative price, or the terms-of-trade factor. Capturing the price effect in international trade, the terms-of-trade factor implicitly captures the impacts of exchange rate fluctuations on export demand. As noted above, another instrumental determinant of export performance is the availability of trade financing. Furthermore, economic crises or downturns have been argued adversely to affect export performance. Incorporating all of these possible determinant factors, the following model specification of the export demand function is derived:

$$\Delta X_t = \alpha + \sum_i \beta_i \Delta X_{t-i} + \sum_i \delta_i \Delta TOT_{t-i} + \sum_i \theta_i \Delta GDPTP_{t-i} \tag{9.1}$$

$$+ \sum_i \eta_i \Delta TCR_{t-i} + \sum_i \chi_i \Delta(DGDP * TCR)_{t-i} + e_t$$

where (Δ) denotes the quarterly growth rate from (t–1) to (t); (X) is the export value in US dollars; (TOT) denotes the terms of trade, measured as the ratio of unit value of exports over unit value of imports; ($GDPTP$) represents the major trading partners' trade-weighted GDP; (TCR) is the trade credit; $\Delta(DGDP*TCR)$ represents the interactive variable of domestic GDP and trade credit; and (e) is the error term and is assumed to have zero mean, constant variance and no autocorrelation.

Theoretically, $\left(\sum_i \delta_i\right)$ is expected to be positive. A rise in the terms of trade (TOT) should have a positive impact on export growth. The inclusion of (TOT) allows us to capture the impact of price, including exchange-rate shocks in the global market. Similarly, fluctuations in external demand would have consequences for export performance. To account for the external demand, ($GDPTP$) the trade-weighted trading partners' GDP is included in the regression model, Equation (9.1). The rise in the purchasing power of trading partners, reflected by a positive growth of ($GDPTP$) should lead to a higher demand for export products. Hence, $\left(\sum_i \theta_i\right)$ is expected to be positive.

The external demand shock has been shown to be highly significant in recent works by Freund (2009) and Freund and Klapper (2009).

Next, a sharp decline in trade credit (*TCR*) is likely to have a number of adverse consequences and to disrupt trade and growth performance (Wang and Tadesse, 2005). As already discussed, the availability of trade credit should enable export producers to meet demand. The loss of liquidity in the trade sector may also force exporters (and importers) to obtain spot foreign exchange to make necessary payments, thereby increasing demand in foreign exchange and possibly creating delays in payment. Furthermore, exports may have high import content in some countries. In these cases, a collapse in import financing could end up adversely affecting exports. Hence, $\left(\sum_i \eta_i\right)$ is expected to be positive.

Finally, the impact of a trade-financing shortage on export performance is likely to be more severe during a financial crisis. As discussed, studies such as Braun and Larrain (2005) have demonstrated that, during recessions, the performance of an industry is heavily influenced by its dependence on the availability of finance. Moreover, the deeper the crisis (higher GDP loss), the further the tightening of credit (including trade credit), which in turn has a much more severe, adverse impact on trade sectors.

To test the effect of trade financing during the crisis on export performance, an interactive variable between the growth rates of domestic GDP and total trade credit $\Delta(DGDP*TCR)$ is introduced in Equation (9.1). The growth rate of domestic GDP (*DGDP*) captures the boom and bust of the local economy. For this study, the GDP growth captures the depth of the economic slowdown/crisis. This series is adopted instead of the frequently applied crisis dummy to allow for a continuous time series. During a period of economic crisis, macroeconomic volatility sharpens and causes severe restrictions to firms' access to external finance, especially from the banking sector (Braun and Larrain, 2005). This situation in turn raises the demand for trade finance and thus enhances the role of trade finance in explaining export performance (Nielsen, 2002).

The adoption of this interactive variable has been reported in many studies, including recent work such as Dell'Ariccia *et al.* (2008) and Iacovone and Zavacka (2009). Finding a positive $\left(\sum_i \chi_i\right)$ suggests that, during a crisis or economic slowdown, the adverse impact of trade credit on the export sector would be more significant. Hence, this variable confirms the existence of a trade-credit channel operating during a period of economic crisis. The case of Brazil in 2002, for instance, demonstrates that the initial impact of a drop in trade credit on export performance created further selling pressure on the local currency. In turn, it worsened external debt payment and increased country risk, leading to further cutbacks in all funding, including trade financing (Mori, 2005). Hence, $\left(\sum_i \chi_i\right)$ is expected to be positive.

Data and empirical testing

Data

Our quarterly observation covers the period from the first quarter of 1993 to the second quarter of 2009. The observation set is dictated by the availability of trade-credit/financing data for each country. The trade-finance data series are all sourced from the respective central banks' databases, namely Bank Indonesia, Bank of Thailand and Bank of Korea. The export series (X) is the total export in US dollars of Indonesia, Korea and Thailand. They are all from the CEIC database. The terms-of-trade series (TOT) is calculated as the ratio of unit value of exports to unit value of imports, gathered from the CEIC Asia database for Korea and Indonesia. The terms-of-trade data for Thailand, on the other hand, are obtained from the Bank of Thailand's database. The real trading partner GDP ($GDPTP$) is the trade-weighted combination of the GDPs of the top three major export destination countries for each country included in our study. The ($GDPTP$) variable is calculated by the following standard formula:

$$GDPTP = \omega_1 GDPTP_1 + \omega_2 GDPTP_2 + \omega_3 GDPTP_3 \tag{9.2}$$

$$\omega_1 = \frac{X_1}{(X_1 + X_2 + X_3)} \tag{9.3}$$

$$\omega_2 = \frac{X_2}{(X_1 + X_2 + X_3)} \tag{9.4}$$

$$\omega_3 = \frac{X_3}{(X_1 + X_2 + X_3)} \tag{9.5}$$

where ($GDPTP_1$), ($GDPTP_2$) and ($GDPTP_3$) are the GDPs for trading-partner countries 1, 2 and 3, respectively. Accordingly, (ω_1,ω_2, ω_3) are the trade weights for trading partners 1, 2, and 3 respectively. Finally, (X_2) and (X_3) are the exports of Indonesia, Korea and Thailand, individually, to each country's respective three major trading partners. For all three countries in our study, the first two major export destinations for our sample period are the United States and Japan. China has emerged as a key trading partner for Indonesia, Korea and Thailand in recent years.[4] However, as a complete set of quarterly GDP data for China is not available, Korea is listed as the third partner for Indonesia and Thailand. For Korea, Germany is the third major export destination. The raw data that are needed to construct the real trading partner GDP are sourced from the CEIC database.

The variable $\Delta(DGDP*TCR)$ is computed as the first difference of the product of the quarterly domestic GDP (*DGDP*) and the quarterly trade credit (*TCR*) for each country included in our study. The domestic GDP series are adopted from the CEIC Asian database. All variables in regression Equation (9.1) are log normalized.

Empirical testing

This study employs the frequently applied autoregressive distributed lag (ARDL) testing with the general-to-specific approach (Hendry, 1976).[5] The ARDL testing includes lags up to four quarters.[6] The combination of the ARDL and the general-to-specific approach allows us to start from the general model by including all key explanatory variables and their time lags, supported by various theoretical frameworks. The general-to-specific procedure is then adopted to reduce the complexity of the model by eliminating the statistically insignificant variables. This process should ensure the consistency of the final, reduced model. The final outcomes of the ARDL and general-to-specific approach should enable us not only to capture the significant determinants and eliminate the insignificant ones, but also to arrive at the number of lags/periods needed for the impacts of changes in the explanatory variables on the dependent variable.

Before conducting the ARDL testing, we test the unit root properties for each of the variables in Equation (9.1). To anticipate the possible presence of structural breaks, we employ Banerjee *et al.* (1992) (henceforth BLS), in addition to standard unit root tests, i.e. the ADF test, the Phillip–Perron test and the KPSS test.[7] Depending on the unit root properties of the series, we then test for the possible cointegration relationship among the variables listed in Equation (9.1) at their levels. If a cointegration relationship is found, then the error correction component series (ECM_{t-1}) will be included in the ARDL testing.

We undertake several test statistics to ensure that our coefficient estimates are valid and robust. In addition to the standard F-statistics to confirm the significance of one or more explanatory variables, we also report the Breusch–Godfrey serial correlation LM-test statistics to verify that autocorrelations in the residuals are not a problem in any of the regressions.

Key results and lessons learned

Based on our set of unit root tests, all relevant series are found to be non-stationary and integrated of order 1 at their level – I(1) series.[8] Hence, we cannot rule out the presence of a cointegration relationship among the variables presented in Equation (9.1) for all three countries. The standard Johansen cointegration test was then carried out. Based on the trace statistics, no cointegration relationship is found at the 5 per cent level of significance. We do, however, find a weak cointegration relationship at 10 per cent for Indonesia. The number of lags included in the cointegration for each country case is determined by the Akaike information criterion (AIC).[9]

The overall ARDL test results are reported in Tables 9.3–9.5. The adjusted R^2 values suggest that the explanatory variables can clarify around 44–55 per cent of the quarterly changes in the export values of these three economies, with Korea having the largest adjusted R^2 and Indonesia the smallest. The F-statistics confirm that one or more of the independent variables is non-zero. In addition, the Breusch–Godfrey serial correlation LM-test statistics confirm that no autocorrelation in the residuals is found in any of the three regressions. All key explanatory factors, namely income, terms of trade and trade financing, contribute, at 10 per cent or more significance level, to the ups and downs of the export values of these countries. In addition, the coefficient estimates of these key factors are theoretically consistent.

Several key lessons from the experiences of these three countries can be highlighted from the ARDL test. First, trade financing has a positive effect on exports, as theoretically expected. However, the size and significance of the estimated parameters vary significantly from one country to another. Based on the sum of the coefficient estimates of (*TCR*), $\left(\sum_i \eta_i\right)$, the role of trade credit on export performance is found to be the largest for Korea and the smallest for Indonesia. This finding supports the claim that exporters in countries with a more developed financial system are perceived to be more reliable and thus have access to more trade credit (Iacovone and Zavacka, 2009). As discussed, the ratio of trade credit to exports for Korea is relatively more significant than that reported for Thailand and Indonesia, as illustrated in Figure 9.4.

Looking at the significant lags of $\left(\sum_i \eta_i\right)$, we can conclude that the consequences of falling trade credit would immediately be felt and would influence the export performance of these economies within the same quarter (t). The results seem also to suggest that the impact of trade finance on exports is most persistent in the case of Indonesia – up to four quarters (t–4).

Among the three primary determinant factors of export performance, namely price, income and trade financing, the income effect has consistently been the most significant determinant in all three countries. The size of the coefficient estimate for (*GDPTP*), $\left(\sum_i \theta_i\right)$, suggests that the full implication of income movement is felt on export demand within the first quarter. Thus, a rise of 1 per cent in a trade-weighted trading partner's GDP would result in an average increase in export demand of about 1 per cent, and vice versa. The most significant income impact is reported in the case of Thailand in Table 9.5, with the size of the coefficient estimate significantly larger than one, at 1.189. This seems to support the World Bank's finding that a major factor explaining the fall in world trade in general (including in Asia) is the falling international demand, or the 'income effect' (Auboin, 2009).

Finally, test results for all three countries confirm the claim that, the deeper the crisis, the more significant the adverse consequences of trade-credit

Table 9.3 Indonesia

Dependent variable: (ΔX)			
Variable	*Coefficient*	*Std error*	*t-statistics*
(ΔTOT_t)	0.713	0.341	2.091**
(ΔTCR_t)	0.744	0.132	5.633***
(ΔTCR_{t-1})	–0.875	0.149	–5.876***
(ΔTCR_{t-4})	0.172	0.077	2.220**
$(\Delta GDPTP_{t-2})$	0.960	0.365	2.633**
$(\Delta DGDP{*}TCR)_{t-1}$	–1.784	0.494	–3.612***
(α)	0.021	0.009	2.369**
Adjusted R-squared: 0.443		Prob (LM-test): 0.409	
F-statistics: 8.677		Prob (F-statistics): 0.000	

Notes: * significant at 10%; ** significant at 5%; and *** significant at 1%.
Source: Author's own calculations

Table 9.4 Korea

Dependent variable: (ΔX)			
Variable	*Coefficient*	*Std error*	*t-statistics*
(ΔX_{t-1})	–0.208	0.114	–1.181*
(ΔTOT_{t-1})	0.725	0.287	2.525**
$(\Delta GDPTP_{t-1})$	0.986	0.481	2.050**
(ΔTCR_t)	0.437	0.195	2.239**
(ΔTCR_{t-2})	0.393	0.195	2.008**
$(\Delta DGDP{*}\Delta TCR)_1$	3.749	1.679	2.231**
$(\Delta DGDP{*}\Delta TCR)_{t-2}$	4.162	1.659	2.507**
(α)	–0.025	0.015	–1.686*
Adjusted R-squared: 0.468		Prob (LM-test): 0.747	
F-statistics: 7.921		Prob (F-statistics): 0.000	

Notes: * significant at 10%; ** significant at 5%; and *** significant at 1%.
Source: Author's own calculations\

Table 9.5 Thailand

Dependent variable: (ΔX)			
Variable	*Coefficient*	*Std error*	*t-statistics*
(ΔTOT_{t-3})	0.572	0.288	1.980**
$(\Delta GDPTP_{t-1})$	1.189	0.240	4.945***
(ΔTCR_t)	0.223	0.075	2.962***
(ΔTCR_{t-1})	0.242	0.074	3.286***
$(\Delta DGDP{*}\Delta TCR)_{t-1}$	–3.874	1.430	–2.708***
$(\Delta DGDP{*}\Delta TCR)_{t-2}$	4.141	1.515	2.734***
(α)	0.004	0.006	0.681
Adjusted R-squared: 0.559		Prob (LM-test): 0.112	
F-statistics: 13.172		Prob (F-Statistics): 0.000	

Notes: * significant at 10%; ** significant at 5%; and *** significant at 1%.
Source: Author's own calculations

collapse ($\Delta(DGDP*TCR)$) for the export sector. It is interesting to note here that the effect of a financial crisis is deeper in countries with a more developed financial system. The sum of the coefficient estimates for variable ($\Delta(DGDP*TCR)$) is the largest for the case of Korea. This result is consistent with Kroszner *et al.* (2007). However, most importantly, this also substantiates the importance of the stage of financial development in linking the financial sector to the real sector, particularly the trade sector.

Our results have confirmed the role of terms of trade in influencing export activities in these major Asian economies. Looking at the sum of the coefficient estimates for the variable (*TOT*) for each country, it is apparent that the price factor is particularly important for Indonesia. The coefficient estimate for this country is not only significant and relatively large, but also suggests that the impacts of global price change on exports are immediately felt within the same quarter. This appears to be consistent with the nature of Indonesian exports, which have predominantly been primary commodities.

Financial crisis and trade-sector linkages: have the stimulus-policy responses been appropriate?

The recent global financial meltdown presented the emerging market economies (EMEs) with two shocks: a 'sudden stop' of capital flows driven by the deleveraging, and a collapse in export demand associated with the global slump. The past episodes of sudden stops have demonstrated that countries with tighter fiscal policy experienced sharper contractions than those with a looser stance (Ortiz *et al.*, 2009). In particular, given the limitation of monetary policy discussed earlier, the role of fiscal stimulus is critical, not only in terms of minimizing the impacts of the crisis, but, more importantly, in stimulating economic recovery. Therefore, it is not a surprise that a similar measure would be pursued during the GFC. However, one of the hallmarks of the GFC is the unprecedented size of the fiscal and monetary policies carried out by countries, which in some cases were done in a coordinated fashion, around the world.

Of the three economies included in this study, Korea has been the most aggressive in its reponse to the GFC. The country's overall fiscal balance remained positive, at 1.2 per cent of GDP, in 2008, but, by the end of the first half of 2009, it reported an overall deficit balance of around 5 per cent of GDP. On the other hand, the governments of Indonesia and Thailand both expanded their stimulus measures in 2009. The Ministry of Finance of Indonesia initially aimed at a very modest budget deficit of around 1.0 per cent of GDP in 2008, but eventually decided to double the stimulus package in early 2009 to a deficit of around 2.5 per cent of GDP. Similarly, Thailand stepped up its fiscal expansion target to –1.7 per cent of GDP in 2009 from a mere –1.0 per cent in 2008. In fact, a number of South-East Asian economies pursued these expansionary efforts in a consistent manner regionally, as illustrated in

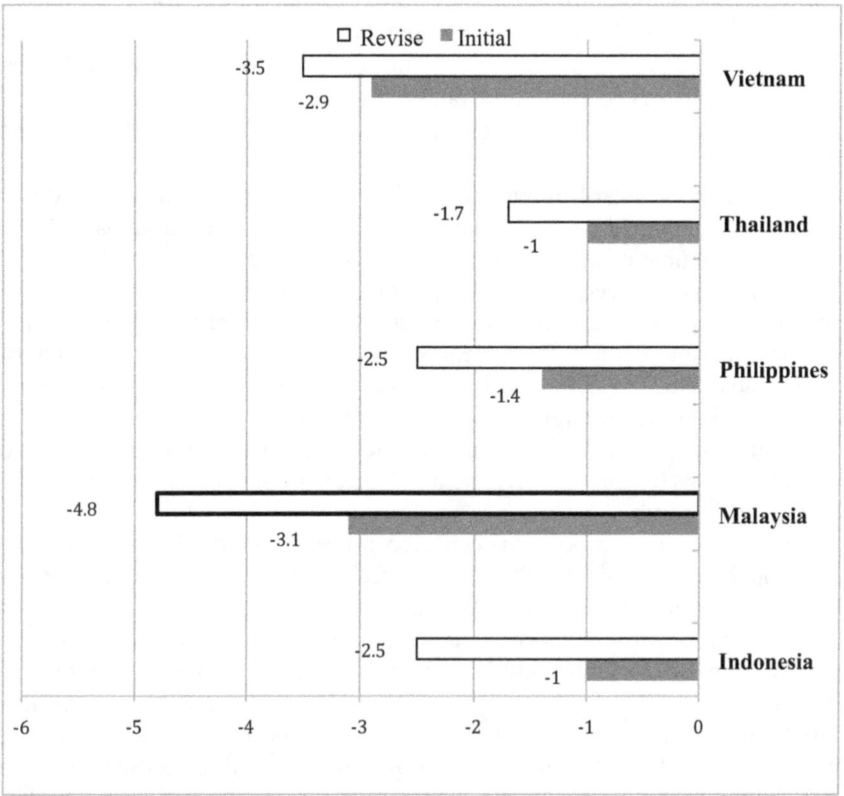

Figure 9.5 Budget deficit as percentage of GDP for selected South-East Asian economies

Source: Bloomberg, CEIC Asia Database

Figure 9.5. In general, the fiscal stimulus of the Asian economies involved both the expansion of the expenditure side and reduction of a number of key tax rates. To support the activities of firms, especially small and medium firms, the governments of these three economies extended tax cuts and other forms of investment fund. A significant number of these small and medium enterprises are export-oriented firms.

In addition, a number of monetary-policy expansionary measures have accompanied fiscal expansion in most emerging markets in Asia. As in advanced economies, the basic thrust of the monetary policy in our three major Asian economies has been to ease the impacts of the deleveraging process in the global economy on domestic liquidity, and to help mitigate the full implications of the GFC on the real sectors of the economy. Most South-East and East Asian economies lowered their policy rates considerably. Indonesia, for instance, reduced its policy rate from 9.5 per cent in December 2008 to 6.5 per cent in August 2009. Similar policy measures were reported in other major SEACEN economies, including Thailand, Malaysia and Korea. For some of these economies, the rates by the end of the third quarter of 2009 hovered around the lowest ranges reported for a long time, at between 1 and 2 per cent.

Beyond the standard interest-rate-policy and reserve-requirement adjustments, to stimulate their credit markets further, the Asian central banks have adopted a number of quantitative measures, including various 'credit-easing' (CE) and 'quantitative-easing' (QE) policies. Korea has been among the most active in employing CE and QE measures. To instil market confidence and financial-sector stability, the Korean government, together with the Bank of Korea, guaranteed repayment of banks' external borrowings; extended foreign-currency liquidity through foreign-exchange swaps; provided liquidity to domestic banks, including Korean branches of foreign banks; and instituted tax exemptions for foreign investment in Korean treasury bonds and monetary-stabilization bonds.

Have these stimulus policies been appropriate to mediate the impacts of the GFC on the exports of these three economies? To address this important policy question, one needs first to review and understand various possible channels of transmission of a financial crisis towards a trade contraction. Borrowing the analyses of Bayoumi and Melander (2008), one common feature of a financial crisis is the presence of much tighter banking credit. Often, this tightened credit can be explained by two sequential factors. The first is due to adverse shocks to a bank's capital position. To avoid further deterioration of their balance sheets, banks often tighten their lending standards, which results in further tightening of credit availability. The drying up of bank lending has been linked to the tightening up of trade credit (Braun and Larrain, 2005; Borensztein and Panizza, 2006; Dell'Ariccia *et al.*, 2008).

The analyses above suggest that the stimulus packages have been appropriate policy responses. With the clear objectives of ensuring continuous flows of bank credit and adequate foreign-exchange supply in the local market during the difficult period of the GFC, the stimulus policies have probably contributed to lessening the severity of the decline in trade financing, especially for Indonesia and Korea, as shown in Table 9.2. However, further in-depth studies are required to examine more closely the components of export credits/trade financing to understand better the role of stimulus policies in mediating the adverse consequences of the recent global financial meltdown for trade financing in our Asian economies.

Concluding remarks

Trade finance has long been an important component of international financial flows, but has often been overlooked in the literature. However, during the AFC, the important contribution of trade credit to export performance was fully appreciated when the major trade-dependent economies of East and South-East Asia saw their trade sectors shrink, which further worsened the balance-of-payment crisis. This study covers the period from 1993 to 2009, covering the period prior to the AFC through to the impacts of the GFC. Extending earlier works, this research study focuses on the experiences of Indonesia, Thailand and Korea, individually. By adopting time-series data for each country's case, and not the panel data of the early works, a number of cross-country experiences can be compared and contrasted.

In general, our findings confirm the critical role of trade credit in explaining the export performance of the three economies. However, the impacts of trade financing on export demand differ from one country to another. The experiences of the three countries included in this study seem to suggest that, the more developed a country's financial sector, the more significant the role of trade financing is likely to be. As expected, the adverse consequences of a fall in trade credit on export performance are amplified during a financial crisis. This last finding confirms the importance of a crisis contagion channel from the financial sector to the real sector of the economy.

Notes

1 The views expressed are the author's only and do not necessarily represent those of the SEACEN entre and its member central banks.

2 One of the few empirical works including the East and South-East Asian economies is Ronci (2005), which works on panel data of ten countries in Asia, Latin America, Turkey and Russia.

3 The countries included in the panel testing are the East and South-East Asian economies (Malaysia, the Philippines, Thailand, Indonesia, Korea), Russia, Brazil, Argentina, Mexico and Turkey.

4 For Indonesia and Thailand, Singapore has also been a key trading partner and a primary export destination. However, as exports to Singapore from these two economies are largely re-exported, and Singapore is not the final main destination of the export goods, we do not include Singapore.

5 The application of the ARDL approach with the general-to-specific approach is common. Recent studies applying the ARDL framework include Siregar and Goo (2010), Campa and Goldberg (2002) and Gagnon and Ihrig (2004).

6 Because of the degree of freedom, we only consider four-quarter lags. Pesaran and Shin (1999) suggested up to two lags for annual data. As we work with quarterly data, we expanded the lags to four.

7 The BLS provides a more in-depth investigation of the possibility that the aggregate economic time series can be characterized as being stationary around 'a single or multiple structural break'. It extends the Dickey–Fuller *t*-test by the construction of the time series of rolling computed estimators and their *t*-statistics. Following the BLS procedure, we compute the smallest (minimal) and the largest Dickey–Fuller *t*-statistics.

8 For the sake of brevity, the test results of the unit root testing are not reported but are available upon request.

9 Based on the AIC, each of the cointegration tests includes around two or three quarter lags. No robust cointegration relationship is reported at the 5 per cent significance level from any of the three countries' test results. For Indonesia, we

do find a weak cointegration relationship at the 10 per cent level when we consider lags for at least four quarters. We included the error-correction component for the case of Indonesia, but did not find the variable to be significant at the 10 per cent level.

References

Auboin, M. (2009) 'The challenges of trade financing', VOX Research-based Policy, see www.voxeu.org/index.php?q=node/2905 (accessed 8 June 2012).

BAFT (2009) Third Benchmark Survey of International Trade Finance Markets, www.baft.org (accessed 8 June 2012).

Banerjee, A., Lumsdaine, R.L. and Stock, J.H. (1992) 'Recursive and sequential tests of the unit-root test and trend break hypotheses: theory and international evidence', *Journal of Business and Economic Statistics*, 10: 271–87.

Bayoumi, T. and Melander, O. (2008) 'Credit matters: empirical evidence of US macro-financial linkages', IMF Working Paper, WP/08/169.

Biais, B., Gollier, C. and Viala, P. (1993) 'Why do firms use trade credit?', mimeo, CEPR Conference in San Sebastian.

Borensztein, E. and Panizza, U. (2006) 'Do sovereign defaults hurt exporters?', RES Working Paper 4447, Inter-American Development Bank, Research Department.

Braun, M. and Larrain, B. (2005) 'Finance and the business cycle: international, inter-industry evidence', *Journal of Finance*, 60(3): 1097–128.

Brennan, M., Maksimovic, V. and Zechner, J. (1998) 'Vendor financing', *Journal of Finance*, 1127–41.

Burkart, M. and Ellingsen, T. (2004) 'In-kind finance: a theory of finance', *American Economic Review*, 94(3): 569–89.

Campa, J.M. and Goldberg, L.S. (2002) 'Exchange rate pass-through into import prices: a macro or micro phenomenon?', NBER Working Paper, no. 8934 (May).

Chor, D. and Manova, K. (2010) 'Off the cliff and back? Credit conditions and international trade during the global financial crisis', NBER Working Paper, no. 16174 (July).

Claudio, R. (2008) 'Credit chains and sectoral co-movement: does the use of trade credit amplify sectoral shocks?', Policy Research Working Paper Series, no. 4525, The World Bank.

Dell'Ariccia, G., Detragiache, E. and Rajan, R. (2008) 'The real effect of banking crises', *Journal of Financial Intermediation*, 17(1): 89–112.

Dornbusch, R. (1988) *Exchange Rate and Inflation*, Cambridge, MA: MIT Press.

Ferris, J.S. (1981) 'A transaction theory of trade credit use', *Quarterly Journal of Economics*, 94: 243–70.

Fisman, R. and Love, I. (2003) 'Trade credit, financial intermediary development, and industry growth', *Journal of Finance*, 58(1): 353–74.

Freund, C. (2009) 'The trade response to global downturns: historical evidence', Policy Research Working Paper Series, no. 5016, The World Bank.

Freund, C. and Klapper, L. (2009) 'Has the decline in the supply of financing affected trade during the crisis?', mimeo, The World Bank.

Gagnon, J.E. and Ihrig, J. (2004) 'Monetary policy and exchange rate pass-through', *International Journal of Finance and Economics*, 9(4): 315–38.

Hendry, D.F. (1976) 'Discussion of "Estimation of linear functional relationships: approximate distributions and connections with simultaneous equations in econometrics" by T.W. Anderson', *Journal of the Royal Statistical Society B*, 38: 24–5.

Hooper, P. and Marquez, J. (1993) 'Exchange rates, prices, and external adjustments in the United States and Japan', International Finance Discussion Paper, no. 456, The Board of Governors of the Federal Reserve System.

Iacovone, L. and Zavacka, V. (2009) 'Banking crisis and exports: lessons from the past', Policy Research Working Paper, no. 5016, The World Bank.

ICC (2009) 'Rethinking trade finance 2009: an ICC global survey', ICC Banking Commission Market Intelligence Report, March.

James, W.E., Park, D., Jha, S., Jongwanich, J., Terada-Hagiwara, A. and Sumulong, L. (2008) 'The US financial crisis, global financial turmoil, and developing Asia: is the era of high growth at an end?', ADB Economics Working Paper Series, no. 139 (December).

Kroszner, R.S., Laeven, L. and Klingebiel, D. (2007) 'Banking crises, financial dependence, and growth', *Journal of Financial Economics*, 84(1): 187–228.

Lane, T. (1999) 'The Asian financial crisis – what we have learned', *Finance and Development*, 36(3).

Levchenko, A.A, Lewis, L. and Tesar, L.L. (2010) 'The collapse of international trade during the 2008–2009 crisis: in search of the smoking gun', NBER Working Paper, no. 16006.

Mian, S. and Smith, C.W. (1992) 'Accounts receivable management policy: theory and evidence', *Journal of Finance*, 47(1): 169–200.

Mori, H. (2005) 'Brazil's approach in the face of export constraints', in *Access to Trade Finance in Times of Crisis*, eds J.-Y. Wang and M. Ronci, Washington, DC: IMF.

Nielsen, J.H. (2002) 'Trade credit and the bank lending channel', *Journal of Money, Credit and Banking*, 34: 226–53.

Ortiz, A.P., Pablo, F., Strurzenegger, F. and Talvi, E. (2009) 'Monetary and fiscal policies in a sudden stop: is tighter brighter?', in *Dealing with an International Credit Crunch: Policy Responds to Sudden Stops in Latin America*, eds E. Cavallo and A. Izquierdo, Washington, DC: Inter-American Development Bank.

Pesaran, H.M. and Shin, Y. (1999) 'Autoregressive distributed lag modeling approach to cointegration analysis', in *Econometrics and Economic Theory in the 20th Century: The Ragnar Frisch Centennial Symposium*, ed. S. Strøm, Cambridge: Cambridge University Press.

Petersen, M.A. and Rajan, R.G. (1995) 'The effect of credit market competition on lending relationships', *Quarterly Journal of Economics*, 60: 407–44.

Petersen, M.A. and Rajan, R.G. (1997) 'Trade credit: theory and evidence', *Review of Financial Studies*, 10(3): 661–91.

Ronci, M. (2005) 'Trade finance and trade flows: panel data evidence from 10 crises', in *Access to Trade Finance in Times of Crisis*, eds J.-Y. Wang and M. Ronci, Washington, DC: IMF.

Siregar, R.Y. and Goo, S. (2010) 'Effectiveness and commitment to inflation targeting policy: evidence from Indonesia and Thailand', *Journal of Asian Economics*, 12(2) (April): 113–28.

Siregar, R.Y. and Lim, V. (2010) 'The role of central banks in sustaining economic recovery and in achieving financial stability', Staff Paper, no. 74, the SEACEN Centre, Kuala Lumpur, Malaysia (February).

Smith, J. (1987) 'Trade credit and information asymmetry', *Journal of Finance*, XLII(4): 863–9.

Wang, J.-Y. and Tadesse, H. (2005) 'Overview', in *Access to Trade Finance in Times of Crisis*, eds J.-Y. Wang and M. Ronci, Washington, DC: IMF.

10 Export credit and export performance

The experience of Indonesia

Reza Y. Siregar
The South-East Asian Central Banks (SEACEN) Research and Training Centre

Anton H. Gunawan
Bank Danamon, Jakarta[1]

Introduction

Having been among the most severely hit economies in the Asian financial crisis (AFC) of 1997–8, Indonesia weathered the global financial crisis (GFC) of 2008–9 remarkably well. The country maintained the third highest GDP growth in the Group of Twenty economies (G-20) and the major Asia-Pacific economies – slower only than China and India – averaging more than 4 per cent quarterly growth during the first half of 2009 (Figure 10.1). Both the fiscal and monetary authorities have coordinated their efforts to maintain price stability. In contrast to the 1997–8 crisis, domestic inflation has been well anchored throughout the height of the GFC (Figure 10.2). Moreover, although the local currency depreciated sharply against the US dollar, it stabilized much quicker in the GFC than during the 1997 currency meltdown, as shown in Figure 10.3.

The strength of Indonesia's financial sector in this recent GFC (also known as the subprime crisis) is in sharp contrast to the financial meltdown of the 1997–8 AFC. Even at the peak period of the global financial slowdown, between the last quarter of 2008 and the first quarter of 2009, banks continued to be profitable and maintained capital adequacy levels well above the Basel requirement. During the first half of 2009, Indonesian banks reported the highest capital adequacy ratio and return on assets among the major South-East and East Asian economies (as shown in Table 10.1).

Despite the relatively strong economic landscape, the Indonesian export sector suffered more severely during the recent GFC than in the AFC. Weak demand, especially from the key export markets of the United States, Japan and Europe, has been identified as one of the main detrimental forces for Indonesian exports. Another possible transmission channel from the financial sector to the real sector meltdown is trade financing. Indeed, Indonesian exporters had access to a wide variety of trade-financing options, including letters of credit and export credits in the forms of working capital and investment capital.

This study examines the link between export credits and export performance in Indonesia. The primary task is to address the following questions: Has the export sector become too dependent on export credit during the past two decades? In particular, did export financing contribute to the boom and bust

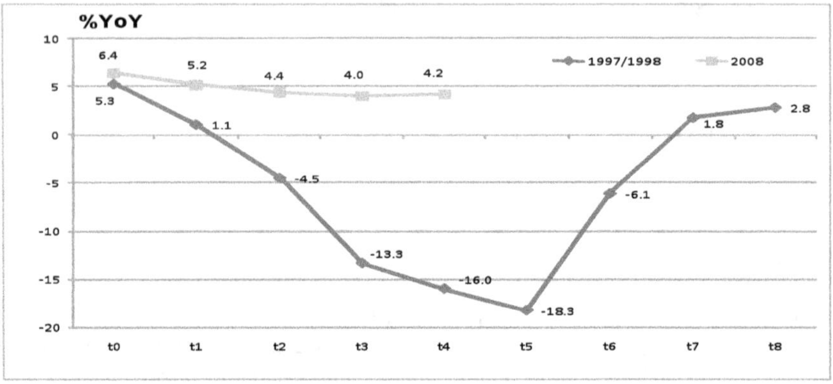

Figure 10.1 GDP growth rate

Notes: (a) 1997–8 AFC: t0 = September (third quarter) 1997 and t8 = September (third quarter) 1999; (b) 2008 GFC: t0 = September 2008 and t4 = September 2009; (c) t1 represents a period one quarter after t0.
Source: CEIC database

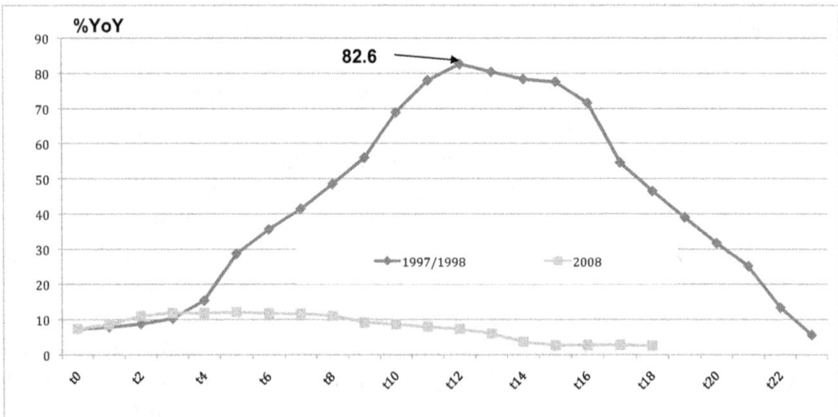

Figure 10.2 Inflation

Notes: (a) 1997–8 AFC: t0 = October 1997 and t23 = September 1999; (b) 2008 GFC: t0 = April 2008 and t18= October 2009.
Source: CEIC database

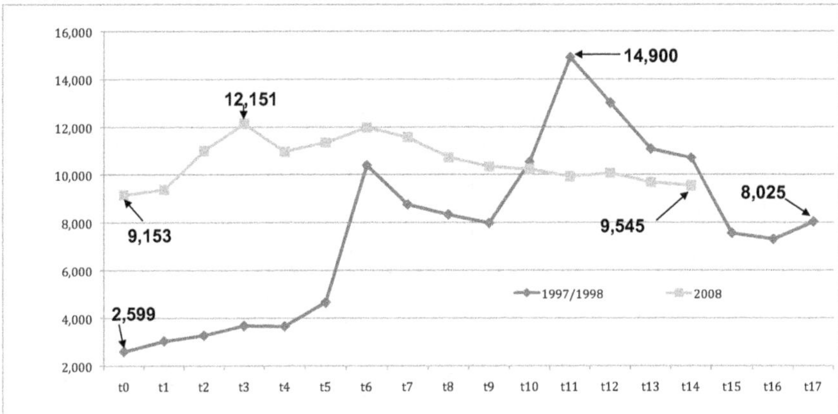

Figure 10.3 Rupiah per US dollar rate

Notes: (a) 1997–8 AFC: t0 = July 1997 and t17 = December 1998.
Source: CEIC database

of the two major export groups, namely manufacturing and mineral exports? Did the recent economic and financial crisis amplify the role of export credit in sustaining exports? Furthermore, was working capital more critical than investment capital in explaining the performance of Indonesia's exports?

To our knowledge, little work has empirically addressed these important questions. Studies such as Brown and Magiera (2000) and Ronci (2005) have either examined the issues qualitatively or considered the Indonesian case as part of a large pool of very diverse panel testing. With the availability of time-series export credit data from third quarter 1993 to first quarter 2009, from Bank Indonesia, our study is in a unique position to look more comprehensively into the role of export financing to explain the performance of the export sector.

In the next section, we present a literature review and analyse key stylized facts. An empirical section follows that includes a discussion of data, model specifications and econometric testing. Key empirical findings are analysed and highlighted in the next section. In the fifth section, a number of policy responses to support the export sector during the recent GFC are presented and discussed. A brief section of concluding remarks ends the paper.

Literature review and stylized facts

Literature review

A number of studies have attempted to address, both directly and indirectly, the question of whether trade financing matters for export activities. However, it is important first to underscore that trade financing, especially trade credit,

Table 10.1 Soundness indicators of Indonesia and selected East and South-East Asian countries

	Non-performing loans (% of bank loans)			*Risk-weighted capital adequacy ratio*			*Bank return on assets*	
	1999	*2007*	*2009*	*1999*	*2007*	*2009*	*1999*	*2009*
Indonesia	32.9	4.02	3.9 Oct/	–6.7	19.18	17.5 Oct/	–8.7	2.7 Apr/
Korea	8.3	0.64	1.2 Sep/	10.8	11.95	14.3 Jun/	–1.3	0.5 Dec 08/
Malaysia	16.6	6.4	4.6 Apr/	12.5	13.2	14.1 Nov/	0.7	1.5 Dec 08/
Philippines	14.6	4.45	3.25 Sep/	17.5	15.93	15.48 Mar/	0.4	0.8 Mar/
Singapore	5.3	1.5	2.3 Sep/	20.6	13.5	16.5 Sep/	1.2	1.1 Dec 08/
Taiwan	4.9 Dec/	1.83	1.38 Sep/	11.2 Dec/	10.8	11.6 Sep/	0.49	0.3 Jun/
Thailand	38.6	7.28	5.31 Sep/	12.4	15.38	16.4 Sep/	–5.7	1.0 Dec 08/

Source: James *et al.* (2008) and Siregar and Lim (2010)

is offered by both financial and non-financial institutions. In particular, the role of non-financial firms in providing trade credits is more important in a country where the quality of financial intermediation is low (Fisman and Love, 2003). In short, trade credit may provide access to capital for firms that are unable to raise it through more traditional channels, such as the banking sector. Why do industrial firms extend trade credit, when financial institutions such as banks can provide this facility? There are a number of possible reasons that have also been theoretically supported (Petersen and Rajan, 1997).

One reason is that imperfect capital markets enable suppliers to finance borrowers at a lower cost than financial institutions (Smith, 1987). In their work, Petersen and Rajan (1995) demonstrate that the supplier of trade credit has a long-term interest in the survival of the borrower. The credit supplier is willing to subsidize borrowers with lower interest rates because they expect to reap a higher return from future activities.

In addition, according to the 'transaction theory' of trade credit, firms can economize on the joint costs of exchange by using trade credits. Many have demonstrated theoretically that trade-credit providers have information advantages that enable them to sort the 'buyers' of their finance (Smith, 1987; Biais *et al.*, 1993; Brennan *et al.*, 1998). Banks can get such necessary information but, through the normal course of business activities, firms may be able to get it faster and more accurately. In addition, the supplier of trade credit has an advantage relating to the collateral. The more durable the goods exchanged in the business transaction, the better collateral they provide, and the greater the credit the supplier can extend (Mian and Smith, 1992). Ferris (1981) has also demonstrated that trade credit may reduce transaction costs for the borrower. Rather than paying bills every time goods are delivered, the firm, for instance, might want to schedule the payment on a monthly basis. Transaction costs could also be lowered, as trade finance could allow the firm to retain inventory and manage it better.

Some empirical works have focused more on the link between the availability of finance and firm/sector performance. These works show that the growth of firms depends heavily on the availability of trade finance. Fisman and Love (2003), for instance, claim that, where the quality of financial intermediation is low, firms relying more on trade finance tend to grow faster. Studies also generally agree that the role of trade finance/credit in export performance is even more formidable during a crisis or recessionary period. Dell'Ariccia *et al.* (2008) show that, during periods of financial distress, external-finance-dependent industries are hurt disproportionately more. In a related study, Borensztein and Panizza (2006) find that industries with a higher propensity to export are more adversely affected during periods of sovereign defaults. Similarly, Braun and Larrain (2005) demonstrate that, during a recession, industries that depend relatively more on external finance get hurt more.

Despite anecdotal evidence that the contraction of trade financing may have affected trade performance, only a few empirical studies have been conducted, particularly on the experiences of emerging economies in Asia. For the case of Indonesia in particular, there has been little empirical research carried out. In addition, past empirical works have largely applied panel testing and, hence, have failed to capture country-specific experiences. Ronci (2005) carried out panel testing on ten countries, covering a number of the South-East Asian (including Indonesia) and East Asian economies. The study examines the impacts of world-trade volume, price factors (export and import prices), trade finance and the banking crisis on export and import volumes.[2]

Brief stylized facts: Indonesian economy and the tales of two crises

As the worst phase of the recent GFC has arguably passed, it is timely to compare its impacts on the Indonesian economy with that of the 1997–8 AFC. In particular, it is worthwhile to extract, where possible, contrasting features of the impacts of these economic slowdowns on the country's export performance. It is safe to conclude, at this stage, that the AFC was far more damaging to the Indonesian economy than the GFC. As shown in Figures 10.1–10.3, a series of primary macroeconomic indicators confirm this conclusion.

During the 1997 crisis, the Indonesian economic growth rate contracted sharply into negative territory a mere two quarters after the onset of the crisis, and it remained a negative growth rate for the following five quarters. In the last quarter of 1998, the economy contracted at an unprecedented rate of –18.3 per cent (year on year). In contrast, the real GDP growth during the GFC slowed only gradually and mildly in the following three quarters and quickly bounced back in the third quarter of 2009. Most importantly, there was clearly no threat of contraction in the country's GDP during the recent GFC.

The severity of the AFC was evident from the skyrocketing inflation rate, hitting over 82 per cent year on year in September 1998. By contrast, inflation remained at single-digit levels for most of the GFC; the inflation rate did rise to a double-digit level, at around 12 per cent year on year in September 2008, but quickly weakened to 2.4 per cent year on year in November 2009. The nominal exchange rate of the rupiah against the US dollar was another key barometer of the severity of the AFC in Indonesia. The currency depreciated very sharply during the 1997–8 crisis, from around Rp2,559 per US dollar in early July 1997 (two weeks before the full-blown speculative attack on the rupiah), to reach Rp14,900 per US dollar by June 1998. The rupiah depreciated during the GFC by slightly over 30 per cent from August to November 2008, but recovered most of the loss swiftly by early January 2009.

Indonesia's export sector suffered substantially, despite the relatively stable income (GDP) and price levels (inflation and exchange rate), as illustrated in Table 10.2. The total export value contracted by around 35 per cent (year on year) within three months of the initial decline in October 2008. The 1997–8 crisis saw a more gradual meltdown of the export sector. It took about fourteen months for the total export value to reach its nadir, reporting a year-on-year

Table 10.2 The tales of two crises

	The Asian financial crisis	*The global financial crisis*
Total exports	–27% (Quarter 3, 1997–Quarter 1, 1999)	–38% (Quarter 3, 2008–Quarter 1, 2009)
Manufacturing exports	–34% (Quarter 2, 1997–Quarter 4, 1998)	–35.6% (Quarter 3, 2008–Quarter 1, 2009)
Mineral and lubricant products exports	–31% (Quarter 2, 1997–Quarter 2, 1998)	–51% (Quarter 3, 2008–Quarter 1, 2009)
Total export credit	–38% (Quarter 3, 1997–Quarter 3, 1998)	–22% (Quarter 3, 2008–Quarter 1, 2009)
Working capital credit	–43% (Quarter 3, 1997–Quarter 3, 1998)	–25% (Quarter 3, 2008–Quarter 1, 2009)
Investment credit	–26% (Quarter 3, 1997–Quarter 3, 1998)	–20% (Quarter 2, 2008–Quarter 1, 2009)

Source: CEIC database, the database of Bank Indonesia

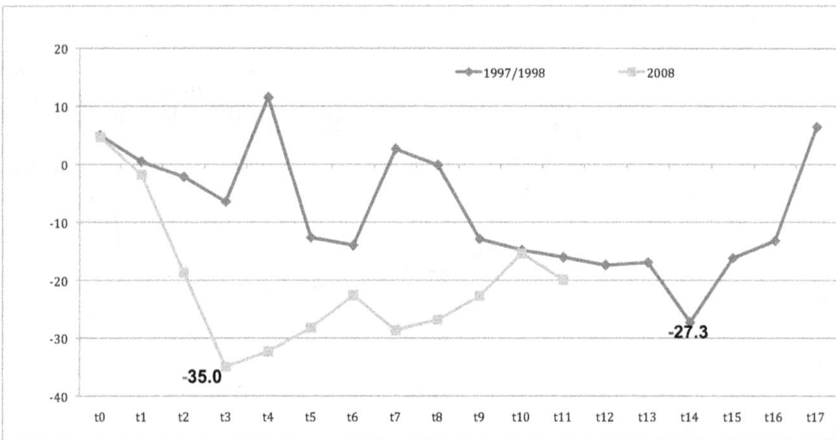

Figure 10.4 Export performance during 1997–8 Asian financial crisis and 2008 global financial crisis

Note: (a) 1997–8 AFC: t0 = October 1997 and t17 = March 1999; (b) 2008 GFC: t0 = October 2008 and t11= September 2009
Source: CEIC database.

contraction of around 27 per cent by the end of 1998. The recovery process was much more rapid during the AFC, once it started, as shown by the steeper curve in Figure 10.4. What explained the severe collapse of exports in the recent crisis? Did export credit decline more sharply during the recent crisis vis-à-vis the 1997 AFC?

Figures 10.5 and 10.6 indicate that the collapse of export credit was much more severe during the 1997–8 AFC than during the GFC. Although the government tried to calm panicked depositors by issuing a blanket guarantee on all banking-sector assets and liabilities in February 1998, social and political shocks in May 1998 led to a near collapse of the Indonesian banking sector. Less than two years after the start of the AFC in Indonesia in August 1997, around sixty-four banks were closed, and a number of big banks, including state banks and large conglomerate-owned banks, were either taken over or bailed out and recapitalized.

This near collapse of the Indonesian banking sector in 1998 greatly compromised the availability of trade finance, and the collapse of many large conglomerates also reduced external trade activities (Brown and Magiera, 2000). Total export credit contracted by as much as 38 per cent in the third quarter of 1998 from one year earlier. Both long-term and short-term financing declined sharply, but short-term financing contracted more, by well above 40 per cent for the same period. In general, the share of short financing (working capital) in the overall export credit averaged around 70 per cent between 1997 and 1999.

The declining trend of export credit may have stabilized by the third quarter of 1998, but the waning trend in fact continued until the first quarter of 2006. The new height of the export credit provisions, at around US$7.4 billion in

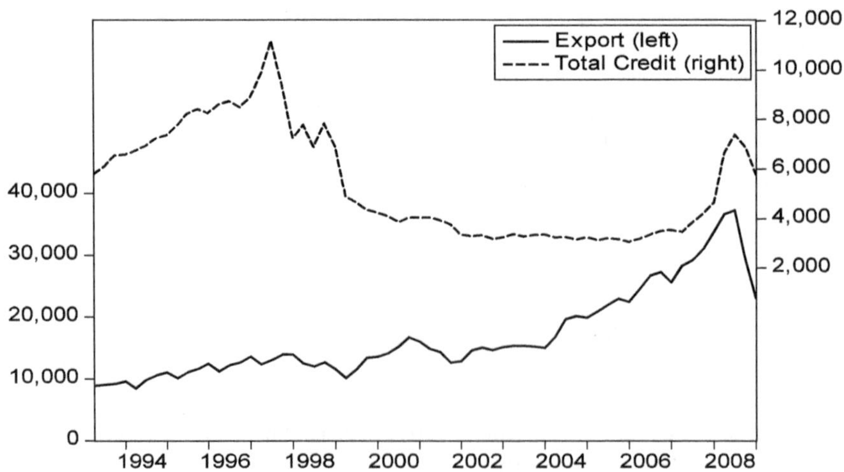

Figure 10.5 Exports and export credit of Indonesia (US$ million)

Source: Bank Indonesia

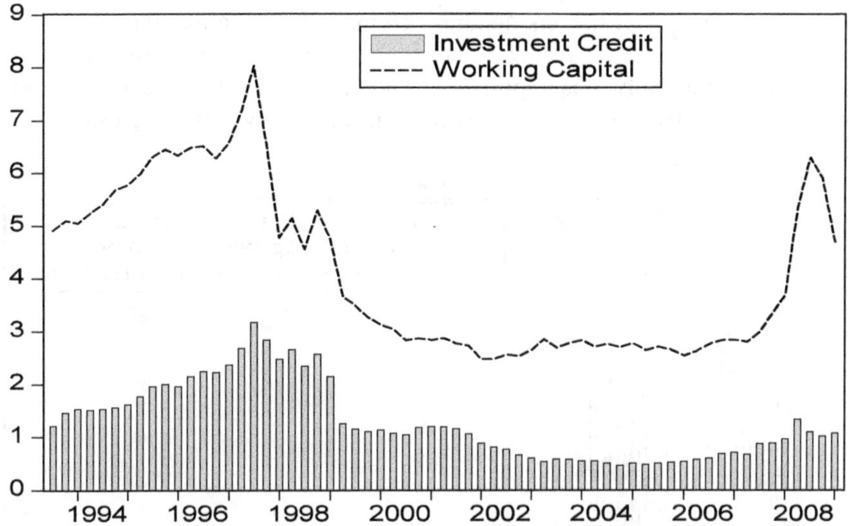

Figure 10.6 Quarterly decomposition of export credit (US$ billion)
Source: Bank Indonesia

the third quarter of 2008, was well below its peak in 1997 of over US$11 billion in the third quarter of 1997. During the GFC, export credit contracted by 22 per cent, well below the sharp fall during the AFC. Figure 10.6 illustrates that the tumble at its highest amounted to slightly over US$1.5 billion, between late 2008 and the first quarter of 2009, compared with about US$4.3 billion from the third quarter of 1997 to the third quarter of 1998. The decline largely resulted from the tightening of short-term financing. The share of working capital in overall export credit was about 80 per cent from the last quarter of 2004, as shown in Figure 10.6.

The analysis above suggests that the role of export credit in explaining recent export slowdowns has weakened. Figure 10.7 reports the ratio of export credit and its main components to total exports. At its height in the third quarter of 1997, total export credit reached around 85 per cent of the country's total exports. By the end of the second quarter of 2007, total export credit amounted to only 12 per cent of total exports. The Indonesian exporters appear to have become less and less dependent on export credit in recent years.

It is interesting to note that there seems to be a strong correlation between the fluctuations of export credit and the flows of the international bank claims to Indonesia from US banks, as illustrated in Figures 10.5, 10.6 and 10.8.[3] Both of these flows dropped significantly during the AFC, followed by a mild increase in 1999 and a declining trend until 2002. The two flows finally showed a substantial upward trend from 2006. Siregar and Choy (2010) reported a similar trend for the total international claims of banks from seven OECD nations to Thailand and Indonesia. This evidence of co-movements between trade finance and international bank claims suggests that, during periods of economic crisis, with bank lending drying up, including that from the international banks, the availability of trade finance should tighten as well in Indonesia.[4] Naturally, it is important to study further the direction of causality between these two flows, if any, before arriving at any firm conclusion.

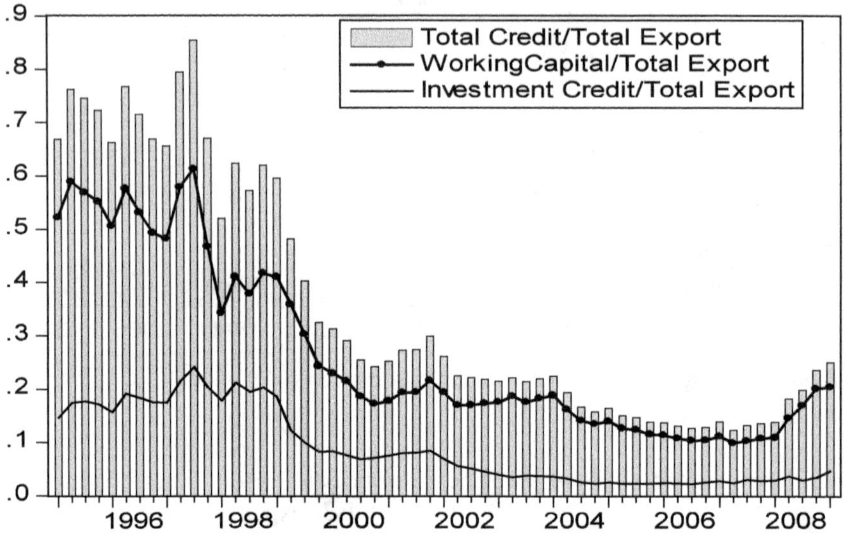

Figure 10.7 Ratio of export credit to total export

Source: Bank Indonesia and author's calculations

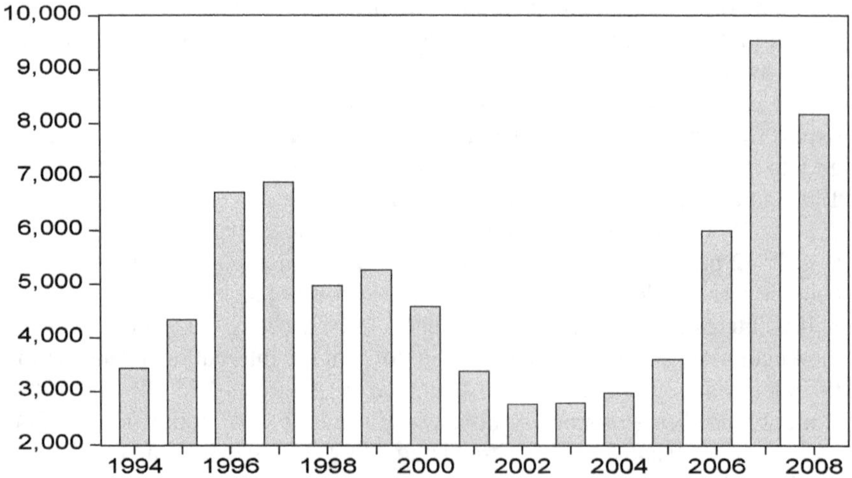

Figure 10.8 Annual lending to Indonesia from the US banks (US$ million)

Source: The World Bank and the Bank for International Settlements' databases

Empirics

Model specification

The methodology we adopt here is similar to the one used in Chapter 9 of this book, and the explanations of the empirical model are given in Chapter 9. The model specification of export demand function is given as:

$$\Delta X_t = \alpha + \sum_i \beta_i \Delta X_{t-i} + \sum_i \delta_i \Delta TOT_{t-i} + \sum_i \theta_i \Delta GDPTP_{t-i} \quad (10.1)$$

$$+ \sum_i \eta_i \Delta TCR_{t-i} + \sum_i \chi_i \Delta (DGDP * TCR)_{t-i} + e_t$$

where: (Δ) denotes growth rate from (t–1) to (t); (X) is the export value in US dollars; (TOT) denotes the terms of trade, measured as the ratio of unit value of export over unit value of import; ($GDPTP$) represents Indonesia's major trading partners' trade-weighted GDP (in US dollars); (TCR) is the total export credit in US dollars; $\Delta(DGDP*TCR)$ represents the interactive variable of domestic GDP and export credit; and (e) is the error term and is assumed to have zero mean and constant variance and is not autocorrelated.

The terms of trade *(TOT)* have a positive impact on export, and, hence, we expect $\left(\sum_i \delta_i\right)$ to be positive, as the rise in the purchasing power of trading partners, ($GDPTP$), will increase exports. Increase in trade credit (TCR) will positive impact on exports, and, hence, $\left(\sum_i \eta_i\right)$ is expected to be positive. To test the role of trade financing during the crisis on export performance, we introduce an interactive variable between the growth rates of domestic GDP and total trade credit, $\Delta(DGDP*TCR)$.

To extend the analysis and to contribute further to the literature in this area, we decompose the export credit into two key components, working capital (TCR^{WK}) and investment capital (TCR^{INV}), and test the following working model:

$$\Delta X_t = \alpha + \sum_i \beta_i \Delta X_{t-i} + \sum_i \delta_i \Delta TOT_{t-i} + \sum_i \theta_i \Delta GDPTP_{t-i} \quad (10.2)$$

$$+ \sum_i \lambda_i \Delta TCR^{WK}_{t-i} + \sum_i \gamma_i \Delta TCR^{INV}_{t-i} + \sum_i \chi_i \Delta\left(DGDP * TCR\right)_{t-i} + e_t$$

The objective here is to examine further which particular kind of export credit Indonesian exporters have been relying on more for delivering their final products. In their papers, Fisman and Love (2003) and Iacovone and Zavacka (2009) claim that long-term financing, i.e. investment credit, tends to harm export performance during a crisis. The latter study looks at panel data for around twenty-three banking-crisis episodes between 1980 and 2000, across twenty-one developed and developing countries, including Indonesia. To our knowledge, however, no empirical study has looked into this issue for the individual case of Indonesia.

Next, we further extend previous research by testing the contribution of investment and working-capital export credits in the overall performance of two major groups of Indonesian exports, manufacturing exports (X^{MAN}) and the export of minerals and lubricant products (X^{MIN}). As the terms of trade for manufacturing and for mineral and lubricant product exports are not available, we exclude the (*TOT*) variable from the following modified export-demand model:

$$\Delta X_t^{MAN/MIN} = \alpha + \sum_i \beta_i \Delta X_{t-i} + \sum_i \theta_i \Delta GDPTP_{t-i} + \sum_i \lambda_i \Delta TCR_{t-i}^{WK} + \sum_i \gamma_i \Delta TCR_{t-i}^{INV} + \sum_i \chi_i \Delta\left(DGDP * TCR\right)_{t-i} + e_t \tag{10.3}$$

Note, for both working models (10.2) and (10.3), the interactive variable, $\Delta(DGDP*TCR)$, is included to capture potential impacts of a crisis on exports and potential structural breaks in the regressions.

Data and empirical testing

Data

In general, the raw data series are sourced from the CEIC database and the IMF–IFS, unless otherwise noted. The observation set included in the empirical testing covers the period from the last quarter of 1993 to the second quarter of 2009. This period is dictated by the availability of export-credit data (*TCR*), which are sourced from the Bank Indonesia database. The total export series (*X*), the manufacturing export (X^{MAN}) and the mineral and lubricant export (X^{MIN}) are in US dollars and were all obtained from the CEIC database. The terms-of-trade series (*TOT*) is calculated as the ratio of unit value of exports over unit value of imports. The real trading partners' GDP (*GDPTP*) is the trade-weighted combination of the GDPs of the top three major export destination countries of Indonesia. The (*GDPTP*) variable is computed by the following standard formula:

$$GDPTP = \omega_1 GDPTP_1 + \omega_2 GDPTP_2 + \omega_3 GDPTP_3 \tag{10.4}$$

$$\omega_1 = \frac{X_1}{\left(X_1 + X_2 + X_3\right)} \tag{10.5}$$

$$\omega_2 = \frac{X_2}{\left(X_1 + X_2 + X_3\right)} \tag{10.6}$$

$$\omega_3 = \frac{X_3}{\left(X_1 + X_2 + X_3\right)} \tag{10.7}$$

where: $(GDPTP_1)$, $(GDPTP_2)$ and $(GDPTP_3)$ are the GDPs for trading partner countries 1, 2 and 3, respectively. Accordingly, $(\omega_1, \omega_2, \omega_3)$ are the trade weights for trading partners 1, 2 and 3, respectively. Lastly, (X_1), (X_2) and (X_3) are the exports of Indonesia to country 1, 2 and 3, individually. The first two major export destinations during the sample period are the United States and Japan. China has emerged as a key trading partner for Indonesia.[5] However, we do not have a complete set of quarterly GDP data for China. Instead, Korea is listed as Indonesia's third major trading partner.

The variable $\Delta(DGDP*TCR)$ is computed as the first difference of the product of the quarterly domestic GDP (*DGDP*) and the quarterly trade credit (*TCR*). All variables in the regression Equations (10.1–10.3) are log-normalized.

Empirical testing

In this study, we employ the frequently applied autoregressive distributed lag (ARDL) testing with the general-to-specific approach (Hendry, 1974).[6] The ARDL testing includes lags up to four quarters.[7] The combination of ARDL and the general-to-specific approach allows us to start from the general model by including all key explanatory variables and their time lags, supported by various theoretical frameworks. The general-to-specific procedure is then adopted to reduce the complexity of the model by eliminating the statistically insignificant variables. This process should ensure the consistency of the final reduced model. The final outcomes of the ARDL and general-to-specific approaches should enable us not only to capture the significant determinants and eliminate the insignificant ones, but also to arrive at the number of lags/periods needed for the impacts of changes in the explanatory variables on the dependent variable.

Before conducting the ARDL testing, we test the unit root properties for each of the variables in Equations (10.1)–(10.3). To anticipate the possible presence of structural breaks, we employ Banerjee *et al.* (1992) (henceforth BLS) in addition to standard unit root tests, i.e. the ADF test, the Phillip–Perron test and the KPSS test.[8] Depending on the unit root properties of the series, we then test for a possible cointegrating relationship among the variables at their levels. If a cointegrating relationship is found, then the error correction component series (ECM_{t-1}) will be included in the ARDL testing.

A number of test statistics will be reported to ensure that the coefficient estimates are valid and robust. In addition to the standard F-statistics to confirm the significance of one or more explanatory variables, we report the

Breusch–Godfrey serial correlation LM-test statistics to verify that autocorrelations in the residuals are not a problem in any of the regressions.

Key results and lessons learned

Based on our set of unit root tests, all relevant series included in Equations (10.1)–(10.3) are found to be non-stationary and integrated of order 1 at their level – I(1) series.[9] Hence, we cannot rule out the presence of a cointegrating relationship among the variables presented in Equation (10.1) for all three countries' cases. The standard Johansen cointegrating test is carried out. Based on the trace statistics, no robust cointegrating relationship is found at the 5 per cent level of significance. The number of lags included in the cointegration for each country case is determined by the Akaike Information Criterion (AIC).[10]

The overall ARDL test results are reported in Tables 10.3–10.6. The adjusted R^2 values suggest that the explanatory variables can clarify around 18–69 per cent of the quarterly changes in the export values of Indonesia. The F-statistics confirm that one or more of the independent variables is non-zero. In addition, the Breusch–Godfrey serial correlation LM-test statistics confirm that no autocorrelation in the residuals is found in any of the three regressions. In general, the coefficient estimates of the explanatory factors are theoretically consistent. Next, we return to the set of policy-relevant issues motivating this study.

We ask: has the Indonesian export sector become too dependent on export credit during the past two decades? In particular, did export financing contribute to the boom and bust of the two major export groups in the country, manufacturing and mineral exports? The evidence is robust that export credit has indeed contributed significantly to the export performance of Indonesia

Table 10.3 The impact of total export credit on total exports

Dependent variable: (ΔX)			
Variable	*Coefficient*	*Std error*	*t-statistics*
(ΔTOT_t)	0.713	0.341	2.091**
(ΔTCR_t)	0.744	0.132	5.633***
(ΔTCR_{t-1})	–0.875	0.149	–5.876***
(ΔTCR_{t-4})	0.172	0.077	2.220**
($\Delta GDPTP_{t-2}$)	0.960	0.365	2.633**
$\Delta(DGDP{*}TCR)_{t-1}$	–1.784	0.494	–3.612***
(α)	0.021	0.009	2.369**
Adjusted R-squared: 0.443		Prob (LM-test): 0.409	
F-statistics: 8.677		Prob (F-statistics): 0.000	

Notes: * significant at 10%; ** significant at 5%; *** significant at 1%.
Source: Author's own calculation

during most of the last two decades. However, the test results also suggest that the size of the contribution of export credit to the boom and bust of the country's exports has been modest. The sum of the total export credit coefficient for total exports $\left(\sum_i \eta_i\right)$ is estimated to be positive or roughly equal to (0.744 + (–0.875) – 0.172), as shown in Table 10.3. Thus, a 1 per cent increase in export credit would only translate into an increase in exports of less than 0.04 per cent. It is worth noting also that the impacts of changes in trade credit on the performance of exports in Indonesia were felt within the same quarter (*t*) and lasted for four quarters (*t*–4).

We also ask: was working capital more critical than investment capital in explaining the performance of the country's exports? When we decompose the export credit into working capital and investment capital, the robust results suggest that Indonesian exporters depend more predominantly on working capital. The importance of working capital is highlighted by the immediate impact (within the same quarter) that it has on exports and the persistence of the impact (lasting up to four quarters). None of the regressions has shown any significant role of investment credit (Tables 10.4–10.6). This finding contradicts the results posted by Fisman and Love (2003) and Iacovone and Zavacka (2009), where they find the importance of long-term financing (i.e. investment credit), but not working capital.

Consistent outcomes for total exports are reported when we consider two major groups of Indonesian exports, namely manufacturing and mineral fuels

Table 10.4 The impact of working and investment export credit on total exports

Dependent variable: (ΔX)			
Variable	*Coefficient*	*Std error*	*t-statistics*
(ΔX_{t-1})	0.293	0.053	5.571***
(ΔTCR_t^{WK})	0.457	0.091	5.042***
(ΔTCR_{t-1}^{WK})	–0.278	0.139	–1.990*
(ΔTCR_{t-2}^{WK})	–0.299	0.135	–2.212**
(ΔTCR_{t-4}^{WK})	0.216	0.101	2.132**
(ΔTOT_t)	0.688	0.210	3.259***
(ΔTOT_{t-3})	0.469	0.251	1.871*
(ΔTOT_{t-4})	–0.489	0.271	–1.809*
$(\Delta GDPTP_t)$	–0.405	0.210	–1.926*
$(\Delta GDPTP_{t-3})$	0.619	0.226	2.738***
$\Delta(DGDP{*}TCR)_t$	1.489	0.364	4.083***
$\Delta(DGDP{*}TCR)_{t-2}$	–1.456	0.436	–3.343***
$\Delta(DGDP{*}TCR)_{t-3}$	1.208	0.415	2.907***
(α)	0.021	0.005	3.963***
Adjusted R-squared: 0.689		Prob (LM-test): 0.601	
F-statistics: 10.572		Prob (F-Statistics): 0.000	

Notes: * significant at 10%; ** significant at 5%; and *** significant at 1%.
Source: Author's own calculation

Table 10.5 The impact of working and investment export credit on manufacturing exports

Dependent variable: (ΔX^{MAN})			
Variable	*Coefficient*	*Std error*	*t-statistics*
(ΔTCR^{WK}_{t-2})	–0.514	0.194	–2.654***
(ΔTCR^{WK}_{t-3})	0.613	0.193	3.182***
$(\Delta GDPTP_{t-1})$	–1.041	0.431	–2.416**
$(\Delta GDPTP_{t-2})$	1.579	0.452	3.490***
$\Delta(DGDP{*}TCR)_{t-4}$	1.017	0.543	1.872*
(α)	0.0009	0.017	0.052
Adjusted R-squared: 0. 341		Prob (LM-test): 0.110	
F-statistics: 6.991		Prob (F-Statistics): 0.000	

Notes: * significant at 10%; ** significant at 5%; and *** significant at 1%.
Source: Author's own calculation

Table 10.6 The impact of working and investment export credit on mineral and lubricant exports

Dependent variable: (ΔX^{MIN})			
Variable	*Coefficient*	*Std error*	*t-statistics*
(ΔX^{MIN}_{t-2})	–0.393	0.140	–2.801***
(ΔTCR^{WK}_{t})	0.313	0.102	3.065***
(ΔTCR^{WK}_{t-1})	–0.262	0.110	–2.373**
$(\Delta GDPTP_{t-2})$	0.641	0.379	1.686*
(α)	0.026	0.015	1.758*
Adjusted R-squared: 0. 175		Prob (LM-test): 0.167	
F-statistics: 4.283		Prob (F-Statistics): 0.004	

Note: * significant at 10%; ** significant at 5%; and *** significant at 1%.
Source: Author's own calculation

and lubricants. Exporters of both groups have been significantly dependent on working capital. As reported for the case of total credit, the role of working capital has been modest. The sums of the coefficients for working capital $\left(\sum_i \lambda_i\right)$ are only 0.10 for the case of manufacturing exports, as shown in Table 10.5, and 0.05 for the case of mineral and lubricant exports (see Table 10.6). As far as the timing is concerned, however, trade-credit fluctuations have more immediate and short-term impacts on the growth rate of mineral and lubricant exports than on that of manufacturing exports.

Next, we ask: did the economic and financial crises amplify the role of export credit in sustaining exports? With the exception of the case of mineral exports, the remaining test results robustly concluded that the economic crises amplified the dependence of Indonesian exporters on export credit. This result confirms the claim that, during economic slowdowns, tightening of liquidity in the economy will also affect the trade sector.

In addition to the above findings, our test results confirm the importance of two primary determinants of export demand, namely income and price factors. The sum of the coefficient estimates for trading-partner income variable (*GDPTP*), as captured by $\left(\sum_i \theta_i\right)$, however, ranges from 0.538 for manufacturing exports to 0.641 for mineral and lubricant exports. The results may fail to capture the true coefficient estimates for income factor (*GDPTP*), as the selection of three trading partners, namely the United States, Japan and Korea, was based on the individual shares of total Indonesian exports to those three countries. It is possible that these three countries are not among the top three destinations of Indonesian manufacturing exports. Regrettably, we do not have detailed breakdowns of Indonesia's manufacturing exports and mineral and lubricant exports by country of destination to select the top three partners more appropriately and calculate their individual weights for each group of exports.

Given the importance of the export of commodities and raw materials in Indonesia's overall export sector, the terms of trade should play a crucial role in explaining the demand for Indonesian exports. As discussed above, we do not have the individual terms-of-trade series for the manufacturing and mineral export groups. Hence, we could not examine the importance of the price factor for those two major groups of exports. The limitation with the data may have contributed to the relatively low levels of adjusted R-squared for the individual groups of exports, as reported in Tables 10.5 and 10.6.

Policy response

Two policy approaches are often implemented in Indonesia to support the export sectors during economic downturns. The first set pays particular attention to ensuring the availability of trade financing. The second set of policies concentrates on areas that enhance the competitiveness of the sector. Given its relevance, we begin by reviewing policy efforts to ensure the adequacy of export financing.

To provide post-shipment guarantees and to reduce the liquidity risks of exporters, commercial banks were allowed to sell (rediscount) export receivables (drafts) to Bank Indonesia, starting in December 2008. Furthermore, to increase the on-shore supply of US dollars and to protect against risk of counterparty default, in January 2009 the Indonesian government issued a regulation

Table 10.7 Types of export payment (US$ million)

Types	*2000*	*2001*	*2002*	*2003*	*2004*	*2005*	*2006*	*2007*	*Jan-08*	*Feb-08*	*Mar-08*	*Apr-08*	*May-08*
1.Letter or Credit	13,294	11,329	10,791	9,976	10,082	10,787	12,498	12,868	1,028	1,031	1,092	1,033	1,153
2. Others	35,189	31,908	34,130	36,582	44,222	55,223	67,594	79,731	7,876	7,237	7,934	7,477	8,362

Source: Bank Indonesia

on mandatory use of a letter of credit (LC) for export payment for certain products (i.e. coffee, crude palm oil (CPO), cocoa, rubber, mining products and tin), stipulating that this payment was to be done through an on-shore foreign-exchange bank.

The effectiveness of these two policies has been somewhat limited. Until late 2009, only a few banks participated and sold their export receivables to Bank Indonesia. Similarly, the implementation of the LC policy has been postponed three times, because it was rejected by the exporters of those commodities. The latest schedule of implementation was scheduled for July 2010. It was unlikely to result in a significant rise in LC payment. Data from Bank Indonesia have, in fact, demonstrated that there has been a decline in the use of LC as an export payment since the first half of 2008, as shown in Table 10.7.

In addition, Lembaga Pembiayaan Ekspor Indonesia (LPEI) was legally established in January 2009 to replace the state-owned Bank Ekspor Indonesia (BEI), which was established in September 1999 to provide financing and co-financing and to guarantee facilities for international trading activities. The BEI, operating as a state bank, was ineffective in giving out loans as, like any other commercial bank, it relied mostly on short-term deposits to fund lending. Hence, the institution faced significant tightening of its third-party liabilities (deposits) during economic downturns.

The LPEI, which operates under the name Indonesia Eximbank, was opened in September 2009. Despite its name, the LPEI is not a commercial bank and thus cannot take third-party deposits. It is a state agency, with government backing to provide financing, insurance, guarantees and consultancy services to exporters. Its authorized capital of at least Rp4 trillion is in the form of government-equity participation. The government is expected to raise its equity participation further. This additional capital can be used as a guarantee for as much as six to ten times additional business credit extension, estimated at around Rp12–20 trillion. This is possible because, besides extending credit directly and export insurance, the LPEI is also allowed to give credit guarantees.

If warranted, the LPEI can raise capital by issuing bonds or borrowing from international multilateral or bilateral agencies. In October 2009, the LPEI received almost Rp1 trillion (or slightly above US$100 million) in a trade-financing loan from the Japanese government through the Japan Bank for International Cooperation (JBIC), with an interest rate of LIBOR plus 230 basis points, maturing in five years, and a grace period of two years. JBIC has committed to extend up to US$500 million of loans to LPEI to support its business credit growth plan. In 2009, the LPEI was estimated to have given trade financing of as much as US$1.35 billion, roughly around 17 per cent of the total national commercial banks' capability. The LPEI has also set a target of trade-related loan growth at 60 per cent in 2010, which was much higher than the overall banking sector loan growth target of 17–20 per cent set by Bank Indonesia.

The injection of capital to the LPEI was part of a series of major fiscal-stimulus packages initiated in 2008–9 (Gunawan and Siregar, 2009). Given the important role of short-term export financing, namely working capital, liquidity provision from fiscal stimulus for export activities has been an appropriate strategy to bridge much-needed temporary financing constraints facing exporters. However, owing to the limited data and information available, further studies are warranted to examine the overall effectiveness of Indonesia Eximbank.

As indicated above, another set of policy efforts concentrated on enhancing the competitiveness of the export sector during the global financial slowdown. One particular policy adjustment, for instance, targeted a key commodity export, namely CPO. Seeking to raise domestic supplies of CPO-based cooking oil, the government imposed a high export tax on CPO when its price skyrocketed between late 2007 and the first half of 2008. However, starting in the third quarter of 2008, the CPO price experienced a sudden and sharp decline. To support the industry, the government eliminated (reduced to zero) the export tax on CPO in November 2008.

Furthermore, the government launched a one-stop service for processing import and export documents/procedures at a number of key ports around Indonesia. Coordinated with twenty-five government agencies, it is known as the National and ASEAN New Single Windows (NSW). The pilot project was completed in 2007 in Batam, followed by a similar undertaking at Tanjung Priok port in Jakarta in 2008. This development involves standardizing documents/business processes for flows of documents and integrating port-clearance procedures for flows of goods. The final target is to have online application, processing and electronic manifests. The government has also been trying to establish a new registration system as part of its NSW programme, leading to a better database system that will benefit the business community. The new system is expected to shorten the registration process to within a seven-day period. By late 2009, the new registration system had approved around 75 per cent of traded commodities.

Concluding remarks

Despite a much stronger overall economic outlook during the recent GFC, Indonesia's export sector suffered a more severe decline than during the 1997–8 AFC. This study evaluates the role of export credit in explaining the performance of the export sector in Indonesia. We are particularly concerned with the role of this financing facility during the economic downturns. The test results found robust evidence that export credit contributed to the boom and bust of the export sector in Indonesia. However, the results also suggest that the size of the contribution is modest at the most. The significance of export credit has indeed been magnified during the crises. Furthermore, it is short-term financing, not investment capital, that has been detrimental to the performance of the export sector in Indonesia. Similar conclusions were reported when we examined the two largest export groups in the country.

Two traditional determinants of export demand remain the most significant contributing factors, namely income and price factors. The slump of the economies of the major trading partners weakened demand for Indonesia's exports. Finally, the country's exports have been highly sensitive to the uncertainties and volatilities in the price of major commodities on the world market.

Notes

1 Reza Y. Siregar (reza@seacen.org) is with the South-East Asian Central Banks Research and Training Centre in Kuala Lumpur, Malaysia, and Anton H. Gunawan (anton.gunawan@danamon.co.id) is with the Bank Danamon, Jakarta, Indonesia. The early draft of the paper was funded by the 2010 ERIA project on 'Linkages between Real and Financial Aspects of Economic Integration in East Asia'. The views expressed are those of the authors only and do not necessarily represent the SEACEN centre or Bank Danamon.

2 The countries included in the panel testing are the East and South-East Asian economies (Malaysia, the Philippines, Thailand, Indonesia and Korea), Russia, Brazil, Argentina, Mexico and Turkey.

3 The total international claims of the US banks to Indonesia ranked among the top three during the period 1990–2004. Japanese banks and UK banks were the other two largest international lenders to Indonesia (Siregar and Choy, 2010).

4 This possible relationship supports the argument extended by previous works, such as Dell'Ariccia *et al.* (2008), Borensztein and Panizza (2006) and Braun and Larrain (2005).

5 For most of the South-East Asian nations, including Indonesia, Singapore has been a key trading partner and a primary export destination. However, exports to Singapore from Indonesia are largely destined for re-export. Hence, Singapore is not the final main destination of the export goods from Indonesia, and thus we do not include Singapore.

6 The application of ARDL testing with the general-to-specific approach is common. Recent studies applying the ARDL framework include Siregar and Goo (2010), Campa and Goldberg (2002) and Gagnon and Ihrig (2004).

7 Pesaran and Shin (1999) suggested up to two lags for annual data. As we work with quarterly data, we expanded the lags up to four.

8 The BLS provides a more in-depth investigation of the possibility that the aggregate economic time series can be characterized as being stationary around 'a single or multiple structural breaks'. It extends the Dickey–Fuller *t*-test by the construction of the time series of rolling computed estimators and their *t*-statistics. Following the BLS procedure, we compute the smallest (minimal) and the largest Dickey–Fuller *t*-statistics.

9 For the sake of brevity, the test results of the unit root testing are not reported, but they can be made available upon request.

10 Based on the AIC, each of the cointegrating tests includes around two or three quarter lags. No robust cointegrating relationship is reported at the 5 per cent significance level from any of the three countries' test results. A weak cointegrating result is found at the 10 per cent level for total export demand (Equation (10.1)). We consider this a weak case because the relationship exists only when we consider lags beyond four quarters. For the sake of completeness, we include the error-correction component in the regression equations. However, we do not find the error-correction component to be significant in all regressions.

References

Banerjee, A., Lumsdaine, R.L. and Stock, J.H. (1992) 'Recursive and sequential tests of the unit-root test and trend break hypotheses: theory and international evidence', *Journal of Business and Economic Statistics*, 10: 271–87.

Biais, B., Gollier, C. and Viala, P. (1993) 'Why do firms use trade credit?', mimeo, CEPR Conference in San Sebastian.

Borensztein, E. and Panizza, U. (2006) 'Do sovereign defaults hurt exporters?', RES Working Paper 4447, Inter-American Development Bank, Research Department.

Braun, M. and Larrain, B. (2005) 'Finance and the business cycle: international, inter-industry evidence', *Journal of Finance*, 60(3): 1097–128.

Brennan, M., Maksimovic, V. and Zechner, J. (1998) 'Vendor financing', *Journal of Finance*, 1127–41.

Brown, M. and Magiera, S.L. (2000) 'Trade finance in Indonesia: structural issues and impact of the financial crisis', Project Report of Partnership for Economic Growth (PEG) for Ministry of Industry and Trade, Republic of Indonesia (March).

Campa, J.M. and Goldberg, L.S. (2002) 'Exchange rate pass-through into import prices: a macro or micro phenomenon?', NBER Working Paper, no. 8934 (May).

Dell'Ariccia, G., Detragiache, E. and Rajan, R. (2008) 'The real effect of banking crises', *Journal of Financial Intermediation*, 17(1): 89–112.

Dornbusch, R. (1988) *Exchange Rate and Inflation*, Cambridge, MA: MIT Press.

Ferris, J.S. (1981) 'A transaction theory of trade credit use', *Quarterly Journal of Economics*, 94: 243–70.

Fisman, R. and Love, I. (2003) 'Trade credit, financial intermediary development, and industry growth', *Journal of Finance*, 58(1): 353–74.

Freund, C. (2009) 'The trade response to global downturns: historical evidence', Policy Research Working Paper Series 5016, The World Bank.

Freund, C. and Klapper, L. (2009) 'Has the decline in the supply of financing affected trade during the crisis?', mimeo, The World Bank.

Gagnon, J.E. and Ihrig, J. (2004) 'Monetary policy and exchange rate pass-through', *International Journal of Finance and Economics*, 9(4): 315–38.

Gunawan, A. and Siregar, R. (2009) 'Survey of recent development', *Bulletin of Indonesian Economic Studies*, 45(1): 7–36.

Hendry, D.F. (1974) 'Stochastic specification in an aggregate demand model of the United Kingdom', *Econometrica*, 42: 559–78.

Hooper, P. and Marquez, J. (1993) 'Exchange rates, prices, and external adjustments in the United States and Japan', International Finance Discussion Paper, no. 456, The Board of Governors of the Federal Reserve System.

Iacovone, L. and Zavacka, V. (2009) 'Banking crises and exports', Policy Research Working Paper, no. 5016, The World Bank.

James, W.E., Park, D., Jha, S., Jongwanich, J., Terada-Hagiwara, A. and Sumulong, L. (2008) 'The US financial crisis, global financial turmoil, and developing Asia: is the era of high growth at an end?', ADB Economics Working Paper Series, no. 139 (December).

Mian, S. and Smith, C.W. (1992) 'Accounts receivable management policy: theory and evidence', *Journal of Finance*, 47(1): 169–200.

Mori, H. (2005) 'Brazil's approach in the face of export constraints', in *Access to Trade Finance in Times of Crisis*, eds J.-Y. Wang and M. Ronci, Washington DC: IMF.

Nielsen, J.H. (2002) 'Trade credit and the bank lending channel', *Journal of Money, Credit, and Banking*, 34: 226–53.

Pesaran, H.M. and Shin, Y. (1999) 'Autoregressive distributed lag modelling approach to cointegration analysis', in *Econometrics and Economic Theory in the 20th Century: The Ragnar Frisch Centennial Symposium*, ed. S. Strøm, Cambridge: Cambridge University Press.

Petersen, M.A. and Rajan, R.G. (1995) 'The effect of credit market competition on lending relationships', *Quarterly Journal of Economics*, 60: 407–44.

Petersen, M.A. and Rajan, R.G. (1997) 'Trade credit: theory and evidence', *Review of Financial Studies*, 10(3): 661–91.

Ronci, M. (2005) 'Trade finance and trade flows: panel data evidence from 10 crises', in *Access to Trade Finance in Times of Crisis*, eds J.-Y. Wang and M. Ronci, Washington DC: IMF.

Siregar, R.Y. and Choy, K.M. (2010) 'Determinants of international bank lending from the developed world to East Asia', *IMF Staff Papers*, 57(2): 484–516.

Siregar, R.Y. and Goo, S. (2010) 'Effectiveness and commitment to inflation targeting policy: evidence from Indonesia and Thailand', *Journal of Asian Economics*, 21: 113–28.

Siregar, R.Y. and Lim, V. (2010) 'The role of central banks in sustaining economic recovery and in achieving financial stability', *Journal of Advance Studies in Finance*, 1(June): 83–9.

Smith, J. (1987) 'Trade credit and information asymmetry', *Journal of Finance*, XLII(4): 863–9.

Wang, J.-Y. and Tadesse, H. (2005) 'Overview', in *Access to Trade Finance in Times of Crisis*, eds J.-Y. Wang and M. Ronci, Washington DC: IMF.

Index